GERMANY'S
FIRST AIR FORCE
1914–1918

GERMANY'S FIRST AIR FORCE 1914–1918

PETER KILDUFF

ARMS AND
ARMOUR

◀ Gotha G V of *Kagohl 3*
being prepared for a raid.
Armourers are checking
the guns, while other
groundcrew pump fuel
and oil into the aircraft.
The aircraft had two 275-
litre fuel tanks fed by a
pump and a 70-litre
gravity tank, as well as a
60-litre auxiliary tank and
a 30-litre oil reservoir to
serve the two engines.

This book is dedicated to the late
HANNS-GERD RABE, former observer with
Flieger-Abteilung (A) 253, and my
long-time friend and German
aviation history mentor

Arms and Armour Press
A Cassell Imprint
Villiers House, 41–47 Strand, London WC2N 5JE.

Distributed in Australia
by Capricorn Link (Australia) Pty Ltd,
P.O. Box 665, Lane Cove, New South Wales
2066, Australia.

British Library Cataloguing in Publication Data
Kilduff, Peter
Germany's first air force, 1914–1918.
1. Germany. Air Forces, history
I. Title
358.400943
ISBN 1-85409-053-4

Jacket illustration: an air action
involving Hanns-Gerd Rabe, from an original artwork
by George Evans.

Designed and edited by DAG Publications Ltd.
Designed by David Gibbons; edited by David
Dorrell; layout by Anthony A. Evans; typeset by
Typesetters (Birmingham) Ltd, Warley, West Midlands;
camerawork by M&E Reproductions, North Fambridge,
printed and bound in Great Britain by
Courier International, Tiptree, Essex.

ALSO BY PETER KILDUFF
*The Red Baron   That's My Bloody Plane
Germany's Last Night of the Air
U.S. Carriers at War   A-4 Skyhawk*

CONTENTS

PREFACE

SOMEHOW, summertime reading during my fifteenth year led me to *The Falcons of France* by Charles Nordhoff and James Norman Hall. That thinly fictionalized account of aerial combat over the Western Front captured my imagination and interest. Before long I was seeking out other books on the then esoteric subject of World War I aviation history.

Then a library and collection of model aircraft began to grow. At the time, 30 years ago, quite a number of World War I aviation personnel were alive and still in good health. And from my first such encounter, with American aviation artist and author Clayton Knight, OBE, I discovered that he and his contemporaries were generally eager to discuss living, flying and fighting during World War I. In a short leap I applied my university German language courses to this avocation and thereby nurtured a special interest in the first German air force.

It was a stroke of the greatest luck that an enquiry about Gustav Tweer, a little-known test pilot, produced a response from *Oberstleutnant der Reserve a D* Hanns-Gerd Rabe, a World War I aviation observer who knew Tweer and many other fliers of that era. Best of all, he maintained a passionate interest in having their deeds remembered. 'They were not the Richthofens and Udets and other highly decorated heroes,' he once told me, 'but they faced the same dangers and are also worthy of note.'

With that thought in mind, my research – and the articles and previous books that resulted from it – has often focused on the 'unknowns', rather than the 'big names'. Hence, in this book the more prominent personalities are duly noted, but within the perspective of other events. For example, there is a whole body of World War I aviation literature devoted to Manfred von Richthofen – but little has been published about his younger brother Lothar, who justly deserves to be the subject of Chapter 6. Many other prominent names – often the subjects of entire works – are noted within the context of overall operations. Likewise, German naval air operations, which deserve a thick volume of their own, are confined to the lesser known subjects covered in Chapter 5. With the prospect of more new material coming out of eastern Germany, it is likely that a multi-volume work on the *Luftstreitkräfte* will emerge one day.

I count as one of the great experiences of my life having come to know – in person or by correspondence – the following World War I German fliers who contributed to this book. It is impossible to place them in order of rank, so in fairness the listing is alphabetical: *Flugkapitän a D* Hans Baur, Oscar Bechtle, *Major der Reserve a D* Carl Degelow, Kurt Delang, *Generalingenieur der Luftwaffe a D* Wolfram Eisenlohr, *Major der Reserve a D* Hellmuth Frank, *General der Flieger a D* Hans Ritter, *Generalleutnant a D* Erwin Jollasse, *Major der Reserve a D Dr* Friedrich Kamfenkel, *Generaloberst a D* Alfred Keller, *Dipl-Ing* John Knauer, *Dr-Ing* Oskar Kuppinger, *Oberstleutnant der Reserve a D* Hanns-Gerd Rabe, and *Major der Reserve a D Dr* Fritz Stormer. In quoting these gentlemen and other original sources for this book, all previous translations have been reviewed and, in many cases, enhanced by virtue of more experience with the language.

Friends and colleagues of mine, as well as relatives of World War I fliers, who have helped with this book include: Wolf-Dieter Braun, Col John A. deVries, A. E. Ferko, *Dipl-Ing* Klaus B. Fischer, Dr Volker Koos, Robert C. Mikesh, Heinz J. Nowarra, Neal W. O'Connor, Annemarie Rieper, Noel C. Shirley, Johan G. H. Visser, George H. Williams, and H. Hugh Wynne. Special thanks go to Dr S. Martin Harwin, whose great care in preparing most of the photographs for this book equals that he has given as pediatrician to my children.

A host of newly gained friends and colleagues (including some who have since retired or died) in many archives deserve thanks. They represented faithfully the following resources: Bayerisches

▲ Author Peter Kilduff and World War I observer Hanns-Gerd Rabe share a light-hearted moment during an interview about the German airman's experiences with *Flieger-Abteilung (A) 253* on the Flanders Front in 1918. In the course of his research over a 25-year period, Kilduff has interviewed or corresponded with well over 100 German aviators or their families to gain an insight into early air operations.

staatsarchiv in Stuttgart, Militärarchiv der Volksarmee der DDR in Potsdam, Public Record Office in Kew, England, and the US National Archives in Washington, DC.

Last, but by no means least, a special tribute to my wife Judy, who has kept things going on the home front while I have spent many hours away in archives or in thought for this book.

Hauptstaatsarchiv in Munich, Bundesarchiv Militärarchiv in Freiburg, Deutsche Bücherei in Leipzig, Generallandesarchiv in Karlsruhe, Haupt-

Peter Kilduff,
New Britain, Connecticut,
July 1990

INTRODUCTION

GERMANY probably owes the establishment of its first military air unit to an Englishman, Henry Coxwell, who demonstrated balloons at exhibitions in Germany in 1848 and 1849. When the Franco-Prussian War started in 1870, the enterprising Coxwell approached German military authorities in Cologne and convinced them that his spherical balloons would give them a tactical advantage over

the French. He sold them two balloons, one of which was used, with minimal success, to reconnoitre Strasbourg. Transportation difficulties and lack of hydrogen kept the balloons from being used during the Battle of Paris. After the war, the fledgling balloon unit was disbanded.[1]

Interest in balloons remained alive in Germany, however, and further development was encouraged. In 1892 *Major* August von Parseval, *Hauptmann* (Captain) Hans Bartsch von Sigsfeld and August Riedinger developed a *Drachen* (kite) captive balloon characterized by a stabilizing fin; it, too, became a successful military reconnaissance resource (as noted in Chapter 7). At about the time von Parseval was experimenting with a motorized, semi-rigid version of his balloon, *General* Ferdinand *Graf* (Count) von Zeppelin was working on a rigid dirigible. Both were viewed with favour by the military establishment, but both could not be supported financially. Eventually, Zeppelin bought Parseval's patents and developed the huge airships that became Germany's first long-range strategic bombing weapon.[2]

The advent of successful heavier-than-air flight was greeted with caution in Germany. It was not until October 1907 that a member of the German Army's new balloon section, Alfred Hildebrandt, determined the feasibility of developing fixed-wing aircraft by visiting the Wright brothers' facilities at Dayton, Ohio. Hildebrandt later arranged for the first aircraft display in Germany, in February 1909, which led to a succession of air shows and competi-

◀ As *Inspekteur der Fliegertruppen* (Inspector General of the Air Service) at the beginning of World War I, Walter von Eberhardt tried to organize the fledgling air arm so that it could assist the overall strategic objectives. He was thwarted by the initial crop of 'old line' generals, who did not want a separate air force beyond their control. Many of von Eberhardt's ideas were later implemented. After the war he became national commander and an honoured member of the *Ring der Flieger* aviation veterans group.

tions that spurred the development of German aviation. Developments were followed with interest by the military establishment.

In 1910 the Army purchased seven aeroplanes and began training officers to be pilots. In May a 'provisional flying school' was established at Döberitz, near Berlin, and by year's end the *Fliegerkommando der Luftschifferabteilung der Verkehrstruppen* (Flying Command of the Airship Section of the Transportation Corps) had been established. On 1 April 1911 that unit became the *Lehr- und Versuchungsanstalt für Militärflugwesen* (Instruction and Research Facility for Military Aviation), and by the end of the year had 170 aeroplanes and 150 pilots.[3]

General der Infanterie Hellmuth *Graf* von Moltke, Chief of the German General Staff, became con-

cerned about the rapid growth of French aviation. He foresaw the military applications of aviation and, on 26 September 1912, he proposed the formation of a separate air arm. On 1 October the existing military aviation structure was converted into the *Fliegertruppe* (Flying Force).[4] German regional interests remained important, despite the union of states welded during the Franco-Prussian War; hence, while essentially a Prussian organization, the *Fliegertruppe* showed a healthy respect for those interests by including contingents from the Kingdoms of Saxony and Württemberg. In typically independent fashion, the Kingdom of Bavaria maintained its own air arm – the *bayerische Militärflieger-Abteilung* (Bavarian Military Aviation Section) – which it agreed to place at the disposal of the Prussian *Fliegertruppe* in the event of war.[5]

▶ *Generalleutnant* Ernst von Hoeppner (centre), the first Commanding General of the air arm when it was reorganized in 1916 as the *Luftstreitkräfte* (Air Force). *Major* Wilhelm Siegert (right), a driving force for an independent air arm and the use of long-range strategic bombing, became *Inspekteur der Fliegertruppen* under von Hoeppner.

With international tensions rising and strengthening alliances turning Europe into two armed camps, von Moltke overrode objections to his plans for the *Fliegertruppe* and continued to nurture the organization. On 1 October 1913 the *Inspektion der Fliegertruppe* (Inspectorate of the Flying Force) and the *Inspektion der Luftschiffertruppen* (Inspectorate of the Airship Service) were formed to oversee further development.[6] *Oberst* (Colonel) Walter von Eberhardt was appointed the first head of the new air service.

When the German Army was mobilized on 1 August 1914, it had 254 trained pilots and 271 observers. The units were:[7]

- 30 Prussian *Feldflieger-Abteilungen* (Field Flying Sections)
- 4 Bavarian *Feldflieger-Abteilungen*
- 6 Prussian *Festungs-Flieger-Abteilungen* (Fortress Flying Sections)
- 1 Bavarian *Festungs-Flieger-Abteilung*
- 8 Prussian *Etappenflugzeugparks* (Home Aircraft Supply Units)
- 1 Bavarian *Etappenflugzeugpark*
- 4 Prussian *Flieger-Ersatz-Abteilungen* (Aviation Replacement Sections)
- 1 Bavarian *Flieger-Ersatz-Abteilung*

For record-keeping purposes, the *Feldflieger-Abteilungen* were supposed to have six aircraft each and the *Festungsflieger-Abteilungen* four each. Thus, when fully deployed, the *Fliegertruppe* had no reserves at a time when it was just beginning to develop the facilities needed to train significant numbers of new aircrews – clearly not an auspicious beginning. (Deployment of the *Luftschiffer-Truppen* is noted in Chapter 7.)

Inspekteur der Fliegertruppen von Eberhardt found that, locked in his command post in Berlin, he had no real contact with the units. Likewise, air officers attached to various Army staffs were not required to leave the capital. Adding to his frustration was the general antipathy towards aviation, as he confided to his diary on 6 August:

'In the Grunewald section [of Berlin] I was almost arrested by cadets who fancy themselves very important as railway sentries. In the Heerstrasse they were shooting like mad at aeroplanes flying from Johannisthal to Döberitz. One battalion in Spandau shot off all its ammunition that way – without getting a hit! The city government of Berlin has issued the unbelievable prohibition against "flying over Berlin". There is no understanding of military aviation.'[8]

Within days *Oberst* von Eberhardt was on the move, making a series of airfield and other visits that showed a *Fliegertruppe* in disarray. His diary entry for 19 August noted:

'Early to Cologne, where workers by the thousands are armed. At the *Flieger-Station* [Air Base] *Hptmn* Volkmann has prepared everything excellently; met *Hptmn* Zimmermann, Kastner and other capable people here. It is a shame that the *Festungs-Flieger-Abteilung* here is not active. Will do everything [possible] to set it right. Then on past Aachen to Lüttich, where at 1600 hours I am at the airfield of [*Feldflieger-*] *Abteilungen 23, 18* and *9*, and *Etappenflugpark 2*. The commander, *Hptmn* Hohl, is at the *Armee-Oberkommando* [Army HQ], he has placed himself at their disposal and lets his aircraft fly to the Front! With that, replacement possibilities cease. Numerous aircraft are already missing.'[9]

In short order, von Eberhardt proposed a new command structure: each *Armee* was to have a staff officer in charge of the aviation units within it and these staff officers would be responsible to a *Chef des Feldflugwesens* (Chief of Field Aviation), a title von Eberhardt had already begun to use, at the senior command level. Even though the plan was blocked by other members of the *Oberste Heeres-leitung (OHL)*, von Eberhardt's ideas did set in motion reporting changes that eliminated much of the individual initiative that he found on his tour.

The early use of aircraft for reconnaissance proved very fruitful. On the Western Front, aircraft alerted commanders of the *1.* and *2. Armees* that French forces were streaming through the gap the Germans had left in their race to reach Paris; the Germans were forced to make an orderly retreat – which was better than a rout. In the East, *General* Paul von Hindenburg gave much credit to aerial reconnaissance for his victory in East Prussia: *'Ohne Flieger, kein Tannenberg!'* ('Without fliers, no Tannenberg'), he said.[10]

The German Army's successful advance to the Channel coast in 1914 allowed both the *Fliegertruppe* and the *Reichsmarine* (Navy) to establish aviation facilities that could interdict maritime traffic and potentially strike England. Chapters 2 and 5 of this book deal with both. But von Eberhardt's failure to convince the *OHL* of the need for a separate air force was no doubt instrumental in the creation of the Army's Flanders-based strategic bombing wing (the subject of Chapter 1), which was responsible to the *OHL*, rather than the local *Armee*.

Oberst von Eberhardt was replaced by another staunch aviation supporter, *Major* Roethe. But he too was unable to provide the organization needed by the *Fliegertruppe*, which was being overwhelmed by its adversaries. *Major* Hermann von der Lieth-Thomsen, a protegé of *General* Ludendorff, succeeded Roethe in the top *Fliegertruppe* post on 11 March 1915. Assisted by *Major* Wilhelm Siegert, Thomsen made a number of changes. He provided

the *Armee-Oberkommandos* with staff officers to ensure proper liaison and communications and diversified the use of the bombing units that were directly under the *OHL*. Assigned to the Russian Front in 1915, they bolstered the relatively few *Feldflieger-Abteilungen* there, although at the loss of crews and equipment to the *Armees*.

Indeed, the 'carrier pigeon' units, initially suggested by *Major* Siegert, evolved into the *Kampfgeschwaders* (Combat Wings) that provided these important developments: *Kampfeinsitzerkommandos* (Combat Single-seater Detachments) that

▼The romantic aura of aviation attracted thousands of young Germans to training centres around the country. A proud *Unteroffizier* (Corporal) Ewald Heidemann poses by an unarmed Pfalz A II parasol during the early days of the war. This Pfalz, a copy of the French Morane-Saulnier Type L, was later fitted with a Spandau machine-gun and redesignated the E III.

▶The image of an aviator wounded in combat was used to appeal for financial support of Germany's wartime efforts, *'Und Ihr? Unterzeichnet Kriegsanleihe'* ('And what about you? Subscribe for War Bonds').

became *Jagdstaffeln* (Fighter Squadrons), and *Kampfstaffeln* (Combat Squadrons) that became *Schutzstaffeln* (two-seat Protection Squadrons) or *Bombenstaffeln* (multi-engine Bombing Squadrons).

Under Thomsen's direction of the *Fliegertruppe* came the development of machine-gun synchronization gear to allow the pilots of single-seat E-type aircraft to fire through the propeller arc, and the development of C-type two-seat aircraft, in which the pilot sat in front and the observer in the back, with a wide field of fire for his flexible machine-gun. The former strengthened the newly formed fighter squadrons, the latter added to the defensive capabilities of the reconnaissance and artillery-ranging *Flieger-Abteilungen*.

With the arrival of the successful Fokker *Eindecker* (monoplane) series in mid-1915, the *Fliegertruppe* gained superiority over British and French aircraft that had outfought and outmanoeuvred the

▲ The observer in this Albatros C V reconnaissance aircraft feigned surrender for the photographer's benefit. In reality, surrender was rarely an option for two-seater crews. With no parachutes in their aircraft – until late in the war – they could only hope to elude a pursuer or fight to the death. Note the mudguards over the wheels to deflect stones at front-line airfields, which were often hastily prepared.

Sperreflüge (barrier flights) of the *Kampfgeschwaders*. The Battle of Verdun, which began on 21 February 1916, was the final proof that *Sperreflüge* made by C-type two-seat reconnaissance aircraft were an inadequate means of local air defence. At the same time, however, the *Feldflieger-Abteilungen* were joined by *Artillerie-Flieger-Abteilungen*, which provided artillery spotting in addition to normal tactical reconnaissance.

Overall, the *Fliegertruppe* expanded its forces, using squadrons for specific missions, and creating units for overseas deployment to Palestine, Turkey and Bulgaria. On 1 April 1916, the front-line aviation organization consisted of:[11]

17 *Stabsoffiziere der Flieger* (Staff Officers for Aviation) for the *1.* to the *17. Armees*; each staff with six aircraft

81 *Feldflieger-Abteilungen (Feldfl-Abt 1 to 81)*, with six aircraft each

27 *Artillerie-Flieger-Abteilungen (Fl-Abt (A) 201 to 227)*, with six aircraft each

5 *Kampfgeschwadern* for bombing and related missions (*Kagohl 1 to 5*), each with 6 *Staffeln* with six aircraft (*Kastas 1 to 30*)

6 *Kampfstaffeln* for bombing missions (*Kastas 31 to 36*), each with six aircraft

17 *Armeeflugparks (AFPs 1 to 17)*, each with twelve aircraft to support each of the *Armees*

2 *Riesenflugzeug-Abteilungen (Rfa 500 and 501)*, each with three to four R-type ('Giant') aircraft for long-range bombing

2 *Versuchs- und Übungsparks* test and training facilities at Tergnier and Warsaw, each with about ten aircraft

2 *Feldflieger-Abteilungen*, each with six aircraft, for Middle East operations under the name *Fl-Abt 300 'Pascha'*

1 *Feldflieger-Abteilung* as *Fliegerkommando Sofia* in Bulgaria

3 *Flieger-Abteilungen* for the Military Mission in Turkey

At this time, dedicated single-seat fighter units were in the process of formation (as described in Chapter 2). In fact, seven *Jagdstaffeln* were created from existing *Kampfeinsitzerkommandos (KEKs)* between 23 and 27 August.[12] Each was equipped with fourteen of the new Albatros, Fokker and Halberstadt D-type single-seat biplane fighters, most of which were equipped with two forward-firing machine-guns. The period of Fokker *Eindecker* supremacy was ended in 1916 by the appearance of Nieuport and other Allied fighter aircraft equipped with single forward-firing machine-guns; the *Jastas* regained that supremacy with better machines and more firepower. By year's end there were 26 fighter squadrons, *Jastas 1 to 26*, and most were proving to be formidable opponents.

The great advances of the *Jagdstaffeln*, however, were not enough to counter devastating German ground and air losses at Verdun. As a result, on 29 August 1916, the architect of the Verdun offensive, German General Staff Chief Erich von Falkenhayn, was dismissed. He was succeeded by *Generalfeldmarschall* Paul von Hindenburg, who had done a masterful job as overall commander of the Eastern Front. Now in charge of all Army operations, Hindenburg called for a number of sweeping changes – including the reorganization of the *Fliegertruppe*.

On 8 October 1916 *Generalleutnant* Ernst von Hoeppner took over the air arm with the new title *Kommandierende General der Luftstreitkräfte* (Commanding General of the Air Force) – abbreviated to *Kogenluft*. He was given a unified command similar to that suggested by *Oberst* von Eberhardt in 1914: 'the scope of what had been under the *Feldflugchef*

◀ *Leutnant* Hinnberg of *Jagdstaffel 59* was prepared for the worst circumstances. Over his all-leather flying suit, he wore a Henecke parachute that was connected by a static line to allow him to bale out of his Albatros D Va fighter, seen behind him, in late 1918. Commonly used by balloon observers since 1915, parachutes appeared in German aircraft two years later.

[Thomsen] for aviation, captive balloons, Army airships and the Army Weather Service, as well as the *Flak* and home defence units'.[13] The only German aviation units not under von Hoeppner's command were the naval airships and aircraft and, of course, the Bavarian air units. As their part in the '*Hindenburgprogramm*', the Bavarians did agree to follow the nomenclature and command structure changes initiated by *General* von Hoeppner.[14]

Aided by *Oberstleutnant* Thomsen, who remained an important presence in the *Luftstreitkräfte*, von Hoeppner proceeded to expand some units, and reassign or consolidate others. He eliminated the *Feldflieger-Abteilungen* and renumbered and redesignated 48 of the old units as long-range reconnaissance *Flieger-Abteilungen*; the other 30 units were redesignated and joined the existing *Artillerie-Flieger-Abteilungen* in performing artillery ranging and infantry support missions. The *Kagohls* were reduced to three (as noted in Chapter 4), and the remaining *Kastas* joined the new *Schutzstaffeln* being organized to protect other two-seater units. The *Jagdstaffeln* were increased to 30 in number, just in time to prepare for the events of April 1917 – called 'Bloody April' by the British in view of the heavy casualties they suffered during that four-week period (see Chapter 6).

Following the United States' declaration of war on the Central Powers on 6 April 1917, an '*Amerikaprogramm*' was begun to achieve a decisive German victory in France before the intervention of US forces could affect the outcome of the war. To bolster the *Luftstreitkräfte*, plans called for aircraft and aircrews to be furnished for seventeen new *Artillerie-Flieger-Abteilungen* and 40 new *Jagdstaffeln*. Meanwhile, the initial success of the three *Kagohls* – especially *KG 3*, which began daytime raids on London and other targets in Britain – led *General* Ludendorff to push for more bombing units. At the same time, the *Kogenluft* staff favoured

▶ As Germany began to run low on supplies and equipment near the end of the war, aircraft were often cannibalized for spare parts. An example is this Albatros B IIa trainer. The right half of the top wing bears the older Cross Patée national marking, while the left half has the late 1918 Greek cross design; both ailerons are decorated with yet another insignia variation.

◀ After the war old aircraft and even old flying suits were put to good use. Here a passenger clad in an observer's heavy suit and crash helmet climbs into an LVG C VI of the new airline *Deutsche Luft-Reederei*, whose logo (DLR) and post-horn insignia of airmail service join the original military insignia on the fuselage.

the proposed increase in the number of *Jagdstaffeln*. A compromise of sorts was reached when the existing *Kastas* were reallocated (except for *Kagohl 3*, which kept its six *Kastas*) and a total of seven bombing units was obtained, followed by an eighth, all-Bavarian, bombing *Geschwader*. Plans for the new *Jagdstaffeln* proceeded.

The British breakthrough at Wytschaete in June 1917 was a clear sign of the coming offensive in Flanders. That area was not only host to *Kagohl 3* and other bombing units, but was also the German Navy's entrance to the Channel. Submarine pens at Bruges, the port at Zeebrugge and other installations were defended by naval artillery, as well as by a concentration of German naval air units (covered in Chapter 5). As far as possible, German Army and Navy air units in Flanders were co-ordinated. For example, the *Kommandeur der Flieger der 4. Armee* (Staff Officer in Charge of Aviation for the 4th Army) routinely reported joint operations to the *OHL*.

To counter the British threat, *Kogenluft* began concentrating his air units so that they equalled those of their numerically superior adversaries. *Jagdgeschwader I*, the first fighter wing, was formed on 26 June and brought together *Jagdstaffeln 4, 6, 10* and *11* under the command of the *Luftstreitkräfte*'s most celebrated fighter ace, *Rittmeister* Manfred *Freiherr* von Richthofen.[16]

While much progress was made on the '*Amerika-programm*', not all of the ambitious goals were reached. Only one new *Artillerie-Flieger-Abteilung* was established, but 36 existing units received additional aircraft (for a total of nine each) and ten *Flieger-Abteilungen* were provided with special cameras to provide 'mosaic' photo maps that proved superior to previous single-shot photo-reconnaissance efforts. Reflecting Germany's success in concluding her war with Russia, seven *Flieger-Abteilungen* were transferred from that theatre to the Western Front. The *Jagdstaffeln* met their goal, with 81 units ready for the Spring 1918 offensive, all but two of them assigned to the Western Front. *Jasta* organization was further strengthened by the formation of *Jagdgeschwaders II* and *III*, each with four *Jastas*.[17]

The Germans' Spring 1918 offensive, set for 1 March, got under way at 0440 hours on 21 March. The objective was for the *7., 2.* and *18. Armees* to break through the British Front at the Somme from Arras to La Fere and drive to the sea, thereby splitting the British and French forces. Despite initial air and ground successes, the assault failed. A second offensive by the *4.* and *6. Armees* in Flanders on 9 April also failed, as did the Aisne offensive by the *1.* and *7. Armees* begun on 27 May. Fourth and fifth drives were also fruitless.

The German air units fought valiantly in all these actions. Above the fray, the *Jastas* began using the outstanding Fokker D VII fighter in May; closer to the ground, *Schlachtstaffeln* (Battle Squadrons) and special armour-protected *Infanteriefliegerdienst* (Infantry Co-operation) aircraft kept the heat on Allied ground forces. Strategic bombing of enemy

capitals was abandoned by the twin-engined bombers, whose units were now called *Bogohls*, and they supported the ground actions in France and Belgium.

By mid-summer, time, material and manpower were running out for the German *Luftstreitkräfte*. The arrival of American airmen and squadrons generated fresh enthusiasm among the war-weary Allies and put additional pressure on German squadron commanders. Added to this was the successful Allied naval blockade, which hindered the delivery of essential raw materials to Germany, thereby exacerbating already hard conditions on the home front. Shortages of petrol and rubber were typical of the supply breakdown that began to affect German air units at the Front. Thus, the Allied counter-attack on 8 August – called 'the black day of the German Army' by General Ludendorff – heralded the beginning of the collapse of the German war effort.

The worldwide influenza epidemic affected soldiers on both sides of the lines, but to the already demoralized German forces, it only added to supply deficiencies and a general disenchantment with the war that finally ended in an armistice at 1100 hours on 11 November 1918.

The absence of a truly decisive victory over the *Luftstreitkräfte* and other German forces led to the myth that they had not been beaten militarily; rather, that they had been 'sold out' by war profiteers and politicians. Indeed, one of the sources for this book is a 1923 volume boldly entitled *In der Luft unbesiegt* ('Unvanquished in the Air'), an anthology of first-hand accounts of stirring deeds by men still convinced of the righteousness of their cause.

Wilhelm Siegert, an *Oberstleutnant* by war's end, wrote shortly afterwards:

> 'Only fliers, airships and submarines had to disappear completely from the sky and from the sea. But no one can tear from our minds and hearts the worthy memory of the creators of the organization, as well as the building of our military aviation and the personalities who carried out the work with their souls and blood.'[18]

The creators of Germany's post-war aviation industry were imbued with a similar spirit and translated it into good works of commerce. Others flew or maintained an interest in flying with a view to the day when a *second* German air force would take to the skies.

I
'PIGEONS' IN COMBAT

IMPERIAL GERMANY entered World War I almost evenly matched with her principal opponents in deployed aircraft. Britain's 48 aircraft and France's 136 faced 180 German aircraft along the Western Front.[1] But the numbers became unimportant when Germany lost the air initiative to the *Entente* forces, which quickly used the new air weapon to go beyond the front-lines and strike the German homeland. On 23 August 1914 French airmen dropped bombs on Müllheim in the Grand Duchy of Baden in south-western Germany.[2] In response, less than a week later *Leutnant* (Second Lieutenant) Ferdinand von Hiddessen, a noted pre-war flier, flew over Paris in an LVG B I and dropped leaflets proclaiming:

'The German Army stands before the gates of Paris. There is no choice but to surrender. /s/ *Leutnant* von Hiddessen.'[3]

While the leaflets were not taken seriously, the 3-kilogramme bombs he dropped caused consider-able concern. Consequently, more raids were launched against Germany and, despite the greater distance involved, the Germans stepped up their efforts to bomb British and French cities. *Ltn* Karl Caspar became a hero after his Christmas Eve 1914 flight in a Gotha-built Taube to Dover, where he dropped what is considered to be the first German aerial bomb to fall on Britain.[4]

The German *Oberste Heeresleitung* (High Command) knew, however, that these sporadic incidents could not achieve a major strategic effect that would lead to a German victory. The objective and the initial means to achieve it were described by *General der Kavallerie* Ernst von Hoeppner, commanding general of the *Luftstreitkräfte*:

'From the beginning [of the war] we sought to increase the effect of our bombing attacks on a target through the combination of several aircraft and, indeed, several *Flieger-Abteilungen* [Flying Sections = squadrons]. This idea of a combined effect was also based on the creation of the first

▶ *Hauptmann* Musset, Commanding Officer of *Feldflieger-Abteilung 9* (left), congratulates *Ltn* Karl Casper after his successful raid on Dover in a Gotha Taube. Casper's one bomb exploded harmlessly in a garden, but he proved that England could be reached by a bomb-laden aircraft.

Flieger-Geschwader [Bombing Group] of the *OHL*. Its cover name *"Brieftauben-Abteilung Ostende"* ["Carrier Pigeon Section at Ostende"] later was changed to its more commonly used designation. Under the command of *Major* [Wilhelm] Siegert, who in peacetime had been a pioneering force for the new air arm, in November 1914 the *Brieftauben-Abteilung* was assembled at Ghistelles near Ostende with a strength of about [four] *Flieger-Abteilungen*. With the advance of the operations of the German Army's right flank, it was supposed to move on to Calais and from there to carry out vigorous bombing attacks against England. When our assault in Flanders was halted, Ostende was taken [and held by the British]. Accordingly, attacks against the central portions of British war industries had to be abandoned because of the great distances; they could be carried out only later with substantially improved aircraft.'[5]

The *Brieftauben-Abteilung Ostende* was conceived by *Major* Siegert, a former infantry officer who learned to fly at the age of 38 with aviation pioneer Hans Grade and who earned *Deutscher Luftfahrer-Verband* (German Air Travellers' Association) licence No 310 in 1912. His extensive pre-war credentials and recent memo on the need for the strategic deployment of an *'Englandgeschwader'* led to his 19 October appointment as adviser to the *OHL* on matters pertaining to military aviation. He proposed that, while each *Armee* directed its own aviation units, there should be a large air unit responsible to the *OHL*, just as the airship fleet was at the disposal of the Navy High Command. Consequently, the *Fliegerkorps der Obersten Heeresleitung* was formed and numbered among its mem-

bers some of the best German military pilots and observers. Siegert was given command of the unit, which was then given an ineffective cover name to mask its true purpose.

Ltn Andre Hug was a pilot with *Feldflieger-Abteilung 26*, attached to the German *7. Armee* near the Vosges mountains in November 1914, when the call came for pilots and observers to volunteer for a confidential assignment. Every army has its own grapevine of unofficial information and, from what Hug heard, the new unit was to be a massive bomber force to strike targets in Britain. The idea appealed to Hug and his observer, *Ltn* Bremer. By the time they joined the *BAO* at Ghistelles, 36 single hangars had been erected to house the variety of aircraft that *Major* Siegert had been able to obtain. Siegert was immensely popular in the *Fliegertruppe* and had little trouble obtaining what he needed for the *BAO*.

To preserve secrecy about the unit, Hug remembered, the aircraft arrived at night and were put into the hangars quickly. Construction of a wooden runway, which could be put down or removed within a few days, gave the unit a sturdy operating platform that could be transported when the unit got closer to its intended launch point. Hug recalled:

'In December 1914 the 31 pilots and 13 observers who had volunteered for the *Brieftauben-Abteilung Ostende* were ordered to the completed airfield. Every pilot had the opportunity to request the type of aircraft that he liked best, such as Albatros, LVG or Aviatik . . .

◀ *Ltn* Andre Hug, in the pilot's cockpit (rear) of an early Albatros assigned to *Feldfl-Abt 26*, and his observer, *Ltn* Bremer, were among numerous aircrews who carried talismans with them. In this case it is the small doll attached to a wire ahead of Bremer's cockpit.

'The . . . [living] accommodation and food [were] in a huge train, which travelled every night, to avoid bombing, to a small railway station some miles away. In the daytime the train returned to the airfield.

'For reasons of security, the mailing address of our new unit was *Brieftauben-Abteilung "O"*, Cologne, Germany. Once a week the outgoing mail of the *Abteilung* was brought to Cologne. One time when I performed this duty, a Cologne post office employee said to me: "You have carrier pigeons. At one time I had been a carrier pigeon corporal in the Army. What does one do today in a war with such pigeons?" I could only tell him what I had once heard about these birds – that they still carry messages in very light, small capsules fastened to [a] leg, and that they were released to their home station. Then I quickly said goodbye before he could ask further questions.'[6]

Provided by a variety of manufacturers, the two-seat aircraft were B-type machines, in which the observer sat in the front cockpit and the pilot in the rear. Andre Hug noted that 'every second or third plane of the *Abteilung* had an observer who was charged with the protection of one other plane that carried no observer. Instead of using automatic pistols and infantry rifles, the observer now carried a Mauser automatic rifle. Every pilot carried two [10kg to 15kg] bombs in his cockpit; the observer . . . carried six more bombs.'[7]

GERMANY'S BOMBER PIONEERS

Major Siegert noted that the 'war diaries of the old *"Brieftauben-Abteilung O"* got lost in November 1918,' but he was able to reconstruct a partial *Abteilung* roster from the menu of a *Kaiser*'s birthday party celebration for 26 January 1915.[8] As expanded and annotated by the author, the following list contains an array of luminaries from bombing, reconnaissance and fighter units that evolved from the *BAO*:

Ltn Leo Pfeifer, *DLV* licence No 303, 9 October 1912.

Ltn Fritz Müller, von Hiddessen's observer; first *BAO* death in combat.

Ltn Egloff *Freiherr* von Freyberg, *DLV* No 355, 24 January 1913.

Ltn Ferdinand von Hiddessen, *DLV* No 47, 17 January 1911.

Ltn Alfred Linke, *DLV* No 332, 23 November 1912.

Ltn Emil Clemens, *DLV* No 435, 17 June 1913.

Ltn Dr Kurt Wegener, *DLV* No 796, 22 June 1914, later leader of *Kampfstaffel 18* of *Kagohl 3*.

Ltn Otto Parschau, *DLV* No 455, 4 July 1913, later fighter ace and recipient of the *Orden Pour le Mérite*.

Ltn Seehagen.

Obltn Hans-Ulrich von Trotha, *DLV* No 243, 20 June 1912, later flight leader in *Kagohls 1* and *3*.

▼ Two Bavarian aristocrats – *Obltn* Hans *Reichsfreiherr* Haller von Hallerstein and *Rittmeister* Hans *Freiherr* von Könitz – showed regional preference in their choice of aircraft. They flew this Otto Type B produced by the Flugzeugwerke Gustav Otto in Munich.

◀ The *BAO*'s airfield at Ghistelles, not far from the Flanders coast, was easily spotted by Allied bombers. By the time this photo was taken in May 1916, the several bomb hits in adjoining fields testified to the Allies' interest – but not to their bombing accuracy.

Ltn von Viebahn.

Obltn Fritz Prestien, later leader of *Kasta 7* of *Kagohl 2*.

Obltn Hans *Reichsfreiherr* Haller von Hallerstein, later active in development of R-class giant bombers.

Ltn Gravenstein, pre-war observer with pioneer Hellmuth Hirth.

Rittmeister Hans *Freiherr* von Könitz, later commander of an R-class aircraft support section.

Ltn Fritz von Falkenhayn, early observer, then pilot.

Ltn Hugo Geyer, *DLV* No 276, 23 August 1912, later commander of *Bomben-Geschawader der OHL 4*.

Ltn Held.

Ltn Kuhn, Geyer's observer in the *BAO*.

Ltn Hell.

Ltn Schwarzenberger.

Obltn Claes, designated military pilot 28 September 1913, later *Stabsoffizier der Flieger, 5. Armee*.

Obltn Hermann Gustav Kastner-Kirdorf, later commander of the *BAO*, the *BAM* and *Kampfgeschwader der OHL 1*.

Ltn Andre Hug, *FAI* licence No 568, 17 October 1913.

Obltn Fritz Groebedinkel.

Ltn Erich Bonde, *DLV* No 419, 27 May 1913.

Ltn Wilhelm *Freiherr* von Ledebur.

Ltn Kurt *'Locken'* ('Curly') Müller.

Ltn Bremer, *Ltn* Hug's observer.

Ltn Paul Henning von Osterroht, *DLV* No 305, 9 October 1912, later Commanding Officer of *Jagdstaffel 12*.

Ltn von Liebermann.

Obltn Wilhelm Emmerich.

Obltn Heinrich von Blanc.

Ltn Wilhelm Blume, *DLV* No 212, 24 May 1912.

Ltn Stenzel, *Major* Siegert's observer.

Ltn Adami.

Ltn Carl Fink, observer.

Ltn Karl Ingold, *DLV* No 114, 13 September 1911.

Obltn Percy *Baron* von Ascheberg, one of the German Army's first nine artillery observers.

Ltn Engwer, von Freyberg's observer.

Obltn Georg Zeumer, later pilot for Manfred von Richthofen (as observer) and then fighter pilot with *Jasta 2*.

Initially, *Major* Siegert planned daylight raids on the targets in Flanders that his assortment of aircraft could reach from Ghistelles. As he later wrote:

'Although we had to rely on 100hp engines against the 160hp [engines] of the British and French, and had to fight with completely inadequate hand-held weapons against machine-guns, in December and January we succeeded in carrying out four major daytime operations against Dunkirk, Nieuport, Furnes and La Panne.'[9]

AIR RAIDS ON DUNKIRK

The operations were not without hazard. During the twelve-aircraft *BAO* raid of 22 January 1915, a mixed flight of British, Belgian and French Maurice Farman MF.11 'pushers' (whose observers were armed with rifles) engaged the German bombers during their run over Dunkirk. Two MF.11s of No 4 Squadron, Royal Flying Corps, closed in on an Albatros and either Captain F. V. Holt or Lieutenant R. P. Mills got off the shot that disabled the Germans' engine.[10] The Albatros landed intact and was taken back to a British aerodrome for examination.

The Albatros B I pilot, *Ltn* Andre Hug, recalled the incident:

'I was attacked from behind by an English plane [while we were still] over the English Channel. After firing two rounds of ammunition at the attacker, Bremer's Mauser automatic rifle jammed. While Bremer tried to clear the stoppage, I fired backwards at the Englishman with my pistol. The English plane shot my engine . . . it grumbled . . . and then finally stopped. Gliding down from 4,000 feet, I could barely reach the dunes of the French coast. To make my plane unserviceable, I let it drop down some yards. Instead of landing smoothly, the plane landed with a crash. Bremer and I were unhurt.

'. . . the English craft that shot at me from behind was a type with which I was not familiar . . . But I realized that his armament consisted of a machine-gun. When I was taken into custody in a prisoner of war camp, the English pilot visited me and asked me to surrender to him my right flying glove, but I refused.'[11]

The loss of Hug and Bremer, as well as the high level of combat damage sustained by the other aircraft, demonstrated to Siegert that his older, underpowered aircraft were too vulnerable during daytime operations. The obvious answer was to fly at night. Siegert later wrote:

◀ The forward-firing machine-gun in Maurice Farman biplanes, such as this F.40, made the French aircraft formidable opponents of the *BAO*, whch had only rearward-firing guns until 1916.

▲ *Major* Hermann von der Lieth-Thomsen (seated left) was well qualified to become *Chef des Flugfeldwesens* on 11 March 1915. Five years earlier, he and *General* Erich Ludendorff had become the first General Staff officers to fly and both recognized the value of aviation. Thomsen was ably assisted by his deputy, *Major* Siegert, seated next to him. Thomsen's leadership and organizational skills were recognized on 8 April 1917 when he received the *Orden Pour le Mérite.*

'The night of 28/29 January 1915 offered favourable meteorological conditions for an attack on Dunkirk. At the rising of the moon, fourteen aircraft of different types were ready, among them the [crew of] Haller von Hallerstein and von Könitz [in an] Otto biplane, an antediluvian apparatus with a pusher engine. During the day the enemy took it for a Farman and left it alone; however, it was a welcome centre of attraction for our own anti-aircraft guns. Despite that, the daring crew remained faithful to their archaeopteryx.

'Light clouds, a cutting gusty east wind. At 2110 hours, I sat – with [*Obltn* Claus] Hempel at the controls – in a 100hp Aviatik biplane in the lead of our small *Geschwader*. We had a combined total of 123 bombs. First we flew in the direction of Ostende; it was recognizable by the vertical beam of its Bamag beacon. Then about a kilometre out to sea: destination Dunkirk. Altitude 1,000 metres, the thermometer showed 25 degrees Celsius.

'The view of Nieuport that emerged in flight made us completely forget our frozen ears, which had meanwhile become brittle as glass, as well as the war and all its noise. The moon illuminated the surf of the North Sea; flames blazed at a factory near Firmeny, the artillery firing on both sides looked like chains of glowing beads, hundreds of thousands of balls of light of all colours were like dancing pearls in black champagne. Between them our star shells to signal our own artillery: "Good people, don't shoot" – and then the countless searchlights.'[12]

Siegert was shaken out of his reverie by an explosion nearby. An engine malfunction? No, Hempel assured him, 'merely' a shell exploding close by. Then they came to Dunkirk, which was ringed by searchlights. Siegert wrote:

'Into this black cone poured the field-grey clumps of iron, each hit as recognizable as lightning as a good shot . . . All the bombs reached the target, none fell on to the wings of one of the aircraft flying below and behind us. And the possibility of that was great.'[13]

Despite a brief moment of disorientation in dense fog that sent them out to sea, the *BAO* flight returned to Ghistelles without loss. On their return petrol-soaked logs were lit and every one of the mixed bag of aircraft – including the Otto Type B 'pusher,' Aviatik B I, Albatros B I and even two-seat Taube aircraft – received a warm welcome.

AIR OPERATIONS OVER VERDUN

Confronted by increasingly superior Entente air units, in late January the *BAO* left Ghistelles. The train used for living quarters transported the personnel, while the aircraft flew on ahead to their new airfield at Metz, in German-occupied Lorraine, near the (then) quieter Verdun Front.

Shortly afterwards, Ghistelles airfield received a warm reaction from British 10cm artillery guns brought up specifically to hit the *BAO* hangars and facilities. On 16 February British air efforts against German naval facilities at Zeebrugge were supported by eight French bombers which attacked Ghistelles.[14]

'It is peculiar that for retaliatory fire one would waste so much gunpowder [Sieger later wrote]. By then we had long since honoured the "open city of Verdun" with our night-time visits, when our harmless 'field at Ghistelles had gone to seed where only a few unserviceable wagons stood in place of our nice train and sleeping cars.'[15]

From their base at Metz, the *Abteilung* also interdicted French aircraft based in the Nancy-Luneville area that were going after targets in the German homeland, and there the unit suffered a prominent loss. On 10 February 1915 the popular *Ltn* Ferdinand von Hiddessen and his observer, *Ltn d Res* Fritz Müller, escaped an attack by French aircraft of *Groupe de Bombardement 1* only to be shot down by anti-aircraft fire over French lines. The pilot was uninjured, but Müller subsequently died of his wounds.

AERIAL MACHINE-GUN DEVELOPMENT

Desperate to improve his crews' defence, *Major* Siegert despatched *Ltn* Hugo Geyer to Berlin to find a machine-gun that could be fitted to the Aviatik B Is coming to the unit. Geyer located a Parabellum 1MG 08 7.92mm gun which weighed only 9.5kg, but he had difficulty in finding a way to have it mounted. At length engineers and mechanics at the Aviatik factory in Freiburg im Breisgau added two gun posts, one left front and the other right rear of the observer's (forward) cockpit, and expanded the outside area for more freedom of movement. It was soon demonstrated that, with practice, an observer could climb up out of his seat, kneel on a platform atop the fuel tank and operate the gun, moving it from one post to the other to defend the aircraft. A guard barrier was added forward of the positions to keep the observer from inadvertently firing into his own propeller arc.

Geyer hastened back to the *BAO* to explain the gun's operation to his observer, *Ltn* Kuhn, and try it. Geyer described their first flight in an Aviatik with the new weapon:

> 'At Hartmannsweilerkopf, on the southern slope of the Vosges mountains, appeared propitiously a French Farman, which attacked us confident of victory with the machine-gun mounted on the front of its cockpit nacelle. We let the opponent get somewhat close to us and, as he shot his first series of 25 rounds at us, he received from my "Franz" a burst of 50 shots. That was obviously so surprising that at first the pilot pulled up on the control column in bewilderment and then "pushed over" as far as he could in a steep dive to escape from this monster which was no longer easy prey.'[16]

This next step in bomber evolution – the addition of flexible machine-gun defence – was added to other *Abteilung* aircraft quickly. Indeed, in addition to its role in individual aircraft defence, the new flexible machine-gun allowed the *BAO* and other groups of aircraft to equip at least one aircraft in the formation solely to ward off attackers in the air. At the time it was the only way to keep 'pusher' aircraft from dominating the skies with a forward field of fire ideal for offensive tactics. Moreover, this capability allowed the *BAO* aircraft to be used for *Sperreflüge* (barrier flights) to prevent an enemy from flying over the German lines.

Hardly settled in at Metz, the *Abteilung* had to pack up and return by rail and air to Ghistelles for what was to be a combined aircraft and airship raid on England, which never took place.[17] From there the *BAO* was ordered to Russia to support Hindenburg's spring offensive there.

In March *Major* Siegert relinquished command to *Hptmn* Hermann Gustav Kastner-Kirdorf and returned to Berlin for an important staff position. Siegert had earlier proposed the creation of the post of *Chef des Feldflugwesens* (Chief of Field Aviation) – abbreviated *Feldflugchef* – to be responsible for all aspects of aerial warfare, as well as equipping and arming the air units. The *Feldflugchef* would direct these matters to the *OHL* and the War Ministry. When the post was filled by the very able administrator *Major* Hermann von der Lieth-Thomsen, Siegert was appointed to the staff as Thomsen's deputy. Also reporting to Thomsen's staff were the two Army inspectorates – *Iluft* for airships and *Idflieg* for heavier-than-air aviation – as well as the front-line Army airships, all the *Feldluftschiffer* (observation balloons) and aviation formations; all aviation supply organizations within Germany also came under the *Feldflugchef*. While Thomsen's staff was responsible for the supply and assignment of the front-line aviation units, they continued to be deployed operationally by the *OHL* or by the Army and Corps Headquarters.

BOMBING ROLE REFINED IN RUSSIA

The *BAO* continued to bear its inappropriate designation when it arrived in Allenstein-Deuten, East Prussia, to support ground units engaged in the massive Eastern Front offensive. A prominent pre-war flier in the unit, *Obltn* Victor Carganico, noted that the unit was now becoming better known as the '*Bombenabwurf-Abteilung der OHL*' (Bomb-Dropping Section of the *OHL*), which also could be abbreviated *BAO*.[18]

From Allenstein (now Olszytn, Poland), north-west of Warsaw, the *BAO* carried out several raids against Russian targets to the east in the German *8. Armee* sector. The *Abteilung*'s bombing role was further refined when its aircraft were divided into three sections, each responsible for a component of the mission as follows: '*Sprengkommando*' (blast detachment), using heavy or light bombs against fixed or mobile defensible ground targets; '*Brandkommando*' (flame detachment), attacking stationary targets vulnerable to fire; and '*Feuerlöschkommando*' (fire-fighting detachment), which made follow-up raids against enemy fire-fighters coping with damage previously caused by the *Brandkommandos*.

Obltn Carganico and his observer, *Obltn* Oskar Knofe, undertook the unit's final mission from Allenstein on 20 April 1915. With fuel for a five-hour flight and carrying 70kg of bombs, they attacked Bialystok, an important railhead, and left the target burning brightly.

Two days later *BAO* aircraft were dismantled, put on railway cars and shipped south to an airfield at Czyzyny, near Krakow, on the Galician Front. The same train included the unit's living quarters, now a common feature of the unit, as noted by Carganico:

> 'Two German dining-cars served as a common *Kasino* [messing facility]. Some Belgian sleeping-cars were appropriately fitted out for the aircrews. Each pilot and observer – "Emil" and "Franz" – had his own washing, sleeping and living space, which altogether was about the size of a servant's quarters. When one sat there, one could feel really cosy, as if in a little doll's house room. When a man

◀ Pre-war flier Victor Carganico, seen here in Albatros MZ 2/1911 of *Fliegerbataillon 4*, was continually in action during the *BAO*'s first tour of duty on the Russian Front. Later he was appointed commander of *Kampfstaffel 8* of *Kagohl 2*, whose members included (then) *Ltn* Manfred *Freiherr* von Richthofen.

returned from a flight, he always had his nice and quiet comfort and his cosy resting place. At the same time, in this way we were always ready to strike and could at any moment – as combat troops of the *Oberste Heeresleitung* – be thrown into any Front wherever [we were needed]. Furthermore, we could go by air under immediate orders to a new front against the enemy, while our living-quarters train rolled after us and, at the latest, had our cosy home ready for us that evening.'[19]

In this instance the *BAO*'s mobility fitted the *OHL*'s plan perfectly. A massively superior aerial

reconnaissance and bombing force could be used in conjunction with the German *11. Armee*'s assault on Gorlice to surprise and overwhelm Russian forces and thereby punch a huge hole in a long thin line on that front. The *kuk* (Austro-Hungarian) *1.* and *4. Armees* to the north of the *11. Armee* and the *kuk 2.* and *3. Armees* to the south could then push forward deep into the Ukraine.

Recently the *BAO* had begun receiving the somewhat smaller but much improved LVG B II and had used these aircraft with great success during the opening of the *11. Armee*'s offensive. At

▶ If nothing else, the *BAO* travelled in style. Veteran bomber crews confirmed for the author that this dining-car scene, including the well-stocked wine tray, was typical of train accommodation provided for the officers. The men had more modest facilities.

0430 hours on 29 April, Carganico and Knofe took off as part of a large flight that went some 35 kilometres behind enemy lines to Jaroslau, site of an important Russian headquarters. Flying at an altitude of 1,600 metres and each carrying 45kg of bombs, the German aircraft hit every important point in the city. By the end of the day 1,000kg of bombs had been dropped and made such an impression on the Russians that the headquarters command was withdrawn hastily.

The following day an early morning aerial assault was launched against Debica, east of Tarnow, which was being attacked by the *kuk 4. Armee*. Again, the combination of ground and air attacks greatly undermined Russian morale and defensive capability.

On Sunday, 2 May the *BAO* participated in a joint action that had a devastating effect on the Russians. A massive artillery barrage was begun late on Saturday evening and continued into the early dawn. Rear area batteries, depots, headquarters buildings and even troops being moved back came under fierce attacks. Then there was a short pause and a flood of German and Austro-Hungarian troops swept over the lines. *BAO* aircraft flew ahead of the infantry, pounding targets along the way. They encountered virtually no resistance. Carganico later wrote:

'We flew over the lines at 1,600 metres. One saw the frightful job that our shells and shrapnel had done, as one shell hole after another had been opened in a burst of fire and a fountain of earth showering around them. Mixed with that sight was the smoke of numerous colossal fires in villages and in the vast forests, surpassed in thickness and unearthly blackness only by the smoke of the numerous crude oil drilling towers near Gorlice. The dense smoke rose to 1,500 metres. Impenetrable in the form of a great column, it reached high up and at the previously noted altitude it sat there like a plate on a table of tremendous expanse. Far below were furious waves of little groups, big groups and masses of retreating Russians in whose midst were repeated explosions and high-rising fountains of earth, the gruesome work of our artillery.'[20]

The *BAO* flight continued on to Jaroslau to drop its murderous load on columns of soldiers and vehicles beyond the reach of artillery. By the end of the day, troops of the *kuk VI. Armeekorps*, which had directly followed the aircraft, had made great advances and had consolidated the Central Powers at noteworthy points eastward. After repeated joint attacks, by the evening 6 May the former Russian positions at Dukla, Jasiolka, Jaroslau and Tarnow had fallen to Austro-Hungarian forces.

The situation was so secure that on 7 May Carganico and Knofe were sent up in an old Albatros 'hack' aircraft to inspect the *BAO*'s proposed new airfield at Tarnow.

Less than a week later, however, the German bomber crews received a grim reminder of the dangers they faced. The *BAO* crew of *Obltns* Wilhelm Emmerich and Erich Leonhardt were shot down, most likely by ground fire.

'Later, during the further advance, Emmerich was found dead and stripped of everything in an abandoned Russian dug-out; the burned-out aircraft lay between the former German and Russian lines and in among the wires of the machine hung the charred body of poor Leonhardt. What is more, it was said that they were tortured to death and then their heads were cut off.'[21]

The success of the Central Powers' offensive led to such an increased demand for air power that the *BAO* began to disintegrate. With demands for air support from many commands, *Abteilungs-Führer* Kastner-Kirdorf had to parcel out aircraft and crews leading to the creation of two new units, *Feldflieger-Abteilungen 66* and *69* – even though that defeated the purpose of the concentrated bombing unit.[22] *Obltns* Carganico and Knofe were temporarily assigned to the *41. Reservekorps* commanded by *General* von Francois, whose experience during the Battle of Tannenberg convinced him of the usefulness of air power. Based on that experience, on 27 May he ordered the aircrew to reconnoitre the area around Przemysl, the major obstacle between *General* August von Mackensen's *11. Armee* and Lemberg (now the Ukrainian city of Lvov). Russian batteries, which had not betrayed their positions previously, opened up when the LVG flew over. Climbing from 1,000 to 2,400 metres, Carganico and Knofe were well out of the guns' range, but noted their positions so that German batteries could deal with them.

During the next few days, *General* von Francois' one-aircraft 'air force' reconnoitred and bombed Russian installations near Przemsyl. The lone LVG encountered no resistance and provided great assistance to the ground forces. Consequently, on 3 June, a massive barrage of Austro-Hungarian heavy mortar fire drove the last Russian troops from Przemsyl.

A few days later a rare event took place. In the early morning hours a Russian bomber – identified by the Germans as a Sikorsky 'Giant Aeroplane' – appeared over Jaroslau and dropped some bombs. For the next few mornings, *BAO* aircrews were kitted up and on the flight line, waiting for word that the interloper had returned. Visions of aerial victories tantalized the crews, but to no avail. It was later learned that the big Sikorsky had crashed on returning from its first mission.

The combined force of the remnants of the *BAO* was employed during the final push toward Lemberg, which fell on 22 June. During the course of the campaign, however, the *Abteilung* was steadily diminished. Since going into action in December 1914, the *BAO* had lost nine of its original complement of 60 officers in combat and, largely during the Galician campaign, some 30 officers had been sent to other units, where their fund of experience

◀ **During airfield changes, most** *BAO* **(and later** *Kagohl*) **aircraft were flown to the new locations. Smaller aircraft,** **such as this Albatros B IIa, were transported by rail at the same time as the ground crews were moved.**

was badly needed.[23] Only 20 original *BAO* officers were with the unit when, on 18 June, *General* von Mackensen hosted a celebration in anticipation of his imminent victory at Lemberg.

Newly promoted *Hauptmann* (Captain) Carganico recalled the end of the campaign:

'On 26 June our last combat flight in Galicia was launched. As far as the weather conditions went, they were the most unpleasant during the entire Galician campaign. It involved only a low-level reconnaissance and even for that the weather was bad enough. We took off in fog, then slipped between fog, rain, clouds and here and there a brief glimpse of the ground during 40 minutes over the Russian front-line at 100 to 900 metres altitude. Apparently, that was so unexpected by the Russians that we again came back without a single hit on the aircraft. It really was "fliers' weather". At times we simply flew blind, as during the many turns the compass could not settle down and was therefore useless. We managed to get our bearings more by luck than by reasoning. As, by luck, we reached our home 'field, there was a thick fog there and first we had to make an emergency landing away from the 'field at the first fog-free area and then set out again. But it worked out. With luck and patience we spied through an opening in the fog a clear spot at the 'field. We whistled through it with the wind at our backs and landed. Then the curtain was drawn shut and we stuck in the fog again.'[24]

A few days later the *Brieftauben-Abteilung Ostende* was packed on to its railway wagons and sent westwards to Ostende to resume its original purpose as a mobile reconnaissance and bombing unit. Most of the LVGs were sent to training schools, which typically used hand-me-down former front-line aircraft. They were replaced by newer C-type reconnaissance and 'light' bombing machines, in which the observer sat in the rear cockpit and was thereby much better able to defend the aircraft. In addition, the *Abteilung* began operating an aircraft much more suited to the bombing role, the twin-engined AEG G II. This early '*Grosskampfflugzeug*' ('Big Combat Aircraft', hence the appellation G-type) offered more than superior performance; the observer/bomb-aimer sat in a protruding, forward cockpit called the '*Kanzel*'

(pulpit), ahead of the pilot, and so had the same forward-firing capability as the Farman.

SECOND 'CARRIER PIGEON' UNIT CREATED

Capitalizing on the experience of the *BAO*, a second *Fliegerkorps der OHL* – called the *Brieftauben-Abteilung Metz* – was established at Metz on 17 August 1915.[25] The *BAM* received a number of officers from the *BAO*, including its commander, *Hptmn* Kastner-Kirdorf, to ensure that the new unit had experienced leadership and aircrews. The new *Abteilungs-Führer* of the *BAO* was *Hptmn* Ernst *Freiherr* von Gersdorff, a pre-war flier (*DLV* licence No 356 on 24 January 1913) who had previously commanded *Feldfl-Abt 32*.

With the lessening of activity on the Russian Front, a stream of new flying personnel joined the *BAO*, including, on 21 August 1915, an observer who went on to become Imperial Germany's most successful fighter pilot: Manfred *Freiherr* von Richthofen. As a *Leutnant*, he had begun his flying career with *Feldfl-Abt 69* after its creation with a *BAO* nucleus in the *11. Armee* sector. Indeed, his first pilot had been an early *BAO* member, *Obltn* George Zeumer, one of the many *Abteilung* members detached to other units during the summer. Zeumer was nicknamed 'the black cat' because recklessness was sure to lead to disaster; he did, in fact, have tuberculosis and had no great expectations of a long life. Zeumer's devil-may-care attitude appealed to the young Silesian nobleman whose great ambitions would be realized through daring deeds.

RICHTHOFEN'S FIRST AERIAL COMBAT

When Richthofen arrived at Ostende, he and Zeumer renewed their partnership. They made an excellent team, Zeumer the skilled pilot and Richthofen a hunter and first-rate marksman. They flew together five or six hours a day, looking for the combat challenge that had eluded them in the east. Then, on 1 September, came the opportunity to test their combat skills in the AEG G II, which Manfred von Richthofen called 'a big apple barge'. They were out on a morning patrol when they encountered a Farman 'pusher' making a reconnaissance flight over German lines.

'My heart beat furiously as Zeumer approached him,' [Richthofen wrote later]. 'I was excited about what would happen. I had never seen an aerial combat and I had only a vague conception of it . . . Before I knew what was happening, both of us, the Englishman and ourselves, were rushing towards each other. I had got, at best, four shots off when the Englishman suddenly got behind us and shot the whole works at us. I must say I did not have the feeling of danger, because I could not really predict the final result of such a battle. We turned around each other time and again until, finally, to our great surprise, the Englishman turned away from us and flew off. I was greatly disappointed and so was my pilot.'[26]

In addition to having his first aerial combat in an AEG G II, Richthofen suffered his first combat wound in one of the big bombers. A few days later he and Zeumer were on a bombing mission in an AEG G II when the observer momentarily forgot about the danger of the big aircraft's two propellers on either side of his 'Kanzel.' In the ace's memoirs he wrote:

'We reached the target and dropped the first bombs. It is, naturally, very interesting to watch the results of such a mission. At least one likes to see the explosion. But my Grosskampfflugzeug, which was well-suited for carrying bombs, had a stupid peculiarity that made it hard to see the explosion of the bombs dropped; for, immediately after the drop, the aircraft moved over the target and covered it with its wings. This always made me angry, since one had so little fun because of it. When the bomb bursts below and one sees the lovely grey-white cloud of the explosion near the target, it is very pleasing. So I signalled to my good friend Zeumer to fly so that the wings were off to the side. In so doing I forgot that my infamous old barge had two propellers which turned right and left near my observer seat. I was showing him approximately where the bomb had hit and – smack! – one of my fingers had been hit. I was surprised at first, but Zeumer had noticed nothing . . . My love for the Grosskampfflugzeug, which at best had been weak, suffered seriously from this episode. I could not fly again for a week.'[27]

In mid-September most of the BAO was sent to the 3. Armee Front to support German Army units engaged in heavy fighting in the Champagne region. Abteilung aircraft were to provide aerial security by working with units in place on the Champagne Front. Thus, initially, four BAO C-type aircraft were joined with two Fokker Eindeckers and moved to Feldfl-Abt 22's airfield at Vouziers to cover the VIII Reserve-Korps sector.[28] Ultimately the BAO also provided two C-types to the X Armee-Korps and the

XII Reserve-Korps and, as a 3. Armee secret directive noted:

'The remainder of the BAO will be in readiness for special missions. Synchronized arrangements of the BAO and the Feldflieger-Abteilung for protecting the aircraft to be covered are required directly and without fail.'[29]

Preparation for the deployment occasioned a number of changes in the BAO. It gave Ltn von Richthofen an opportunity to fly in a smaller, more manoeuvrable C-type aircraft and to satisfy his growing desire for aerial combat. It also afforded two-seater pilots such as Georg Zeumer a chance to try their hand at the controls of the nimble Fokker monoplane fighters. To Zeumer the single-seat fighter was a better way to meet his destiny; he therefore devoted all his time to mastering the smaller, more manoeuvrable aeroplane, and left his friend to find a new flying partner.

Eventually Richthofen was assigned a mission with Obltn Paul Henning von Osterroht, a pre-war flier and an original BAO member. Osterroht, who went on to command Jagdstaffel 12, shared Richthofen's interest in aerial combat. Their flight in an Aviatik C I equipped with a Parabellum 7.9mm machine-gun, that could be moved from one mounting to another on either side of the observer's cockpit, was recorded in the 'Red Baron's' memoirs:

'About 5 kilometres behind the Front we approached a Farman two-seater. Osterroht calmly approached him, and for the first time I saw an opponent in the air within reasonable distance. Osterroht skilfully flew so close that I could easily bring him under fire. The enemy had not noticed us at all, for he did not begin to return fire until my gun jammed. I shot my cartridge case of a hundred rounds, and then I could hardly believe my eyes: suddenly the enemy aeroplane went down in a curious spiral. I followed it with my eyes and tapped Osterroht on the head. It fell and fell and then dropped into a huge bomb crater; we saw it standing upright, tail pointing to the sky. According to the map, it lay 5 kilometres behind the Front, on the other side of the lines. At that time aircraft shot down behind enemy lines did not count; otherwise, I should have one more on my victory list today. But I was very proud of my success, for the main thing is that a fellow is brought down, not that one is credited with doing it.'[30]

On 23 September a massive French artillery barrage along the Champagne Front initiated a three-day offensive designed to break through the German lines. Strong German counter-actions thwarted that plan, but, to be safe, more German units were called in. The *Brieftauben-Abteilung Metz*, still building to full strength, sent a detachment to the *6. Armee* Front in Flanders, even though the *BAO* was closer to that front. *Hptmn* Leo Leonhardy, commander of *Feldfl-Abt 25*, went to the Champagne Front with a *5. Armee* strengthened section of 22 aircraft and crews from his own unit, as well as *Feldfl-Abt 19* and the *BAM*. Adding to this large number of C-type combat aircraft opposing the French, elements of the *BAO* remaining in Ostende entrained for Rethel, some 30 kilometres north-east of Vouziers, on 1 October.

A VISITOR NAMED BOELCKE

Manfred von Richthofen, who participated in that deployment, later wrote about the aspect of the train ride to Rethel that changed his life:

'In the dining-car a young, unpretentious *Leutnant* sat at the table near mine. There was no reason to take special note of him except that, of all of us, he was the only one who had shot down an enemy and, indeed, not only one but four. He was even mentioned by name in the Army Reports. He impressed me because his experiences were quite exciting. Even though I had tried so hard, I had up to that point bagged none; in any case, I had not been credited with any. All too gladly I wanted to learn how this *Leutnant* [Oswald] Boelcke had really done it. So I asked the question: "Tell me honestly, how do you really do it?" He laughed in amusement, even though I had asked him quite seriously. Then he answered me: "Yes, good God, it is quite simple. I fly in as close as I can, take good aim, [and shoot and] then he falls down." I simply

shook my head and thought to myself that I had done the same thing, but [the adversary] had not simply fallen down. The difference surely was that he flew a Fokker and I flew my *Grosskampfflugzeug*.

'I took the trouble to get better acquainted with this nice, modest man who had impressed me so much. Often we played cards together and took walks [during which] I would question him. Thus within me blossomed the decision: "You must learn to fly a Fokker yourself and then perhaps things will be better." '[31]

The would-be ace persuaded Zeumer to teach him how to fly in one of the *Abteilung*'s old two-seaters used for training purposes and by 10 October Richthofen was ready for his first solo flight. He was safe in flying an unarmed aeroplane for a short course behind the lines. And all went well, except for the landing. Just as Richthofen touched down, the machine nosed over and ended up a wreck, to the amusement of the ground crew.

Richthofen persisted, however, and continued to fly when he was not involved in combat missions over the Front. As the German ground units recovered lost ground and had to regroup, he was less in demand for observation duties and was able to log more flight time. On 5 November the remainder of the *Brieftauben-Abteilung Metz* was ordered to be deployed with the *BAO* on the *3. Armee* Front, adding even more air strength to the area.[32] The French sustained heavy losses in the Champagne fighting and were forced to halt their attacks. Consequently, the *BAO* returned to Ghistelles and the *BAM* went back to Metz, both to carry out training programmes for newly arriving aircrews.

The *BAO* could easily give up one experienced observer and so Manfred von Richthofen's request

▶ The Albatros C I that the *BAO* received on its return to the Western Front proved to be among the best of the armed two-seaters. The Parabellum gun was ring-mounted to give the observer a good field of fire.

▶ *Unteroffizier* Paul Witte and the Rumpler C I that he flew with *Kagohl 1*. In 1916 the *Geschwader* used a combination of Roman and Arabic numerals to identify aircraft and their units. Under this system Witte's 'I.2' indicates that it was the second aircraft in *Kampfstaffel 1*.

for formal flight training was approved. On 15 November he was sent to the training unit *Flieger-Ersatz-Abteilung 2* at Döberitz. No doubt the thought was that he would return to the *BAO* as a pilot for its C-type or G-type aircraft and use his observer's knowledge in a broad way; for plans were already afoot to transform the inappropriately named 'Carrier Pigeon Sections,' each then equipped with 24 C-type aircraft, into an even stronger mobile strike force for bombing and air combat missions.

THE *KAGOHLS* EMERGE

On 1 December 1915 *Feldflugchef Major* von der Lieth-Thomsen ordered the establishment of two *Kampfgeschwader der OHL* (Combat Wings deployed at the discretion of the High Command) – identified by the acronym '*Kagohl*'. On 20 December the *BAO* became *Kagohl 1* and the *BAM* became *Kagohl 2*. With the thought of eventually having a separate aviation service – equal to the Army and Navy – Thomsen used this development as an organizational model of force deployment. Each *Kagohl* consisted of six *Kampfstaffeln* (Battle Squadrons) of six aircraft each, which could be deployed as units and still report to the *Geschwader-Kommandeur*, who was responsible through Thomsen to the *OHL*. Subsequently three additional *Kagohls* (each with six *Staffeln*) and six single *Staffeln* were formed. Clearly there was to be no repetition of the deployment during the Galician Campaign, when aircrews were detached as needed, thereby weakening the unit structure.

The formation of fourteen *Artillerie-Flieger-Abteilungen* in the latter part of 1915 also aided development of a dedicated bomber and aerial defence force. Assigned to artillery-ranging and reconnaissance duties, their presence freed the *Kagohls* to concentrate on bombing missions and *Sperreflüge* to ward off enemy aircraft.

A pilot new to *Kampfstaffel 10* of *Kagohl 2*, Ltn Erwin Böhme, commented on the slow pace of activity during the winter months in a letter dated 22 December 1915:

'I have not yet encountered the enemy. Here we are at the disposal of the *OHL* for special assignments and we have to restrain our courage. Our base at the moment is in Saarbrücken. Wonderful pictures arise up out of the landscape: the Vosges mountains, the Black Forest, [and] in clear weather the long Alpine chain – up there it is easy to forget that, down below, petty squabbling goes on . . .'33

From an airfield at Mörchingen, closer to the Front, Böhme wrote on 14 January 1916:

'One has a curious mixture of feelings during the often many-hours-long patrol flights over the Front. I go up to fight, but when I am up there, many times it happens that my own situation disappears from consciousness and that everything visible is perceived as only a picture. That is, to be sure, magnificent enough. At 3,000 metres altitude one no longer sees the miseries of the defensive dug-outs. But one does see, as if on a big map, the different lines of the fortifications on this side and the other side of the battlefront, and one can gain quite a good picture of the individual bases [used in] positional warfare . . .

'You may be interested to know that the famous Boelcke belongs to my *Geschwader*. His older brother [Wilhelm] is the chief of my *Staffel* and my room-mate on the train.'34

On 21 February the German offensive against Verdun began and the two *Kagohls*, each strengthened by the temporary addition of two *Kastas* from other *Armees*, played a key role. By the time he wrote on 16 March, Böhme had seen the advances made by tactical use of *Kagohl 2*:

'After three weeks of carrying bombs from Metz to the railheads at Bar-le-Duc, Ligny and Verdun, now

we have moved closer to Verdun. Here we reside between Landres and Marville in our comfortable train-home (it even has a piano!) near an abandoned mine, in which we have set up an exceptionally sumptuous *"Heldenkeller"* [heroes' cellar = bomb shelter] as our *Kasino*. The villages around us look like Pompeii . . .

'Now we have been entrusted with a new mission, which is more to my liking than that awful bomb-flinging: it is *"Sperreflüge"* opposite Verdun. I must explain the word to you. Often our infantry and artillery have had to grit their teeth that French fliers have been unhindered in bothering them from above and directing enemy artillery fire against them. Now that is prevented by our aircraft, flying back and forth over the Front and hindering them . . .'[35]

RICHTHOFEN RETURNS

By now Manfred von Richthofen had completed his pilot training and been assigned to *Kagohl 2*. During a *Sperreflug* on 26 April, he scored his first aerial victory as a pilot when he shot down a Nieuport near Fort Douaumont; as with his earlier observer victory, this one was behind enemy lines and Richthofen did not receive official credit for it.

But the value of individual *Sperreflüge* came into question just three days later, when he saw how quickly the French responded to the challenge. Once again, Richthofen was over Fort Douaumont, then the object of intense shelling by the Germans, when he saw three French Caudrons in the distance. A lone Fokker *Eindecker* appeared and began to attack one of the French twin-engined aircraft. It was obvious that the single-seater would pick off the slower reconnaissance machines one at a time.

Suddenly, ten more French aircraft showed up and turned the tables on the small monoplane. A strong west wind kept Richthofen from aiding the *Eindecker* and he could only watch as his countryman dived into a cloud with a French swarm in hot pursuit. Richthofen hoped that the clouds provided the cover needed to elude the French flight.

After Richthofen reported the incident over Fort Douaumont, he learnt that the Fokker pilot had been a squadron mate of his in Russia, *Rittmeister* Erich *Graf* von Holck. Now a fighter pilot attached to *Flieger-Abteilung (A) 203*, Holck had been shot through the head and killed. What opposing French units lacked in individual aircraft performance they made up for in numerical strength and organization – lessons not lost on Manfred von Richthofen, who became a vigorous proponent of the deployment of single-seat fighters in group attacks in *Staffel* strength.

GERMAN AIR PROTECTION FAILS

The lessons were reinforced on the morning of 22 May, when the French counter-attack against Fort Douaumont was augmented by the deployment of a superior number of aircraft. At 0815 hours, *Hptmn* Wilhelm Boelcke, leader of *Kasta 10*, and an aerial gunner went up on a *Sperreflug* to protect German observation balloons in the vicinity of Fort Vaux. They were at 3,000 metres when Boelcke spotted a formation of 'several Nieuports', which suddenly split up. Two headed for him, to keep him busy, while the rest went after the balloons with air-launched rockets. Each time Boelcke sought to engage one of the Nieuports, it flew westwards back to Verdun. Then to the south he saw two more Nieuport 11s heading for a balloon site near Etain. He flew back at top speed, but the Nieuports got there first and set fire to the sinking balloons. Quickly flying to a neighbouring balloon site, *Staffel-Führer* Boelcke had just started to circle it protectively when the balloon blossomed into bright flames. Then, off to the west, near the River Meuse, Boelcke saw Nieuports attacking a captive balloon that was vigorously defended by *Ballon-Abwehr-Kanonen* (Balloon Defence Guns). Despite the considerable risk that *BAK* fire would hit his own machine, Wilhelm Boelcke flew straight to the scene and chased off the Nieuports. In his report Boelcke stated:

> 'From the experience of these events, I come to the opinion that our [two-seat] aircraft are too slow for the combat mission assigned them and that a *Sperre* [barrier against the enemy] would be carried out more effectively by single- and two-seaters with the reliable stationary engines, which only for this purpose are more suitable against the French Nieuports, which are light and manoeuvrable, have good climbing ability and can withstand steep dives. Furthermore, co-operation with the *BAK* leaves much to be desired . . .'[36]

This sequence of events is typical of the problems – approaching crisis proportions – facing the German air arm during the Battle of Verdun. Their aircraft were being outclassed by newer and better Entente machines and the aircraft they had were not deployed in sufficient numbers.

The problem was compounded a month later, when the Russians launched the so-called Brusilov offensive and the British began the massive attack that became The First Battle of the Somme. Both events strained the *Kagohls* so that the combined elite force – which was meant to deliver bombs far behind enemy lines, while denying the enemy access to German rear areas (via the *Sperreflüge*) – did not achieve both of those primary objectives. Indeed, at the end of June 1916, the bombing units were split again: *Kagohl 2* went to help the *8. Armee* in Russia and half of *Kagohl 1* (*Kastas 1, 4* and *6*) went to the German *2. Armee* Front on the Somme. *KG 1*'s *Kastas 2, 3* and *5* went to Romania and then on to the Macedonian Front.

During those deployments *Kagohl 1* units in France took a step backwards in their development when their aircraft resumed previously discarded infantry and artillery co-operation missions. The *KG 1 Staffeln* in Romania and *KG 2* in Russia adhered more to their original purpose. As Manfred von Richthofen wrote: 'Compared with the Western Front, in any case, the Eastern Front is like a holiday.'[37] And, never happy with inactivity, he had already begun flying one of the Fokker *Eindeckers* attached to his *Geschwader*. For despite the loss of his friend *Graf* von Holck, and the loss on 19 June 1916 of *Hptmn* von Gersdorff, also in an *Eindecker* while battling against superior numbers of enemy aircraft, Richthofen knew that a change to a more proper use of single-seaters would have a dramatic effect on the air war.

And change was coming. The poor use of air power by the German Army units and the dwindling success of German air units all reinforced *Feldflugchef* Thomsen's contention that total reorganization of the *Fliegertruppe* was needed. A realignment of units and their missions was required to make German air power effective.

EMERGENCE OF THE *JAGDSTAFFELN*

A glimpse of that change was seen when, in August 1916, the celebrated ace *Hptmn* Oswald Boelcke visited *Kagohl 2* at its airfield in Kovel. Following the death in combat of *Obltn* Max Immelmann, Boelcke had been withdrawn from the Front and sent on an extended tour of military facilities all the way to Turkey. On the way back, he had stopped to see his brother Wilhelm, and also review the performance of some of the *Kagohl 2* pilots he had met earlier. Oswald Boelcke was ordered to establish a new type of single-seat fighter unit – a *Jagdstaffel* – and he was allowed to select pilots he considered suitable for the new unit. One of those pilots was *Ltn* Manfred *Freiherr* von Richthofen who, under Boelcke's tutelage, would refine his aerial hunting techniques and gain the highest score of confirmed aerial victories of any pilot in World War I.

In addition to the new *Jagdstaffeln*, other elements of organization and better use of German air power would be prepared under the direction of the old *BAO*'s founder, *Major* Wilhelm Siegert, for whom the month of August 1916 meant a change of position to *Inspekteur der Fliegertruppen* (Inspector General of the Air Service). With the air-fighting role to be assumed by the *Jagdstaffeln*, the mobile *Kampfgeschwadern* could be developed as the effective bombing force originally envisaged for the 'Carrier Pigeon' units.

2
FOKKER FRENZY

WELL BEFORE the *Brieftauben-Abteilungen* had completed their evolution into *Kampfgeschwaders*, it had been apparent to *Fliegertruppe* leaders that dedicated aerial protection aircraft were needed. The *BAO* and *BAM* B- and C-type (and especially the G-type) aircraft could do little more than stave off immediate threats to themselves. As *General* von Hoeppner later pointed out:

'. . . the necessity, first of all [for the observer] to have to turn around, in order to have a free field of fire, gave the C-type aircraft [only] the temporary character of an attack weapon . . . The true *Kampfflugzeug* [combat aircraft] originated first with the utilization of the invention of Fokker, which made it possible to fire through the propeller arc. The fixed [forward-firing] machine-gun was now operated by the pilot himself. The omission of the observer produced in this new [single-seat] E-type aeroplane extraordinary speed, manoeuvrability and climbing ability; these attributes marked the pure [dedicated] *Kampfflugzeug*. In the

hands of a determined pilot the Fokker *Eindecker* [monoplane fighter] very soon became the great fear of our enemies . . .'[1]

The 'invention', of course, was the interrupter gear developed by Heinrich Lübbe, Fritz Heber and other engineers and craftsmen at the Fokker Aeroplanbau in Schwerin. Challenged by *Lieutenant* Roland Garros' Morane-Saulnier Type L parasol monoplane, captured on 18 April 1915, the engineers considered anew the idea of shooting through the propeller arc. The French aircraft was powered by an 80hp Le Rhône rotary engine similar to the 80hp Oberursel engine used in the Fokker M 5K (M = *Militar*, 5 = fifth Fokker type, K = *kurz* or short wingspan) monoplane currently in service. The Fokker staff were told to copy or improve the methods of the Frenchman, who had shot down five German aircraft within three weeks. The crude device used by Garros, steel wedges on the pro-

▼ Even from a distance Allied airmen could spot the short, thick black 'line' on the cowling of a Fokker *Eindecker*, which was the single machine-gun synchronized to fire through the propeller arc, thereby giving the *Eindecker* a great tactical advantage.

▼ Fokker E III 635/15 was one of 36 produced in 1915. Problems with the 100hp Oberursel engine led to a few E IIIs being fitted with captured 80hp Le Rhône rotary engines, which produced a much better performance. There was no attempt to use captured engines for the line, but this event did emphasize the need for the production of reliable engines.

peller blades to deflect bullets that did not pass through the arc, inspired a much better push-rod gear that interrupted the gun's firing sequence when the propeller blade was in front of the muzzle.

SYNCHRONIZED MACHINE-GUN DEVELOPED

Anthony Fokker had the device and an air-cooled Parabellum 1MG 14 machine-gun mounted on an M 5K. That aircraft, *Werknummer* 216, was first demonstrated for the *Feldflugchef's* staff at Döberitz, west of Berlin. Initially designated M 5K/MG (for *Maschinengewehr* = machine-gun), the armed monoplane entered Army service with the military order number E I/15. A second M 5K, *Werknr* 258, was fitted with a 1MG 08, as were two single-seat fighters, designated E 2/15 and E 3/15, which Fokker used during a demonstration and sales promotion tour for operational units beginning at Stenay on 23 May.

The following month Fokker's efforts were aided by the arrival of a talented demonstration pilot, *Leutnant* Otto Parschau. A pre-war flier (*DLV* licence No 455 on 4 July 1913), Parschau had already flown front-line missions with *Feldflieger-Abteilungen 22* and *42*, as well as with the *BAO*. The impression he and Anthony Fokker created at the front-line units was recorded in a letter of 25 June 1915 written by Max Immelmann, then a *Fähnrich* flying LVG B-types with *Feldfl-Abt 62* at Douai:

> 'Recently, we received two small combat monoplanes from the Fokker factory. Primarily to see these fighting machines, yesterday the Crown Prince of Bavaria visited the 'field and inspected us and [*Feldfl-*] *Abteilung 20. Direktor* Fokker, the constructor of the combat aircraft, was presented to

him. He [Fokker], as well as a *Leutnant* Parschau, flew the aircraft and fired from the air at the ground. Fokker especially amazed us with his skill.'[2]

While Fokker was impressing the front-line fliers with his new aeroplane, word was received of the first *Eindecker* victory. On 1 July *Ltn* Kurt Wintgens of *Feldfl-Abt 67* shot down a Morane-Saulnier Type L parasol monoplane east of Luneville. That success and the demonstrations prompted quick production of the versatile new machine. By the time Fokker left *Feldfl-Abt 62* at Douai airfield on 12 July and returned to Schwerin, eleven German front-line pilots were flying Fokker *Eindeckers*.[3] In all, 54 E Is were produced, 48 for the Army and six for the Navy.[4]

Initially, one or two single-seat fighters were assigned to most of the *Feldflieger-Abteilungen* to protect their two-seat reconnaissance and artillery co-operation aircraft. One of the first demonstration *Eindeckers*, E 3/15, went to *Ltn* Oswald Boelcke, a senior pilot in *Feldfl-Abt 62*. Initially, he shared the Fokker with the newly promoted *Ltn* Immelmann and was understandably chagrined when the junior man achieved the *Abteilung*'s first aerial victory with a Fokker, on 1 August.

IMMELMANN'S FIRST AERIAL VICTORY

At 0445 French time (0545 German time) on that day Immelmann was awakened by an awful clatter. At first he thought that it was just a storm outside, but, looking out of a window, he saw about ten enemy aircraft buzzing around over the airfield and dropping bomb continuously. Neighbouring *Flak* batteries opened up, but with little effect. Immedi-

◄ The Austro-Hungarian *Luftfahrttruppen* ordered eleven Fokker E IIIs, of which 03.43 was the third example. Three E Is were also ordered, but by the time Fokker production was able to meet the demand, the *Eindecker* series had been outclassed by the new Allied biplane fighters equipped with forward-firing machine-guns.

▲ *Ltn* Kurt Wintgens, who scored the first victory with a Fokker *Eindecker*, was one of three prominent German aces who wore glasses while flying. The others were *Obltn* Fritz Bernert (27 victories) and *Ltn* Otto Kissenberth (17 victories). An 18-victory ace, Wintgens was shot down and killed in a fight with *Lieutenant* Alfred Heurtaux of the French *Escadrille Spa 3* on 25 September 1916.

▼ Armourers at *Kampfeinsitzerkommando* Habsheim, on the Vosges Front, load the Spandau 7.92mm machine-gun on a Fokker E III. The gun fired at the rate of 400–500 rounds per minute, which in short well-aimed bursts was enough to disable or knock out an opponent.

ately, he called for a car, got dressed and headed for the flight line. Along the way he met Boelcke, who was heading out on a motor-cycle to go up and drive off the enemy with his *Eindecker*. Immelmann followed but, at the airfield, his observer, *Ltn* von Teubern, said he considered it hopeless to go up because the visibility was so poor.

Not to be dissuaded, Max Immelmann had the other Fokker pulled out of the hangar and took off after Boelcke and the intruders. He described the ensuing combat in a letter:

'When I got to 2,000 metres, two enemy aircraft passed over me at about 2,600 metres. They flew in the direction of Arras, from whence I had just come. I was glad that they had not attacked me, for at 600 metres below them I would have been defenceless. When I was almost at Douai, I was at 2,400 metres, once again I encountered two enemy [aircraft], as well as Boelcke. They were at 3,200 metres. All three flew in the direction of Arras. I too flew towards Arras in the hope that once I got up there I could help Boelcke, for I heard the clatter of machine-gun fire.

'Suddenly, I saw Boelcke going down in a steep dive. As I learned later, his gun had jammed badly and he could no longer fire. I was just halfway between Douai and Arras when I saw a third flier far ahead of me. We were at about the same altitude. I could not see whether it was an enemy or one of ours. I flew towards him. Then I saw him drop bombs over Vitry. Now it was clear: [he was] an enemy. I climbed a bit and flew towards him. I was about 80 to 100 metres higher than him and about 50 metres away in a straight line. I could see the French [*sic*] emblem big and clear: blue-white-red rings. Now there was no longer any doubt. The other two came at me now, although they were still a bit higher. Like a hawk, I dived on the one and fired my machine-gun. For a moment I believed I would fly right into him. I had fired about 60 shots when my gun jammed. That was quite awkward, for to clear the jam I needed both hands; also I had to fly completely without hands, without being able to operate the control column. This was new and strange to me, but it worked. In the course of the fight that happened to me twice.

'Meanwhile, the enemy headed towards Arras. Quickly, I came up alongside him and cut off his way back, in which he was forced to make a left turn, that is, in the direction of Douai. We came down about 400 metres. During my respite from firing, I heard only softly the machine-gun clatter of the enemy [aircraft] still above me. I kept myself constantly perpendicular to my victim because no biplane can fire perpendicularly upwards. After 450 to 500 shots, the battle had lasted about eight to ten minutes, the enemy went down in a steep glide. I followed him. I could no longer fire, [as] the machine-gun had broken down. When I saw that he had landed, I landed near him immediately.'[5]

Boldly, Immelmann got out of his Fokker and, although unarmed, approached the enemy aircraft and announced, first in French, that the fallen pilot was his prisoner. The pilot raised his hands and answered in English, to which Immelmann responded in the same language: 'Ah, you are Englishman? You are my prisoner.'

The British pilot, 2nd Lt William Reid of No 2 Squadron, Royal Flying Corps, had been wounded in the left arm during the fight. He was taken to a field hospital, while Immelmann walked about, counting the more than 40 holes in the downed B.E.2c. No mentioned is made of the fate of the observer, 2nd Lt J. F. Lascelles.

With that first aerial victory Max Immelmann became noteworthy. Two days later, he was presented with the *Eisernes Kreuz I. Klasse* (Iron Cross 1st Class), quite a distinction at that time. He was also the object of praise in a lengthy report by *Feldfl-Abt 62*'s commanding officer, *Hptmn* Hermann Kastner (not to be confused with *Hptmn* Hermann Gustav Kastner-Kirdorf, the commander of the *BAO*). And, having demonstrated the *Eindecker*'s effectiveness so well, Immelmann was responsible for the *Abteilung*'s being assigned newer and better versions of the aircraft.

The first batch of *Eindeckers* were, in fact, a hastily assembled group of unrefined and often unreliable aircraft. Three *Eindecker*-related fatalities at the Döberitz flying school in July and August led to a general grounding of the type in early September. But rapid developments at the Fokker factory in Schwerin quickly led to the improved 100hp-engined Fokker E II and the even better E III. At one point all three *Eindecker* types were at the Front at the same time, but the E II and E III types were preferred by front-line pilots.

Ltn Boelcke, who had scored his first victory flying an LVG C I on 15 June, achieved his second success with a Fokker E I; he shot down a Bristol two-seater on 19 August. In late August *Feldfl-Abt 62* received another Fokker *Eindecker*, at a time when many other *Feldflieger-Abteilungen* had only one, and soon traded one of them for Fokker E II 37/15, which became Boelcke's new machine.

An interesting problem posed by the new *Eindeckers* at this time was noted in August 1915 by the

▲ Max Immelmann was an *Oberleutnant* and a celebrated *Eindecker* ace when he posed for this photo in front of Fokker E 3/15, one of the demonstration aircraft. Note the wartime censor's zeal in retouching the cowling area to eliminate the (then) secret machine-gun, as well as the rotary engine.

3. *Armee* officer in charge of balloon anti-aircraft defence, who pointed out the effect on anti-air gunners in his sector, who were accustomed to firing at Morane parasol monoplanes:

'[Feld] *Flieger-Abteilung 53* in Monthois now has three Fokker *Eindeckers*, which have a great similarity [in appearance] to French aircraft and also have a very similar engine sound. They are *Kampfflieger*, which fly very fast and are *not* in a position to fire signal flares, as the sole occupant must operate the controls along with the machine-gun. These aeroplanes go up only to repel French aircraft that have broken through [our defences]; they have orders to not cross the lines under any circumstances.'[6]

EINDECKER TACTICS

Often the Fokkers did fly low enough to be mistaken for enemy monoplanes, so the caution was worth noting. Generally, however, the *Eindeckers'* mode of operation was hawklike, to gain altitude and then, ideally with the sun at their backs, dive down on their prey. A popular Royal Flying Corps squadron ready-room poster warned the unwary to 'Beware the Hun in the Sun'. The swift attack was accompanied by a long burst of machine-gun fire at the target, followed by a dive which was continued until the attacker was well out of range. If the intended prey did not fall, the attack was repeated.

Even that tactic was refined, as RAF Historian H. A. Jones recorded: 'Then came the famous manoeuvre, introduced by Lieutenant Max Immelmann, which made it possible for the Fokker pilot to strike again and again with little loss of time. In the Immelmann turn the aeroplane rears up as if to loop, turns sideways over the vertical, and then comes out in the opposite direction. This mano-uvre, in which height is gained at the same time as direction is changed, took the British pilots by surprise and added to the losses which the Fokker[s] inflicted.'[7]

Boelcke and Immelmann were creating the text-book for future *Jagdflieger* (literally 'hunting fliers', or fighter pilots), but the techniques were not perfect, as seen in their encounter on 9 September. That day Immelmann and Boelcke attacked a big twin-engined aircraft just inside German lines and almost forced it down. When the French pilot managed to make for his own lines, however, they had to let him go. The German High Command did not want to risk the loss of their new air fighting advantage, as the French had done by allowing Roland Garros to cross over into enemy territory.

The following day Immelmann fought with two more enemy aircraft. The second was a biplane that had got on Boelcke's tail and, when the two Fokkers turned to deal with the intruder, Boelcke's gun jammed. Immelmann closed in and finished the job. On 10 September the Kingdom of Saxony awarded Ltn Immelmann its *Albrechts-Orden Ritter II. Klasse mit Schwertern* (Order of Albert, Knight 2nd Class with Swords) and eight days later he was promoted to *Oberleutnant*.

The friendly rivalry continued as Boelcke gained his third victory, over a Morane, on the day of Immelmann's promotion. Immelmann's third victory was achieved on 21 September. Shortly after

that, when ten French bombers attacked Metz, one fell before Boelcke's guns near Pont-à-Mousson – his fourth victory. As the numbers of victories rose, so did the awards. After Boelcke's sixth victory on 30 October, attaining the highest score of any German pilot at that time, he became the first *Fliegertruppe* member to receive the *Ritterkreuz des königlichen Hausordens von Hohenzollern mit Schwertern* (Knight's Cross of the Royal Order of the House of Hohenzollern with Swords). Immelmann's sixth victory, on 7 November, led to his becoming the second airman to receive that high Prussian honour.

FIRST AVIATION *POUR LE MÉRITES*

Ultimately, after both Boelcke and Immelmann had achieved eight confirmed victories, they were pre-sented with Prussia's highest award for bravery, the *Orden Pour le Mérite*, on 12 January 1916. The hand-some deep blue enamel and gold trim badge, a Maltese Cross worn at the neck, is said to have reflected a

▲The *Orden Pour le Mérite*, Prussia's highest decoration for bravery, was awarded only to commissioned officers. During World War I, 687 *Pour le Mérites* were awarded and of that number, 81 went to aviation personnel.

▶ Two members of the four-pilot team of *KEK* Habsheim that fought off French bombers which threatened German-held Alsace: *Uffz* Udet (left) and *Vzfw* Weingärtner.

Unsuccessful with the *KEK*, Ernst Udet went on to become Germany's second highest-scoring ace, with a final total of 62 victories.

blue cast against Immelmann's pale skin and led to the award's being nicknamed 'The Blue Max'.

By then the *Eindecker* series had undergone considerable development. During a visit to Fokker's factory at Schwerin in November 1915, Oswald Boelcke tested the E IV prototype, powered by a 160hp Oberursel twin-row rotary engine. His favourable report on it prompted Max Immelmann to order an E IV with three machine-guns – with which he promptly shot off the propeller. Even with two guns, there were problems with the E IV. The added weight and increased gyroscopic effect of the rotary engine made it less manoeuvrable than its predecessors (despite a lengthened wingspan to compensate for the more powerful engine). In addition, the 160hp engine was produced in only limited quantities, resulting in only 49 E IVs being built, 48 for the Army and one for the Navy. In the hands of the right pilot, however, the E IV was effective and so Boelcke, for example, continued to fly the E IV longer than other pilots.

ORGANIZING *EINDECKER* UNITS

In late 1915 the *Armee-Oberkommandos* began using *Eindeckers* as operational sub-units to support broader objectives. In the *6. Armee* area one of the better-known plans was developed by *Major* Friedrich Stempel, one of the founders of Bavaria's pre-war military air arm. At the time, Stempel was *Stabsoffizier der Flieger* (Staff Officer in Charge of Aviation) for the *6. Armee*, commanded by Crown Prince Rupprecht of Bavaria. To ensure protection for the *Armee*'s reconnaissance aircraft at all times, Stempel devised a command structure of *Kampfeinsitzerkommandos* (Combat Single-seater Detachments) – abbreviated as *KEK*s.[8] Three *KEK*s drew

▶ *Obltn* Ernst *Freiherr von Althaus* alongside the Fokker E I he flew with *Feldfl-Abt 23*. He scored his 8th confirmed aerial victory on 22 July 1916 and five days later was awarded the *Orden Pour*

le Mérite. His final total was 17 victories. Even though he suffered eye problems that later led to total blindness, von Althaus served with *Jagdstaffel 10* and commanded *Jasta 4*.

on the *Eindeckers* assigned to Prussian and Bavarian *Feldflieger-Abteilungen* to perform *Luft-wachtdienst* (Aerial Guard Duty) in shifts. In its ultimate form, taking 28 July 1916 as an example, Stempel's plan provided *6. Armee* units this coverage,[9] in which the Bavarian units are identified by the suffix 'b':

	Time of Day	Unit	Responsibility of
KEK I	Morning	FFl-Abt 5b	Commander of FFl-Abt 5b
	Afternoon	FFl-Abt 24	
KEK II	Morning	FFl-Abt 2b	Commander of FFl-Abt 18
	Afternoon	FFl-Abt 18	
KEK III	Daybreak to 1000 hours	FFl-Abt 13	
	1000 to 1600	FFl-Abt 5b	Commander of FFl-Abt 9
	1600 to Darkness	FFl-Abt 9	

Other *Armees* took similar organizational approaches to group their *Eindeckers* to maximize their use. On the *2. Armee* Front, for example, *Feldfl-Abt 32*'s monoplanes became the nucleus of an effective fighter aircraft command structure that became the lineal antecedent of the first *Jagdstaffel*:

'As soon as the first double sheds are completed at the new airfield in Bertincourt, expected to take place on Wednesday, 17 November 1915, the *Abteilung* intends to transfer both Fokker *Kampf-flugzeuge* and attendant personnel and materiel there.'[10]

The unit had been assigned Fokker E III 86/15, which *Ltn d Res* Gustav Leffers picked up from *Armee-Flugpark 2* on 5 November. On returning to *Feldfl-Abt 32*'s airfield at Cambrai, however, Leffers crashed and totally ruined the new aircraft. Three days later he had to go to *Feldfl-Abt 27* to pick up E III 84/15 as a replacement. When Leffers returned to Cambrai on the 11th, he found that *Obltn d Res* Ernst *Freiherr* von Althaus and another E III had been detached temporarily from *Feldfl-Abt 23* to help form a *KEK* at Velu, just north of Bertincourt. *Freiherr* von Althaus, who went on to become the eighth aviation recipient of the *Orden Pour le Mérite*, returned to his unit at Roupy shortly after Leffers' arrival at Velu.

On the afternoon of 5 December the lone pilot of

KEK Bertincourt used the classic *Eindecker* attack method:

'About 1500 hours I happened to be over Bapaume and, through our artillery's shell bursts, became aware of an enemy aircraft almost over Martinpuich at 1,500 metres, flying northwards. I gave chase immediately. Between Grevillers and Achiet-le-Grand I was 600 metres away and opened fire, which was returned immediately. I was 200 metres higher than the enemy machine and went into a dive, continuously firing with my machine-gun until I went right on past the aeroplane. Now I noticed that the pilot was hit and the machine began to waver. Until this moment I had been under intense machine-gun fire from the opponent. Suddenly I received a strong blast of air from the prop wash of the enemy aircraft, whereupon my machine was thrown on its side and sideslipped about 150 metres. I recovered quickly, however, and tried to cut off the opponent's route to the Front. But now he went down into a steep dive from 300 metres and crashed, totally demolishing the aircraft. Both crewmen of the British BE biplane were killed immediately.'[11]

The B.E.2c, probably one of two aircraft from No 13 Squadron, RFC, brought down that day, was the first of nine victories achieved by Leffers, who was awarded the *Orden Pour le Mérite* on 5 November 1916.

Before 1915 ended, however, he scored his second victory. On 29 December, three B.E.2c's were spotted heading for the *KEK* at Velu and Leffers went up to head them off. He caught up with them over Bertincourt, where the local *BAK* were firing at them. The *BAK* gunners ceased firing when they recognized Leffers' *Eindecker*, and he closed in on one of the BEs, as he reported:

'Both aircraft, which stayed close together, fired at me with their [combined] four machine-guns. Coming in [and] at 400 metres away, I likewise opened fire with my machine-gun at one of the enemy aeroplanes, while the [observer in the] other attacked me from the side by firing his machine-gun. Closing in to only a short distance, suddenly my gun jammed, although with the last shots I had got a good hit, for at the same moment the enemy aircraft went into a steep spiral and from 300 metres went straight down and crashed.

'The second British machine, which had fired at me vigorously from the side and behind, turned away immediately and soon disappeared from my field of vision, as I had to follow the falling aircraft until just before it hit the ground.

'The pilot of the aeroplane shot down was killed instantly by a shot through the heart. The observer

is severely wounded. The machine had two machine-guns with ten ammunition drums on board.'[12]

Coincidentally, Leffers was nearly matched by his former *KEK* colleague *Freiherr* von Althaus, who 'through courageous and determined attacks on 5 December near Bapaume and 28 December near Douilly, north of Ham, each [time] caused a British aircraft to crash.'[13]

EINDECKERS FORCE NEW RFC TACTICS

Given the mounting level of success of the Fokker *Eindeckers* – in the hands of established aces Boelcke and Immelmann, as well as such rising stars as Leffers, von Althaus and Rudolf Berthold – the British and French air arms were forced to make a drastic change away from the single- and double-aircraft flights that had previously been so successful against German *Sperreflüge* flown by C-type aircraft. On 14 January 1916 RFC Head-quarters issued this order:

◀ Often mistaken for a Fokker *Eindecker*, the rotary-engined Pfalz E I 'shoulder-wing' monoplane was a slightly modified Morane-Saulnier Type H. This machine, E I 215/15, was one of 44 such aircraft produced by the Pfalz Flugzeugwerke GmbH of Speyer.

▼ The secrets of the Fokker *Eindecker* became known when some of their pilots inadvertently crossed the lines and had to land in Allied territory. This aircraft, which had its original serial number and national markings overpainted, fell into French hands and was evaluated.

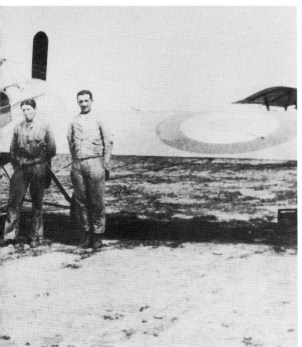

'Until the Royal Flying Corps are in possession of a machine as good as or better than the German Fokker, it seems that a change in the tactics employed becomes necessary. It is hoped very shortly to obtain a machine which will be able successfully to engage the Fokkers at present in use by the Germans. In the meantime, it must be laid down as a hard and fast rule that a machine proceeding on reconnaissance must be escorted by at least three other fighting machines. These machines must fly in close formation and a reconnaissance should not be continued if any of the machines become detached. This should apply to both short and distant reconnaissances. Aeroplanes proceeding on photographic duty any considerable distance east of the line should be similarly escorted. From recent experience it seems that the Germans are now employing their aeroplanes in groups of three or four, and these numbers are frequently encountered by our aeroplanes. Flying in close formation must be practised by all pilots.'[14]

This change in tactics effectively cut RFC strength. The need for reconnaissance and other missions remained at the same level but, since it took more aircraft (including required escorts) to perform them, the number of flights had to decrease. Furthermore, even increased numbers of existing aircraft – now called 'Fokker fodder' – did not ensure successful flights over the lines. As recorded in *Feldfl-Abt 32*'s war diary for 5 February 1916:

'About 1000 hours four British BE aircraft appeared twice at short intervals. Unfortunately, the flight was reported so late that our defensive aircraft – Fokker E III 84/15 with *Ltn* Leffers, Fokker E III 400/15 with *Ltn* Lehmann and Pfalz E I 220/15 with *Ltn* Rouselle – could not catch up with them. However, a BE was forced to land near Irles by *Ltn* [Rudolf] Berthold of *Feldfl-Abt 23*. The British aircraft was recovered by *Feldfl/Abt 32*.'[15]

Feldfl-Abt 32 KEK's one Pfalz E I is worthy of note. Similar in general appearance to the Fokker *Eindecker*, the Pfalz was in fact a licence-built Morane-Saulnier Type H mid-wing monoplane powered by an 80hp Oberursel engine. It too was fitted with a synchronized machine-gun, but was not the equal of the later Fokkers alongside which it was used in front-line service.

Indeed, the real question about the overall effectiveness of the Fokker *Eindecker* frenzy is: were they more myth than substance? According to one account:

'The British losses were exaggerated. There were actually very few Fokkers opposite them. The German Army had only about 40 monoplane fighters at the end of 1915 scattered along the entire front. There were only about 16 to 20 machines being delivered every month, and early in 1916 a majority were concentrated in the Verdun sector opposite the French.'[16]

EINDECKERS DE-MYTHICIZED

Despite being prohibited from crossing the lines, *Eindeckers* did find their way into Entente hands for evaluation – and de-mythification. On 8 April 1916 the RFC received an intelligence bonanza when factory-fresh Fokker E III 210/16 was delivered into their hands inadvertently. Earlier that day a 24-year-old *Gefreiter*, whose identity was not revealed in official reports, went to *Armeeflugpark 6* at Valenciennes to collect the new aircraft for his unit, *Feldfl-Abt 5*. He was supposed to follow the railway line to Lille, heading in a north-westerly direction to his own airfield at Wasquehal. The pilot became disorientated along the way, stopped at two German airfields to get directions and, instead of following the canal north-east to Lille, he followed the La Bassee canal along its course to the west. He did not realize that he had crossed the lines until engine failure forced him to land at Renescure, 9 kilometres east of St Omer. There, British soldiers appeared and prevented him from destroying the aircraft.

Eindecker 210/16 was tested at least twice at St Omer. The results were surprising, as noted by eight-victory ace Capt Cecil A. Lewis, MC, in his recollection of what was probably the first British test of an *Eindecker* against current RFC aircraft:

'Great excitement in the Depot! A Fokker has been captured undamaged. Early in 1916 the Fokker was the menace of the RFC. Hearsay and a few lucky encounters had made the machine respected, not to say dreaded, by the slow, unwieldy machines then used by us for Artillery Observation and Offensive Patrols.

'A sort of mystery surrounded the Fokker . . . Rumour credited it with the most fantastic performance! It could outclimb, outpace, and outmanoeuvre anything in the RFC. You were as good as dead if you as much as saw one . . . and so on. In short, our morale wanted bucking up . . .

'[Despite rumours] . . . it was perfectly orthodox, and there remained only to put it up against a British scout to judge its performance. The Morane Bullet was chosen and the two machines were run

▲ Successful early fighter pilots were often decorated by Prussia and their home states. A native of Oldenburg, 9-victory ace *Ltn d Res Gustav Leffers* posed for this formal portrait wearing Prussia's *Orden Pour le Mérite*, just over the top jacket button, and on his medals bar: Iron Cross 2nd Class, Knight's Cross of the Royal Order of the House of Hohen- zollern with Swords, and the Friedrich-August Cross of Oldenburg 2nd Class; and below these: Friedrich-August Cross 1st Class, Army Pilot's Badge, and the Iron Cross 1st Class. On 27 December 1916, just a few days short of his 22nd birthday, Leffers was killed in combat over Cheresy on the Somme Front.

out on the aerodrome, side by side. All the General Staff assembled to watch the tests. Both machines took off together, and it was immediately clear that the Morane was all over the Fokker. It climbed quicker, it was faster on the level, and when the two machines began a mock fight over the aerodrome, the Morane had everything its own way. The bogey was laid. A description of the machine, its size, power, [and] capabilities, was circulated at once to every one in the [Royal Flying] Corps. It did a great deal to raise the morale and prepare the way for the Allied air supremacy later that year.'[17]

Thus the *Eindecker*'s advantages were not speed, power and great height so much as manoeuvrability and climbing ability. The proof of those capabilities had been seen when Gustav Leffers flew Fokker E III 84/15 in an attack on four BEs on 20 February 1916. He was at the same altitude, 2,500 metres, when he opened fire on the rearmost aircraft. Suddenly his engine stopped. Desperately Leffers tried to re-start it, all the while taking heavy fire from the two-seat biplanes. When the engine finally came to life, he regained height quickly and resumed firing at the last aircraft in the formation.

'Through careful manoeuvring, the other aircraft succeeded in attacking me from the side. At this moment I administered the fatal shot to the aeroplane I was attacking, whereupon it went down in a steep dive and crashed.'[18]

Even though he had further engine trouble with E III 84/15 and had to make a forced landing on 13 March, Leffers flew the same machine the next day and went after two B.E.2c's of No 15 Squadron. Closing to within 100 metres, he succeeded in shooting down one of them only after pushing his own machine to the absolute limits:

'. . . At this distance I opened fire, but from the first shots the pilot understood that it would take skilful and steep turns to evade my fire. This fight lasted some minutes. Many times both machines were so close to each other that I clearly saw the pilot shake his clenched fist at me. Shortly afterwards an unpleasant moment for both machines occurred. At a distance of about 30 metres both machines suddenly turned and at exactly the same altitude came towards each other. I then had my opponent right in my sights and did not want to swerve aside. On their side, at this moment the crew of the enemy aeroplane were shielded by their forward-mounted engine and also did not swerve. At the last moment I tried to dive beneath the enemy machine to get by to the other side and at the same instant the opponent tried the same thing. Now a collision was

unavoidable and I let go of the control column, whereby my machine bolted upwards, [and] a brief shock went through my machine, [as] the wheels brushed against the opponent's wings. Thereby set off balance, the opponent dived suddenly in order to increase the distance between us and to return closer to the Front. Consequently, he came within the field of fire of my machine-gun and went down in a steep spiral. From 500 metres he went straight down and on impact began to burn. Pilot and observer were incinerated.'[19]

A few weeks later Leffers received a brand-new machine – Fokker E IV 161/16 – and added to his successes. But on 30 April his *KEK* comrade *Ltn* Otto Schmedes was killed in the crash of an E III at Combles. According to the official report: 'Apparently the lower bracing struts of the Fokker were severed by machine-gun fire.'[20]

BOELCKE EVALUATES THE E IV

In this case previous combat damage to the aircraft seems to have been the cause of the crash, but enough other *Eindeckers* had been lost to raise concerns in *Oberstleutnant* von der Lieth-Thomsen's office. With the advent of a variety of new, improved Entente fighter aircraft, the *Feldflugchef* was particularly interested in Oswald Boelcke's report on the Fokker E IV. Boelcke had experienced problems with what should have been the best of the *Eindeckers* and, in his usual methodical manner, he analyzed the aircraft in the light of existing combat conditions. His report, written while he was with the *KEK* at Sivry, north of Verdun, and dated 23 March 1916, was as follows:

'I. Flying Technical Qualities:
(a) The speed of the 160hp Fokker *Eindecker* is sufficient for the demands at the Front, especially in level flight; in climbing it loses speed rapidly, so that many times Nieuport biplanes get away from me.
(b) Climbing ability decreases very much at great height (over 3,000 metres). This could well be avoided by the construction of a lightweight biplane.
(c) Turning ability of the 160hp machine is substantially inferior to that of the 100hp and 80hp machines, as the kinetic energy of the heavy engine has to be overcome. A really fast sharp turn can be achieved only by switching off the engine. As, in the natural order of things, one always loses altitude doing this, an aerial combat with an opponent at the same altitude or even higher is very dangerous with the 160hp machine.

▶ The Royal Aircraft Factory's F.E.8 single-seater was intended to provide RFC fighter pilots with a forward-firing machine-gun to counter the *Eindecker* threat. By the time the F.E.8 reached France, however, the new German *Jagdstaffeln* were using Albatros D I and D II fighters which were far superior to the little 'pusher'. This machine, 7624 of No 40 Squadron, was forced down near La Bassée by aircraft of *Jasta 8* on 9 November 1916. The pilot, Capt T. Mapplebeck, was taken prisoner and his machine was evaluated bearing German markings to avoid being shot down by German ground and air units.

'II. Engine:

The performance of the 160hp engine is good at the beginning, also at great height, when the [rotary] engine in comparison with the stationary engine loses [about 40 to 50] rpms. After longer use at greater heights it loses 100 or more rpms.

'III. The machine-guns work perfectly with careful treatment. Engaging the cam was very unsatisfactory on newly arrived machines and thus many breaks occurred in the small couplings. The material for the rocker arms was hardened too much [and] they often broke.'[21]

The ace completely discounted any thought of having the forward-firing machine-guns mounted at a 15deg angle for attacking enemy aircraft from below. Boelcke noted that that method of attack was used much less frequently than engaging a target directly in the line of flight. The main point of his report was that, until the development of a good light biplane fighter, comparable to the French

Nieuport 17 then entering service, German single-seater pilots had to learn to develop tactics to work around certain inherent problems in their *Eindeckers*. One such tactic was the now widespread practice of grouping the monoplanes together.

In most cases the various *Armee* commands continued to organize the Fokkers to support their reconnaissance aircraft. Apparently the 7. *Armee* tried to substitute Fokkers for C-types in the *Sperreflüge* that defended ground and balloon positions. As that mission was not suited for the Fokkers, in March 1916 the 7. *Armee* followed the example of neighbouring units and began grouping the Fokkers assigned to its *Feldflieger-Abteilungen* based on this assessment:

'Use of the Fokker *Kampfeindeckers* for *Sperreflüge* has not been approved because the engines are very delicate and suffer very much under the strong demands and must be repaired frequently. Conse-

new *Staffeln*, the *Stofl 7. Armee*, *Hptmn* Bauer, ordered:

'It is not the mission of the Fokker *Staffeln* to barricade [our lines]. The Fokker aircraft are, as before, forbidden to fly over our own lines, thereby keeping details of the construction of our machine-guns from falling into enemy hands.'[23]

Hptmn Bauer need not have worried about the German machine-gun interrupter gear being acquired by his adversaries, even though that would take place within a few weeks. Spurred by the Fokkers' success, Entente engineers set out to equip their aircraft with the same capability. In Britain alone three mechanical gears were available for use with the fixed, forward-firing 0.303in Vickers-Maxim machine-gun: Vickers, Scarff-Dibovsky, and Arsiad. Eventually, the Vickers-Challenger gear became the RFC standard. It was first applied to Bristol Scout serial 5313, which went initially to No 12 Squadron 'and then to No 11, where it was flown by Lt Albert Ball in combat on 15 May when he drove down an Albatros two-seater.'[24] With the development of fast, manoeuvrable single-seat 'pushers' such as the Airco D.H.2, which was not intended to be a fighter aircraft, Britain had aircraft well qualified to engage *Eindeckers*.

EINDECKER USE REDEFINED

These developments caused Thomsen to re-think the short-term tactical use of the *Eindeckers*, for which replacements were already being sought. Therefore, in May the *Feldflugchef* issued this directive:

'Many commands at the Front have expressed the wish that E-type aircraft be released for flights over our own lines.

'As the opposition has acquired knowledge of the device to fire through the propeller through E-type aircraft that have landed undamaged in his terri-tory, I will permit a more relaxed interpretation of the previously strictly drawn boundaries for flights over our own trenches.

'But in this regard I point out emphatically that, strategically, the E-type aeroplanes are a purely defensive weapon, under no conditions to be allowed to perform reconnaissance missions, [and] arbitrary enlargement of the fuel tank is forbidden and pursuit of the enemy may be carried out [only] when the fuel supply assures a completely certain return flight to the home airfield.'[25]

Recognizing the newly defined defensive role of the *Eindeckers*, in late May the *Stofl 2. Armee. Hptmn*

quently, the combat aircraft will be withdrawn [and returned] to their actual purpose of attacking enemy aircraft when they come behind our lines.

'Accordingly, it will be arranged for:
'The barrier protection [flights] to be taken over in the Corps sector by the *Korps Flieger-Abteilungen* with biplanes; in this they will be supported by the *Armee Flieger-Abteilungen*.

'The Fokker aircraft, as from 1 April 1916, will be assembled into two *Staffeln* (East and West). Airfield of the West-*Staffel* will be at le Faux Ferme, north-east of Coucy. Airfield of the East-*Staffel* will be just west of St Erme.

'To *Fokker-Staffel*-West will go: the aircraft of [*Feldflieger-*] *Abteilung 7, 11* and *39* – four aircraft.

'To *Fokker-Staffel*-East will go: the aircraft of *Abteilung 26* and *29* – five aircraft.

'The Fokker *Staffeln* come under the direct orders of the *Stabsoffizier der Flieger* to whom they are allocated.'[22]

To reinforce the point, in his first order to the

▶ Aware that his *Eindecker* series could not be developed beyond the E IV, Anthony Fokker began work on a biplane in 1915. The family resemblance is apparent, but the new D types were hardly better than the E types and were far out-classed by the emerging Albatros fighters. For a brief period *Hptmn* Oswald Boelcke flew this D III (352/16, *Werknr* 784) fitted with a twin-row 160hp Oberursel rotary engine, but turned it in.

Mahnke, expanded the *KEK* at Velu (Bertincourt), which then consisted of these *Feldfl-Abt 32* men and machines: *Ltn* Lehmann, E III 400/15; *Ltn* Leffers, E IV 161/16; and *Ltn* Dittrich, E III 411/15. Mahnke added *Ltn d Res* Hendrichs and E III 238/15 from *Feldfl-Abt 59*, as well as this contingent from *Feldfl-Abt 1b*: *Ltn* Diemer, E III 414/15; *Offizierstellvertreter* (Warrant Officer) Müller, E III 211/15; and *Unteroffizier* (Sergeant) Ehrentaller, whose aircraft had not yet arrived. Together, the group became the *Abwehrkommando Nord* (Defence Unit North), abbreviated *AKN*.[26]

This assignment was the first of two that *Offstlv* Max Müller would serve with the Fokker unit derived from *Feldfl-Abt 32*. In neither case, however, did he initiate the air combat successes that later led to his leading a *Jagdstaffel* in the air and receiving the highest bravery awards from both Bavaria and Prussia. Indeed, these were lean times for the *AKN*. On several occasions over the next few weeks the Fokkers took off to defend the reconnaissance aircraft, but made no contact with the enemy. Meanwhile, the *AKN* continued to grow and to rely on *Eindeckers* – mostly E IIIs – for its strength. In fact, by mid-June, its one E IV, 161/16, was assigned to the unit's most experienced pilot, *Ltn* Gustav Leffers. When *Gefreiter* (Lance Corporal) Hermann Keller was detached to the *AKN*, he was assigned Fokker E III 346/16, a new arrival.[27]

At that time British preparations for the First Battle of the Somme were presaged by increased air activity. One of the units responding to that build-up was *KEK III* (also known as *KEK Douai*) on the 6. *Armee* Front, commanded by *Obltn* Max Immelmann. On 12 June the *KEK* had been detached from *Feldfl-Abt 62*, which was then being transferred to the Eastern Front. Shortly afterwards, Immelmann's unit was attached to *Feldfl-Abt 5b* commanded by *Obltn* Johann Moosmeier (DLV No 631 on 19 December 1913),[28] with whom the great ace had been discussing the formation of his own *Jagdstaffel*,[29] reflecting yet another development in the use of single-seat fighters.

IMMELMANN'S LAST FIGHT

On the afternoon of 18 June Immelmann flew a Fokker E IV to intercept a flight of eight F.E.2b aircraft from No 25 Squadron, RFC, heading for Arras. He had encountered the new two-seat 'pusher' biplane before and was aware of its flexible Lewis machine-gun in the front cockpit and a second Lewis gun on a telescopic mounting to enable the observer to fire backwards over the top wing. Indeed, Immelmann's 12th victory, scored on 29 March 1916, had been an F.E.2b of No 23 Squadron. Hence, on this June afternoon he knew how to use the strengths of the E IV and make good use of the more powerful engine. In short order he achieved his 16th victory, F.E.2b 6940; the pilot, 2nd Lt C. E. Rogers, was killed during the fight and the observer, Sgt H. Taylor, was wounded and taken prisoner.

▶ The ultimate *Eindecker* was the Fokker E V (later known as the D VIII) produced near the end of the war. This high-wing monoplane with its tubular steel construction and 140hp Oberursel rotary engine had great potential, but scarcely had time to prove itself.

That day also marked the fourth victory for *Ltn* Max Mulzer, an old *Feldfl-Abt 62* comrade. Immelmann was at a celebration dinner hosted by Mulzer's Bavarian comrades when word was received that a flight of seven enemy aircraft had crossed the Front near Sallaumines. Mulzer and *Ltn* Oesterreicher had already engaged the intruders by the time word reached the dinner. *Obltn* Immelmann and *Uffz* Wolfgang Heinemann left the celebration and hastened to join their comrades in the air. At the Douai hangars, however, Immelmann discovered that his E IV had received several hits in its wing ribs during the afternoon fight and was still being repaired. He and Heinemann took off in E IIIs.

They caught up with their quarry, more F.E.2b's from No 25 Squadron, over Lens. *Ltn* Mulzer and *Vzfw* Prehn were busy with targets of their own when Immelmann came on the scene and shot down F.E.2b 4909; the pilot, 2nd Lt John R. B. Savage, was killed and his observer, 2/AM Robinson, was wounded and taken prisoner.

Next, Immelmann engaged an F.E.2b crewed by Lt G. R. McCubbin and Cpl J. H. Waller. He closed to about 1,000 metres and then:

'Suddenly Immelmann's Fokker reared up, sideslipped down to the left, straightened out again and flew straight ahead with an odd seesaw movement of the tail.
'But now Heinemann had to turn back to the

enemy, for three Vickers [sic] had dived on Prehn, who was already in a fight with one Englishman. Thus he [Heinemann] was not able to look back on the end of his *Staffelführer*.'[30]

Max Immelmann's Fokker E III broke up and fell 2,000 metres to the ground. Immelmann was dead at the scene of the crash. The wreckage was examined in an attempt to determine whether structural fatigue or enemy bullets had caused the *Eindecker* to break up in the air. Neither answer was good for the morale of the pilots of *Eindeckers* still in service or for Anthony Fokker, who was already at work on a biplane successor to the E-types.

The day after Immelmann's death, another prominent pilot went down in a Fokker, *Hptmn* Ernest *Freiherr* von Gersdorff, commander of *Kagohl 1*. In an odd twist of fate, Gersdorff, a native of Strasbourg in German-held Alsace, was flying an *Eindecker* when he was shot down over Neuburg in the German-occupied Lorraine sector not far from Verdun.

Oswald Boelcke, who had been involved with testing the 120hp Mercedes-powered Fokker D I, was ordered off flight status. *Kaiser* Wilhelm himself determined that the *Fliegertruppe* could not risk losing another great '*Fokkerflieger*', so Boelcke was sent off to the Balkans on an 'inspection tour'. On the way back to the Western Front, he selected a number of pilots – including Erwin Böhme and Manfred von Richthofen – to join the new unit, *Jagdstaffel 2*, to be established in August 1916.

Meanwhile, troubles continued to plague the *Eindeckers*. Less than two weeks after Immelmann's death, *Uffz* Leopold Reimann of the *Abwehrkommando Nord* was shot down in Fokker E III 347/15 after a fierce fight near Bapaume; he received hits in the engine and bracing cables which destabilized the aircraft and sent it into a dive. Reimann was lucky to walk away from the crash.

The *AKN* received two Halberstadt D II biplanes in June 1916 and, although intended to work with reconnaissance squadrons, they were assigned to the *Kampfeinsitzerkommandos* to bolster the weakening Fokker *Eindeckers*. A review of *AKN* operations, however, showed no successes achieved by the Halberstadts. Indeed, on 1 July, the day after Reimann's near-fatal crash, *Vzfw* Dittrich was flying an E III when he encountered an F.E.2b over Grevillers and shot it down. The following day *Eindecker* pilot *Ltn* Max Mulzer scored his seventh victory. On 8 July Mulzer brought down a B.E.2c of No. 4 Squadron near Miraumont. And on 9 July the *AKN* was joined by master *Eindeckerflieger Ltn* Otto Parschau and another seasoned veteran of *Kagohl 1*, *Lt* Werner Schramm. On that day Parschau shot down a balloon near Laneuville, for his eighth and final victory.

At the time there was a tacit understanding that, with the attainment of eight aerial victories, an ace would be awarded the *Orden Pour le Mérite*. Thus, on 10 July, Otto Parschau received the coveted honour. It was as much a statement about the effectiveness of the *Eindecker* – in the hands of a highly skilled pilot – as a recognition of Parschau's talent and courage. Four days later Parschau was

named commander of the *AKN*, which was given the new designation *Kampf-Einsitzer Staffel B* (signifying its proximity to Bertincourt), made independent of *Feldfl-Abt 32* and placed directly under the command of *AOK 2. Armee*.[31] The unit was further strengthened by the arrival on 20 July of *Obltn* Karl Grieffenhagen, another former *Kagohl 1* pilot.

All along the Front the Fokkers were up in force on 21 July. On the *6. Armee* Front, 22 aircraft of the 9th Wing, RFC, attacked the railway bridge over the canal at Aubigny and were driven back by aircraft from *KEKs I* and *III*. One aircraft, described as a 'Vikkers' (but more likely B.E.2c 2100 of No 12 Squadron), was forced to land near Haucourt, south of Vitry. Later that day *Vzfw* Wolfgang Heinemann – Immelmann's companion during the ace's last fight – was himself shot down and killed during a fight over Haucourt. And for *KESt B* it was the blackest day imaginable: *Ltn* Werner Schramm was hit by shrapnel over Combles and killed, and *Ltn* Otto Parschau was mortally wounded in a fight; he made it back to the airfield, but died in a field hospital in Grevillers.

Despite these losses, *KESt B* had to continue to rely on Fokker *Eindeckers*. At the end of July the unit noted the arrival of another experienced *Kagohl 1* pilot, *Offstlv* Hesse, and the return of *Offstlv* Max Müller; *KESt B* also listed five E IIIs powered by 100hp Oberursel engines in a ready status. But no string of aerial victories followed that infusion of men and machines. The lack of success clearly demonstrated that more aircraft and more pilots could not overcome the *Eindecker*'s loss of superiority.

◄ Master airfighter *Hptmn* Oswald Boelcke's funeral in Cambrai. He was killed when his Albatros collided with that of Erwin Böhme, a colleague in *Jasta 2*, while closing in for a kill on 28 October 1916. The top wing of Boelcke's Albatros D II came loose and the aircraft plummeted to the ground. In this scene, just ahead of the guard of honour, *Ltn* Manfred *Freiherr* von Richthofen can be seen

carrying the *Ordenskissen* (Cushion with Decorations) of the fallen 40-victory ace.

► Boelcke's *Ordenskissen* bore an array of high honours. At the top, *Orden Pour le Mérite*. First row from left: Army Pilot's Badge, Iron Cross 2nd Class, Knight's Cross of the Royal Order of the House of Hohenzollern with Swords, Prussian Life-Saving Medal, Anhalt House Order of Albert the

Thus the history of *Kampfeinsitzer-Staffel B* seems to trail off to an unspectacular ending, with *Hptm* Schregel succeeding to the *Staffel-Führer* vacancy left by *Ltn* Parschau and with a number of other promising pilots joining the unit – but with no further air successes being recorded. On 23 August *KESt B* and fourteen pilots and other support personnel were attached to *Fl-Abt (A) 210* at Sains-lez-Marquion, west of Cambrai.[32] But, as one source notes: 'After what amounted to only a few hours' association with *ArtFl-Abt 210*, *KESt B* was dissolved and authorization came forth establishing *Jagdstaffel 1* of the *1. Armee*.'[33]

JAGDSTAFFEL ERA BEGINS

Commanded by former *Kagohl 1* pilot *Hptmn* Martin Zander, *Jagdstaffel 1* recorded its first victory on 24 August. *Vzfw* Leopold Reimann's quick transition from a Fokker E III to a Halberstadt D II enabled him to shoot down Sopwith 1½-Strutter A879 of No 70 Squadron. The following day *Hptmn* Zander in another Halberstadt attacked F.E.2b 4285 of No 22 Squadron and forced it to land near Guedecourt. On 29 August *Jasta 1*'s third victory was scored when *Obltn* Hans Bethge, a former *Eindecker* pilot, shot down B.E.2e 5836 of No 34 Squadron near Auchonvillers. Two days later *Jasta 1* intercepted a flight of Martinsyde G 100 'Elephants' of No 27 Squadron over Havrincourt Wood; *Ltn* Hans von Keudell shot one down at 0800 hours, *Obltn* Bethge scored his second victory 15 minutes later, and *Ltn* Gustav Leffers achieved his and the *Staffel*'s sixth victories at 0840.

In the days ahead *Jasta 1* added to its roster the former *Eindecker* pilots and *Pour le Mérite* recipients *Ltn* Kurt Wintgens and *Ltn* Walter Höhndorf, both of whom added to their victory lists. Zander's unit shared Bertincourt airfield[34] with *Jasta 2*, which was commanded by *Hptmn* Oswald Boelcke and staffed by a pride of eager young lions recruited from throughout the *Fliegertruppe*. Together the *Jastas* worked to regain the German air superiority first achieved by the Fokker *Eindeckers*. Looking for the Fokker 'magic,' *Jasta 1* switched from using its successful Halberstadt fighters to Fokker D I biplanes, but found the new Fokkers were no match for the new Allied biplanes. As late as November 1916 *Jasta 12*, commanded by *Obltn* Paul Henning von Osterroht, had fourteen Fokker D Is on strength despite their poor performance.[35] Indeed, Fokkers would not reappear as front-line fighters until the advent of the successful Fokker Dr I triplane series of 1917.

In the interim, the 'Fokker Scourge' was succeeded by various types, of which the most successful was the series of single-bay biplane fighters produced by the Albatros-Flugzeuwerke of Johannisthal and Schneidemühl. With their faster climb rate and superior fire power, the Albatros D I and D II helped turn the tide back in Germany's favour. The D III, with its high-compression engine and improved performance, enabled the *Jagdstaffeln* to make 'Bloody April' 1917 the month of the worst RFC casualties of World War I.

The Albatros fighters were the worthy successors to the Fokker *Eindeckers* that enabled German fighter pilots to go on the offensive.

Bear Knight's Cross 1st and 2nd Classes with Swords, Anhalt Friedrich Cross, Bavarian Merit Order 4th Class with Swords and Ottoman Empire Pilot's Badge. Second row from left: Bulgarian Bravery Order 4th Class 2nd Degree, Württemberg Knight of the Military Merit Order, Ottoman Iron Half-Moon, Iron Cross 1st Class, and Ottoman Imtiaz Medal in Silver.

3
OVER THE RUSSIAN FRONT

A S THE CERTAINTY of armed conflict increased in the summer of 1914, the German *Oberste Heeresleitung* prepared for a two-front war. But, having to commit so many of its resources to the Western Front, the *OHL* faced an extremely difficult situation in the coming struggle with Czarist Russia. Even with Austro-Hungarian forces waging a massive campaign along the southern part of the Eastern Front, German cities in East Prussia were vulnerable to an anticipated two-pronged assault: one from along the River Niemen in Lithuania and one from the area between the Bohr and Narew rivers in Poland.

The German *8. Armee* commanded by *General-oberst* (Colonel General) Max von Prittwitz was charged with holding the line. In the worst case, the fall-back position was to be the west bank of the River Vistula. The latter course would have ceded all of East Prussia to the enemy and been a resounding blow to the German war effort. The defensive nature of the action, however, offered the fledgling *Fliegertruppe* an opportunity to display its ability to keep track of and harass a numerically superior enemy which had a number of operational options.

Available to *Generaloberst* von Prittwitz were: *Feldflieger-Abteilung 16* at *8. Armee* Headquarters in Allenstein; *Feldfl-Abt 14* at the *I Korps* in Gumbinnen; *Feldfl-Abt 17* at the *XVII Korps* in Deutsch-Eylau; and *Feldfl-Abt 15* at the *XX Korps*, also in Allenstein. (No air unit was attached to the *I Reserve-Korps* at Nordenburg, south of the *I Korps*.) Assigned to principal cities were so-called 'fortress' flying sections and those within the *8. Armee* were: *Festungs-Flieger-Abteilung 4* at Posen, *Fest-Fl-Abt 5* at Königsberg, *Fest-Fl-Abt 6* at Kulm (as well as Graudenz and Marienberg), and *Fest-Fl-Abt 7* at Lotzen.[1]

The eight units had a total of only 40 aircraft, which were augmented by three dirigibles: Schütte-Lanz *SL.2* at Liegnitz, to assist Austro-Hungarian forces, and the German Army's oldest Zeppelin-built airships, *Z.IV* at Königsberg and *Z.V* at Posen.[2] For all practical purposes, the airships had little value; for example, *Z.IV* had no radio, as the added weight kept it from climbing to maximum height.[3]

NUMERICALLY SUPERIOR RUSSIAN AIR ARM

At the beginning of the war the Imperial Russian Air Service had 224 aeroplanes, 12 airships and 46 kite balloons.[4] Despite this numerical superiority, there is no record of any of these aircraft being deployed in the invasion of East Prussia. The

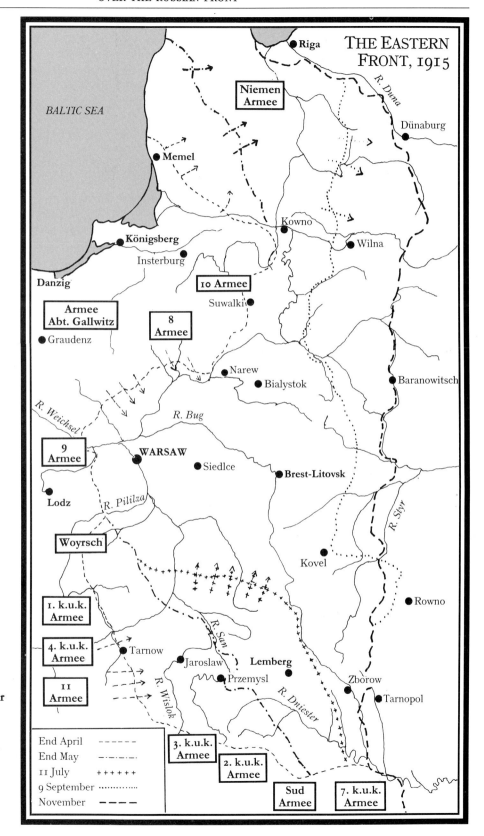

THE EASTERN
FRONT, 1915

BALTIC SEA

R. Duna

Riga

Dünaburg

Niemen
Armee

Memel

Kowno

Wilna

Königsberg

Insterburg

Danzig

10 Armee

Suwalki

Armee
Abt. Gallwitz

8
Armee

Graudenz

Narew

Bialystok

Baranowitsch

R. Weichsel

R. Bug

9
Armee

WARSAW

Siedlce

Brest-Litovsk

R. Styr

Lodz

R. Pililza

Woyrsch

Kovel

Rowno

1. k.u.k.
Armee

R. San

4. k.u.k.
Armee

Tarnow

Jaroslaw

Lemberg

Zborow

11
Armee

Przemysl

Tarnopol

R. Wislok

R. Dniester

End April ───────
End May ─·─·─·─
11 July ++++++
9 September ·············
November ── ── ──

3. k.u.k.
Armee

2. k.u.k.
Armee

Sud
Armee

7. k.u.k.
Armee

◀ Czarist Russia entered
World War I with an air
force numerically superior
to the aircraft its Central
Powers opponents could
muster on their Eastern
Front. A large number of
imported aircraft was
used, such as this
Morane-Saulnier Type H
in which the pilot was
armed with a pistol.

Russians' reliance on traditional reconnaissance by ground forces and the Germans' use of aerial reconnaissance became a critical difference in the outcome of this initial encounter in the east.

General von Prittwitz deployed aircraft to reconnoitre the broad front he had to defend, even to the extent of ordering flights over Russian-held Warsaw. Little activity was reported during the first week of August, but on the 11th forces of Russian General Pavel Rennenkampf's 1st Army were spotted in positions that appeared poised to strike Prittwitz's *8. Armee* from the south. Prittwitz then prepared to trap the Russians between three of his four corps. But he did not know that his aerial reconnaissance had missed a major enemy troop concentration north of Suwalki that would have indicated the true, more northerly, thrust of the first Russian attack. Bad weather on 15 and 16 August made impossible any further aerial reconnaissance. Thus, when Rennenkampf's forces entered East Prussia on the 17th, *General* Hermann von Francois' *I Korps*, counter to orders, hastily engaged the enemy and upset what should have been a skilfully executed counter-attack. In subsequent fighting, the *I Reserve-Korps* and the *XVII Korps* were drawn into the action and away from the point where aerial reconnaissance indicated that General Aleksandr Samsonov's 2nd Army would attack.

General von Hoeppner later wrote:

'The main force of the *8. Armee* was gathered east of the Masurian Lakes; however, their battle with [General] Rennenkampf had to be broken off since, according to fliers' reports, by this time the Narew Army [of General Samsonov] had begun to move and on 22 August with at least two Army Corps had crossed the line from Prasnysch to Ciechanow. It was now of prime importance to determine whether Rennenkampf would remain where he was, rush to help the Narew Army or head for the fortress at Königsberg.'[5]

As these events were unfolding, *General* von Prittwitz sensed that he was caught in a trap by a Russian pincer movement that he had underestimated (in fact, had *over*estimated). On 20 August he informed the Chief of the General Staff, *Generaloberst* Helmuth *Graf* von Moltke, of his intention to withdraw to the Vistula, where he would need additional forces to hold off a further Russian advance.

HINDENBURG'S AERIAL RECONNAISSANCE

Moltke immediately relieved Prittwitz of his command. *Generaloberst* von Prittwitz and his chief of staff, *Graf* Waldersee, were replaced by one of the best command teams of the war: (then) *General* Paul von Beneckendorf und Hindenburg and his Chief of Staff, *Generalmajor* Erich Ludendorff. Called out of retirement, the 66-year-old Hindenburg directed several brilliant strokes which, during the next few days, drastically changed the course of the campaign in East Prussia. Using aerial reconnaissance to keep himself apprised of the movements of his

◀ Pre-war stunt flier Gustav Tweer enlisted in the *Fliegertruppe* and for a short time flew with the *Brieftauben-Abteilung Ostende* during its tour of duty on the Russian Front in 1915. Tweer carried out a number of reconnaissance flights in this unarmed Fokker A II. He was decorated with the Iron Cross 2nd and 1st Classes while in Russia and was then assigned to be Chief Test Pilot at the Hannoversche Waggonfabrik. While flying a new machine on 1 November 1916, Gustav Tweer's aircraft suffered a structural failure and crashed, killing him instantly.

adversaries to the south and east, Hindenburg directed the bulk of his forces to deal with General Samsonov and the Russian 2nd Army's threat from the south; if unchecked, Samsonov would have pushed on to the Gulf of Danzig and cut off the entire *8. Armee*.

With only a small force left to delay General Rennenkampf's 1st Army, Hindenburg pulled the *XX Korps* back to a pocket at Tannenberg to trap Samsonov's 2nd Army. He had the *I Korps* draw behind the bulk of the 2nd Army in a thin line from Neidenburg to Willenburg. To help keep that line secure, Hindenburg and his Corps commanders relied on fast and accurate aerial reconnaissance. Thus, in response to a *Feldfl-Abt 14* report on the 29th that a troop column was heading from Mlawa to the north-east, *General* von Francois brought a reserve force to Neidenburg.

On the morning of 30 August a critically important piece of intelligence was brought back by the *Feldfl-Abt 14* crew of *Obltn* Körner (observer) and *Ltn* Hesse (pilot). They flew from Deutsch-Eylau, base for *General* August von Mackensen's *XVII Korps*, along the westernmost edge of the Russian forces, south to Soldau, then to the Russian staging area at Mlawa and north-east to the front-line at Neidenburg. Their report at 0910 hours of the advance of a brigade-sized relief force only 4 kilometres from Neidenburg countered the prevailing sense that little immediate danger existed from the south.

That information reinforced a similar observation gathered at 0600 hours during the morning mist by *Ltns* Mertens and Canter of *Feldfl-Abt 14*. The critical difference is that the latter crew went straight to *I Korps* headquarters in Neidenburg and reported to the Chief of Staff, *Major* von Massow, who was drafting refined battle plans. When a Russian artillery shell knocked out the Corps'

phone lines, von Massow sent Mertens and Canter to *8. Armee* Headquarters to make a personal report to *Generals* von Hindenburg and Ludendorff.

In his memoirs, Hindenburg wrote:

'On 30 August the opponent attempted to break out of our encirclement by sending in fresh and regrouped forces from the east and south. From the direction of Ostrolenka [to the south-east] he led a new, strong force against Neidenburg and Ortelsburg, where our troops had completely ringed the Russian central [force] and from which [we] held off the opposition approaching from the rear. The danger was all the more imminent because the columns approaching from Mlawa were 35 kilometres long, according to the fliers' reports, and therefore would have been very strong.'[6]

VICTORY AT TANNENBERG

Ultimately success at Tannenberg was determined by *General* von Francois' being able to contain the main Russian 2nd Army element within the pocket and being able to hold off the relief columns. The latter withdrew into Poland on 31 August, thereby confirming the German victory.

Following the Battle of Tannenberg, Hindenburg was promoted to *Generaloberst* and became the hero of the nation for leading the campaign that drove the invaders from German soil. Hindenburg was lavish in his praise for his Corps commanders, but paid special tribute to his aviation crews. He told an Italian war correspondent:

'But the most remarkable people are my fliers. I cannot begin to tell you the remarkable things they have accomplished on their reconnaissance flights.'[7]

Hindenburg next turned his attention to Rennenkampf's 1st Army, which still threatened East Prussia and was expected to make a strong drive for the fortress city of Königsberg. Anticipating that Hindenburg would follow up his success with a drive southwards, towards Warsaw, General Ivan Zhilinsky, overall commander of the 1st and 2nd Armies, reinforced the remnants of the 2nd Army of General Samsonov, who had committed suicide after the defeat at Tannenberg. In fact, the Austro-Hungarian armies were bogged down with their Galician campaign, along the southern part of the Eastern Front, and urged an attack on Warsaw to take some of the pressure off them. But Hindenburg was resolute in his determination to secure the borders of East Prussia.

Once again Hindenburg called on reconnaissance aircraft to help him locate an elusive adversary in the Masurian lakes area, where the final battle for East Prussia took place. For the most part, enemy locations were identified, but aerial reconnaissance was still imprecise. *Obltn* Elard *Baron* von Löwenstern, an observer with *Feldfl-Abt 15*, described one such flight with his pilot, *Ltn* Wittke, in an unarmed Jeannin Taube:

'Around 7 to 8 September our command was not clear as to whether the Russians were withdrawing or preparing for a decisive battle. Thus the order was issued to determine the enemy's whereabouts and to carry out a reconnaissance of the country-side and the roads that led to the line Wirballen, Kalwarija and Suwalki. We had already flown and determined that the battle was in full swing along the line of Lyck, Angerburg, Nordenburg and northwards, but that the barracks near Angerburg had been demolished and a strange quietness prevailed in the countryside just behind the front-lines.'[8]

It was apparent that the Russians were preparing for a major thrust by Hindenburg's forces. *Hptmn* Hans Donat, Commander of *Feldfl-Abt 15*, briefed von Löwenstern and Wittke: 'Under [cover of] strong rearguard actions the main Russian force has been detached. You must positively establish their whereabouts. I will go immediately to Darkehmen, which will be taken today, and lay out directional signs for you.'[9]

When the *Abteilungs-Führer* proceeded with the advance party, von Löwenstern and Wittke were already over the lines:

'We were at 900 metres over Nordenburg. Before us lay Darkehmen – but, no, surely that could not be Darkehmen? To all appearances, a fierce battle raged here. Lichterloh burned ahead of us. Wide, thick smoke clouds covered the place. I had to reorientate myself, as a train crossed below in a way that was quite different from what the map showed. Should I let my pilot know? But that would make me look foolish. Was I about over Gerdauen? But Gerdauen did not lie alongside a brook. The big place off to the right must have been Goldap [not far from the Lithuanian border]. In any case, it was not quite clear to me, but I said nothing and was happy when Wittke eased up on the throttle and headed for what we presumed was Darkehmen. Just beneath us some shrapnel shells exploded. What was that supposed to mean? "A place to land? They are still fighting," I wrote on my tablet [and showed the pilot]. Wittke nodded vigorously. Coming out of a turn we approached Lake Goldap.

'As everything there was free of the enemy, we curved northwards. No enemy, no forest encampments were recognizable. As far as we could see, there was no movement at all. And we were supposed to look for the Russians!? What now? My pilot went down slowly. We crossed roads leading to Gumbinnen, Goldap and Stalluponen. Nothing! Now we flew along the edge of the Rominten Heath. For the most part we got a good look at the heath. How small this great forest looked from 800 metres . . .

'There I was startled back to reality by a clatter of machine-gun fire, followed by a thud as a shot

◀ The Russians also used captured German aircraft, such as this DFW B I fitted with skis for winter operations.

hit the wings. Instinctively I pointed out the hits to Wittke and then rode along as if electrified. A machine-gun did not simply wander alone around the countryside. Where there were shots there must have been troops.

'I bent way overboard to look. Right – there at the edge of the woods were horses. Finally, finally the Russians! Just then I bent down inside the aeroplane to look for the writing tablet I had dropped in the excitement and something cracked nearby, popping in my face, smashing into my goggles. I reeled back. Hits! Wounded? Nervously I felt around on my head. Everything seemed to be all there! Just as I took my hand away from the edge of the fuselage the steel tubing there splintered into pieces. A few seconds' delay and my hand would have been gone. Faster than I can describe it, my brown fur coat was ripped to pieces. Instinctively, when Wittke heard the racket, he turned our bird into the wind. We rose up. We were already in a machine-gun's field of fire. The move with which Wittke reacted saved us.

'Now it meant that we had to fly back over this terrible place, so as not to lose the contact with the Russians. There below us along the northern edge of the Rominten Heath rode the Russian cavalry, without a doubt heading home. My pilot flew a course along the German border and around Lake Wyschtyt.'[10]

As they headed home, von Löwenstern and Wittke saw signs of a general Russian retreat. When this information was relayed to *8. Armee* Headquarters, *Generaloberst* von Hindenburg followed up with a strong push to keep his adversaries on the move. By 10 September the Battle of the Masurian Lakes was recorded as another great victory for Hindenburg and Ludendorff.

Detailed studies of these early battles show that the Russians lost one opportunity after another to defeat a smaller, thinly deployed German force. No doubt the greatest mistake General Zhilinsky's forces made was to send uncoded messages that provided the Germans with a clear intelligence advantage. The next big Russian mistake was their failure to use aircraft that were available to front-line forces. As *Baron* von Löwenstern reported:

'In the evening we reported . . . what was especially interesting to us, a Russian aerodrome at Neidenburg occupied by three biplanes and a monoplane; there were also six aeroplanes at Soldau. We had seen none in the air. The Russians used aircraft chiefly for orderly duty.'[11]

FIRST RUSSIAN AERIAL VICTORY

The lone Russian aerial success of this early period occurred on the Galician Front when, on 8 September 1914, Staff Captain Petr Nikolaevich Nesterov achieved his nation's first aerial victory. Flying an unarmed Morane Type M monoplane, Nesterov went after an Austrian three-aircraft formation bombing the Russian airfield at Sholkiv. Nesterov singled out the flight leader, *Ltn Baron* von Rosenthal, and rammed him. The collision sent both aircraft to the ground and resulted in the deaths of both pilots.[12]

▶ With a flexible forward-firing machine-gun, Russian Voisin LA crews could harass early German aircraft. The 120hp Canton-Unne engine allowed the aircraft to carry considerable weight, but at slow speed and so restricted the machine's ability to engage in long encounters.

Poor tactics and missed opportunities by Austro-Hungarian *Generalfeldmarschall* (Field Marshal) Franz *Baron* Conrad von Hötzendorf required the creation of the German *9. Armee* to reinforce the Galician Front and to keep the Russians from invading the south-eastern German province of Silesia. As it turned out, the *9. Armee* was heading south at a time the Russians were preparing another thrust into Germany and so, in October, the two armies clashed in a battle around Warsaw.

Again, aerial reconnaissance played an important role, but, as *Baron* von Löwenstern noted, both aircrews and ground commanders did not yet appreciate their working relationship:

'. . . the results [of reconnaissance] were not fully utilized because there was no authority to appraise them in their entirety. Thus, the *Korps* commanders received only fragments of the overall observations. Yet they were only superficially interested in the latter. For example, the *XX Korps*, for which *Feldfl-Abt 15* flew, primarily wanted to know if and where the Russians were crossing the Vistula. Everything in the field of strategic reconnaissance . . . only indirectly interested the individual staffs under whom we served because the enemy reported in another sector might in the course of its further advance go somewhere else.

'On the other hand, the commanders of the *Feldflieger-Abteilungen* did not yet understand how to evaluate systematically the reports in collaboration with General Staff officers assigned this duty . . . [After weather and other delays] it was difficult to determine which troops we were observing. Were they the same seen a few days ago? Or were they new? The answer could only be determined from prisoners, reports and spies or some other information. To analyze reports correctly was not always an easy task right up to the end of the war. But it was very responsible work that had to be studied, and that demanded a great deal of practical experience. It was not easily done in the heat of mobile warfare.'[13]

Expansion of the war in the east led to Hindenburg's being named *Oberfehlshaber der gesamten deutschen Streitkräfte im Osten* (Commander-in-Chief of All German Forces in the East) on 1 November. Following the successful rebuff of the Russian push toward Silesia and the important Polish city of Lodz, on 27 November Hindenburg was promoted to *Generalfeldmarschall*. Using his successes and now considerable prestige, Hindenburg and his faithful Chief of Staff, Ludendorff, convinced *Kaiser* Wilhelm that a vigorous Spring

1915 campaign in the East would force the weakened Russians to sue for peace. If successful, the campaign would have freed enormous resources for use on the Western Front, and so the *Kaiser* accepted the idea.

NEW GERMAN AIR UNITS CREATED

As part of the expansion of forces, many new air units were created at the *Flieger-Ersatz-Abteilungen* which were training aircrews. *Ltn* Oskar Kuppinger, a career officer who transferred to aviation in April 1915, described the creation of one such unit at Hannover:

'In May 1915 *FEA 5* was ordered by the highest aviation authority within Germany, the *Inspektion der Fliegertruppen*, to form a squadron for front-line service. I was immediately assigned to the unit, which was designated *Feldflieger-Abteilung 64*. Commanding the new unit was *Hptmn* Hermann Pohl, a veteran aviator who was known as *"Adler"* ["Eagle"] Pohl.

'Six pairs of airmen [from the new unit then] proceeded to the aviation depot at Berlin-Adlershof to pick up the six LVG B II aircraft . . . allotted to *Feldfl-Abt 64*. They took off in the new machines from nearby Berlin-Johannisthal airfield, attained an altitude of 3,000 metres after an hour's flying time and landed safe and sound at Hannover three hours later.'[13]

The unit was sent by train to Kielce, in southern Poland, to support the *Preussisches Landwehrkorps* (Prussian Militia) commanded by *Generaloberst* Remus von Woyrsch. Kuppinger recalled that:

'The first mission was a bombing flight over enemy troops encamped in the Lysa Gora mountains. Each aircraft carried two 10kg pear-shaped bombs . . . hung outside the fuselage, near the pilot's seat, [and] tied with a strong cord which the observer had to cut with a knife before the bombs would drop.

'Some aircraft had bombs placed near the observer's seat, lying on the floorboard. In order to drop these bombs, the observer first had to place them on his seat, turn and, while kneeling on the seat, drop the bombs overboard – without damaging the wing in the process. By using either of these primitive methods of bomb-dropping, a direct hit on the designated target was clearly accidental. Success was moderate.'[15]

The aircrews soon found that their LVG B IIs were inadequate for the task in hand. They were awkward and underpowered, and often difficult to control. Replacements of tired, hand-me-down Albatros B IIs were little better and results did not

▲LVG B I aircraft such as this example were slow, underpowered and had a short career at the Front. They were used for a time on the Eastern Front by such units as *Feldfl-Abt*

64. When replaced by LVG B IIs the new aircraft were just as sluggish and underpowered as the B Is, observed *Ltn* Oskar Kuppinger and other aviation personnel.

improve until the Eastern Front air units began to receive C-type aircraft later in 1915.

While the Eastern Front campaign was not as swiftly decisive as Hindenburg and Ludendorff had assured the *Kaiser* it would be, the German armies were quite successful. Infantry and artillery brought in from the Western Front helped make the 2 May offensive another triumph, leading to the capture of Lemberg, south of Warsaw, and setting up the successful assault on Warsaw. The Polish capital fell on 5 August, the key Ukrainian city of Brest-Litovsk was taken on 25 August, and the Germans were ready to swing northwards into Lithuania and then into the Russian homeland.

Oskar Kuppinger participated in these advances, flying in one of the older Albatros B IIs, and recalled:

'The Austrian *kuk 1. Armee* was deployed to the right of the *Preussisches Landwehrkorps*. In our army orders many references were made to the fact that German fliers on reconnaissance duty should pay attention to the right flank of the *Landwehrkorps*, as [our] allies were known to move further back to where it was more peaceful. With the frontline of the German Army storming forward, it was not easy to keep pace with it or its flanks.

'After changing airfields from Kielce to Radom, in the second week of August we were at the banks of the River Vistula. The *Landwehrkorps* went further north, over the River Strom, following the fall of Ivangorod. Our ground personnel followed the army. The next airfield that we reconnoitred east of the Vistula was at Zelechov, where we arrived in the middle of August 1915. Reconnaissance flights were begun immediately. The sun had already burned for weeks on the Russian plains. So, by early morning the air masses were moving vigorously due to the heat rising off the plains. Our aircraft pitched up and down in this very turbulent air. Some of our observers were always "seasick".

'Our next airfield was near Siedlce, from whence our entire *Abteilung* carried out a raid on Brest-Litovsk. Since my Albatros was much too slow compared with the C-type aircraft, I took off about 80 minutes before they did. As usual, there was not a cloud in the sky. I still had half an hour to go before reaching the target when the other aeroplanes were already over Brest-Litovsk. With my binoculars I could observe very well the fire of the Russian anti-aircraft guns. My comrades later told me that they flew at 3,000 metres altitude. My tired Albatros bird did not get above 800 metres. The Russian defenders were, of course, all ready when I flew over the fortress and dropped my bombs. The Russians fired like mad, but shot too high and hit nothing. My pilot then turned back and, unmolested by Russian fliers, we flew back to our own airfield, where we subsequently met the other aircraft of the unit.'[16]

RUSSIAN WINTER FLIGHTS

Feldfl-Abt 64 continued to move north and east, first to a field just south of Brest-Litovsk and then in October to Slonim, which was also home to the Headquarters for the *9. Armee*, now commanded by *Prinz* Leopold of Bavaria. There the Russian winter began to close in. Flight operations were curtailed by the weather, but not totally halted, as Oskar Kuppinger remembered:

'During flights it was not rare to see temperatures of −40° Celsius. Despite the heavy felt boots and the warm flying clothing we wore, we had to break off all flights after two to three hours due to the cold. The aircraft radiators, which were attached to the fuselage near the pilot's seat, had to be wrapped with cloth for every flight to keep them from freezing.'[17]

In early December 1916 *Feldfl-Abt 64* detached two LVG C IVs to operate from a forward airfield at Baranowitschi and *Ltn* Kuppinger was one of the observers assigned to the advance unit. The crews' primary task was to range heavy artillery fire in the hope of opening a way for the German Army to push north-east to Minsk and thereby place greater pressure on the Russians. As *Feldfl-Abt 31*, also based at Slonim, was the only unit in the area with a wireless-telegraphy set, it took an order from *Hptmn* Streccius, then *Stabsoffizier der Flieger* for the *9. Armee*, to effect the transfer to Kuppinger's aircraft. With the set, the observer could transmit messages to artillery units and help them improve the accuracy of their guns.

'The first ranging by aerial observation went off with no trouble [Kuppinger wrote to the author]. Right up until the last shot was fired we had communication in a very direct way with the artillery. In this way *Feldfl-Abt 64* supported nearby artillery units on more than 25 occasions until April

▲ *Ltn* Werner Chomton and his pilot, *Ltn* Schwartzkopf, of *Fl-Abt 4* shot down a Russian Farman south of Drywiaty 1916. on 14 October 1917. Before leaving the scene, the observer photographed the vanquished aircraft.

Since wireless telegraphy was so new at the time, many visitors from the *OHL* came to the artillery position to witness the arrangements.'[18]

In early 1916 *Feldfl-Abt 64* received its first defensive aircraft, a Fokker *Eindecker*. That type had become outclassed on the Western Front, but it was a valuable addition to a unit in Russia. To prove its worth, shortly after his arrival, pilot *Vzfw* Erich Camphausen forced down a Farman pusher biplane near the railway station at Baronowitschi.

While there was a limited demand for fighter aircraft, the German armies on the Eastern Front did need experienced combat aircrews. Hence, Max Immelmann's *Kampf-Einsitzer-Kommando III* remained in France, while the rest of *Feldfl-Abt 62* went to Russia in June 1916 in response to the great offensive launched by the Russian South-West Army Group commanded by General Aleksei Alekseievich Brusilov. The so-called Brusilov Offensive was intended to draw German forces away from France and Austro-Hungarian forces away from their Italian Front campaign. For a time it was very effective.

One pilot who joined *Feldfl-Abt 62* in May and was with the unit in France just long enough to

meet and become inspired by Immelmann was fellow Dresden native *Uffz* Rudolf Windisch. When he arrived in Russia, Windisch was determined to prove himself, even on a Front not known for extensive air activity.

In France he had been well paired with an aggressive observer, *Obltn* Maximilian von Cossel. They remained together and on 25 August shot down a Russian observation balloon just south-east of Brody, an important front-line position in the Russian 11th Army's drive to recapture Lemberg.

Windisch, who had been promoted to *Vizefeld-webel* in July, received the *EK I* for his role in the balloon attack. He and von Cossel also received the *Ehrenbecher dem Sieger im Luftkampfe* (Cup of Honour for the Victor in Aerial Combat), a heavy silver drinking cup presented to German airmen on the occasion of their first aerial victory.

LANDING BEHIND ENEMY LINES

Windisch and von Cossel continued to look for other missions and targets of opportunity. Their reconnaissance flights took them far behind Russian lines and made them aware of the delicate state of enemy supply trains. They knew that if they could get a good solid hit on a section of track just before an important train came through, the derail-ment would tear up more track, as well as wreck the train, and result in a considerable disruption of Russian supplies. But they also knew that they did

▲ **The rotary-engined Maurice Farman MF.7, based on a 1913 design, saw service in the Russian Imperial Air Service right** up to the end of hostili-ties in 1917. Despite its primitive design, it was highly regarded by its crews.

not have the capability or opportunity to try precision bombing; for, if nothing else, the train to be attacked could simply stop and run in reverse to a safe, well-defended block station. Eventually the two fliers thought, why not risk a landing behind the Russian Front; then the right train could be blown up with charges planted on the tracks. Later von Cossel wrote:

'Risk was the right term, for a landing on unknown terrain could be made on a grass-covered trench, a tree stump, [or] a frozen-hard mole tunnel, and the aeroplane could go over on its nose. All that had to happen was for the propeller to break and we would sit there until enemy search parties and the enemy population seized us. But Windisch and I were quickly in agreement that, with sufficient prepara-tion and some luck, the mission must succeed.'[19]

As the Brusilov Offensive began to run out of steam in September, German army commanders looked for more ways to hamper the Russian effort. In view of the importance of the railway line from Rowno to Brody, the *AOK* Litzmann now pressed its request to have the railway line cut. Windisch and von Cossel brought their plan to their *Abteilungs-*

Führer, Hptmn Kastner, and he authorized them to begin preparations.

During daily reconnaissance flights, a suitable landing place was identified 100 kilometres behind the Russian lines. Only 10 kilometres from the railway line, it was a stubble-field cut out of the woods in such a way that an aircraft landing there would not be visible from three sides.

Von Cossel and Windisch were given explosives and, after some wrangling with Army engineers, an electric detonator. Saying nothing to their comrades – for fear of being overheard by Russian spies – they practised on fox holes in the woods near their airfield. By the end of September they were ready for their special mission.

It was still pitch-dark when von Cossel and Windisch were awakened early on the morning of 2 October to have a light breakfast before starting out. Their supplies and the explosives were stowed in a knapsack weighing 50kg (110lb).

They were assigned an LFG Roland C II *Walfisch* ('Whale') which, being slightly nose-heavy, was not popular with many crews. But it was a rugged, small, single-bay biplane that was ideal for the task in hand. *Feldfl-Abt 62*'s airfield at Perespa, near Sokal, was only 40 kilometres due west of the Front, but Windisch had to take a south-easterly course for about 100 kilometres to ensure that they crossed the Front at a point covered by extensive, thick woods. The darkness, density of the woods and the 1,000 metres altitude all combined to mask them from Russian ground forces. Von Cossel wrote:

'As we approached the chosen landing place, a fiery red sun rose over the morning mist of the Wolhyny Marshes . . . [A short time later Windisch] backed off on the throttle. We glided along [until] Windisch executed an absolutely perfect landing. The *Walfisch* set down like a feather and rolled across the millet stubble to the edge of the woods. Then it was out of the old barge! Sacks into the woods! The heavy stuff firmly strapped to my back so it wouldn't shift; every minute lost was a chance for the Cossacks to swoop down on us. Now with only myself to hold on to one wing, the engine was revved up so the aeroplane could turn around. A handshake. Good hunting! And away! Windisch flew home. I noticed that during the take-off he had to steer around a *Muschik* [Russian peasant] and barely missed him. The horse bolted, the peasant fell backwards into his cart. In his fright he surely did not see the black crosses on the undersides of the wings and would not have betrayed us.'[20]

Safe for the moment, *Obltn* von Cossel disguised himself enough not to be immediately recognizable, but not so completely as to be taken for a spy (and

◀The LFG Roland C II *Walfisch* was man-oeuvrable enough to have been used as a fighter early in its career. Pilot Rudolf Windisch capital-ized on the aircraft's small size and speed to slip in and out of Russian territory.

Following their successful raid of 2/3 October 1916, *Obltn* Maximilian von Cossel (left) and *Vzfw* Rudolf Windisch became national heroes. This photo, showing them wearing their new awards, became the subject of a popular postcard series which glorified the growing number of German aviation personnel who performed noteworthy deeds.

a loud roar, the tracks and nearby telegraph line went up in smoke. The locomotive and many wagons tumbled off the tracks and on to their sides.

Quickly, von Cossel reeled in his ignition line so as to leave no clue to his presence. To confuse the Russians further, he left behind the latest issue he could obtain of *The Times*. Then, despite the rain that followed, he was off at a brisk pace to his rendezvous with Windisch.

'Carefully, I stalked the woods around the landing site [von Cossel wrote]. Everything was clear! Yesterday's landing had not been noticed, [and] the peasant had betrayed nothing. I laid out the landing sign in the hope that there were better weather conditions on our side of the Front and that Windisch would have taken off as soon as possible. And then it really happened! First barely perceptible off in the distance, then it died away, then there was clearly a distant, soft droning sound. It got stronger. With my good Zeiss telescope I saw just beneath the clouds, buffeted by strong winds, the *Walfisch* was approaching. Windisch had not abandoned me. He saw my sign, throttled back [and came in] and soon after that we were shaking hands.

'"Three trains were backed up there," he said.

'In spite of the rain, Windisch had taken a look at the situation. In very cosy fashion, we enjoyed a cigar. Windisch gave me letters and newspapers to read on the return flight. We packed up everything and gave it the gas – homewards.'[21]

The two fliers became national heroes and, two days later, when *Kaiser* Wilhelm was on a tour behind the Front, he used the occasion to honour them. He personally presented *Obltn* Maximilian von Cossel with the *Ritterkreuz des königlichen Hausordens von Hohenzollern mit Schwertern* and to *Vzfw* Rudolf Windisch went Prussia's *Kronen-Orden IV. Klasse mit Schwertern* (Crown Order 4th Class with Swords), the first such award in World War I to an NCO. The men's home states also accorded them suitable recognition: *Fürst* (Prince) Friedrich of Waldeck-Pyrmont awarded von Cossel the princi-

executed) if caught. He removed his woollen flying suit, donned a wooden water cask and covered his uniform with a half-length fur waistcoat that made him look like a local farmer. He smeared mud on his shoulder straps to conceal them, dirtied his boots and removed the insignia from his cap. Carrying explosives in his knapsack and armed with a pistol and a knife, he set out for the railway line and his mission of sabotage.

Along the way von Cossel encountered local residents and soldiers, none of whom questioned him. Indeed, when he camped out on a haystack not far from the railway line, he was joined by Russian travellers who shared their bottles of local brew with him. He was careful not to overindulge.

As soon as it became dark, with the moon and the stars hidden by clouds, von Cossel managed to steal away from the group and begin planting explosives. He had to stop several times for trains heading for the Front with supplies. Finally, at about midnight, he spotted the approaching lights of an obviously long train and decided that it would be his target. As the locomotive approached, von Cossel ignited the explosives. In a brilliant flash and pality's *Verdienstkreuz III. Klasse mit Schwertern* (Cross of Merit 3rd Class with Swords) and his pilot a non-commissioned officer's award connected with the order, the *Ehrenkreuz mit Schwertern* (Cross of Honour with Swords). Later that month Windisch, a native of Saxony, received his home kingdom's *Militär-St-Heinrichs Silberne Verdienstmedaille* (Silver Medal of Merit associated with Saxony's highest bravery award, the Military Order of St Henry).

Windisch later gained wider recognition as a fighter pilot on the Western Front and as commander of *Jagdstaffel 66*. Promoted to *Leutnant* on 5 December 1916, he received the *Ritterkreuz I. Klasse des Albrechts-Ordens mit Schwertern* (Knight's Cross 1st Class of the Order of Albert with Swords) on 4 November 1917 and, after scoring his 20th aerial victory, Prussia's highest bravery award, the *Orden Pour le Mérite*, effective 2 June 1918.

Here the Rudolf Windisch story took a strange turn. He had been shot down or forced to land behind French lines after scoring his 22nd victory on 27 May 1918. The German Army and the German Red Cross were informed that *Ltn* Windisch had been taken prisoner and was not wounded. The *Pour le Mérite* was not awarded posthumously, so it seemed that it would be a matter of waiting for his repatriation before Windisch would receive the high honour. But he was never returned to his homeland and French authorities have no record of his having died in a prison camp. The fate of *Ltn* Rudolf Windisch is one of the unsolved mysteries of World War I.

The ultimate failure of the Brusilov Offensive to make extensive gains (and thereby offset the huge losses of men and matériel) contributed to rebellion in Russia. On 12 March 1917 Czar Nicholas II was forced to abdicate and was succeeded by a liberal provisional government headed by Aleksandr Feodorovich Kerenski, who remained sympathetic to Russia's allies. In April the German *OHL* sought to destabilize the Kerenski government and disrupt the Russian war effort by returning Bolshevik leader V. I. Lenin and his closest supporters from Swiss exile.

On 1 July 1917 the Kerenski government tried to fulfil its obligations to the Allies by launching one more offensive against weakened Austro-Hungarian forces on the Galician Front. It failed and *General-feldmarschall Prinz* Leopold of Bavaria, who had

▲ Uffz Carl Bücker in the cockpit of the LFG Roland D II *Haifisch* in which he shot down a Russian balloon on 16 June 1916. Even though he achieved that distinc-tion, under the strict *Fliegertruppe* rules Bücker did not receive his Pilot's Badge until he had completed all qualifica-tions on 3 August of that year.

succeeded *Generalfeldmarschall* von Hindenburg as commander of all German forces in the East, led an advance that moved relentlessly against the Russians to knock them out of the war.

GERMAN BALLOON-BUSTERS

Russian preparations for General Brusilov's last offensive – including the use of defensive aircraft – were countered by a strengthened German force that could see victory within its grasp. *Dr* Wilhelm Bormann, then an *Unteroffizier* with *Fl-Abt (A) 230*, flew an LFG Roland D II *Haifisch* ('Shark') in support of the *Südarmee* (Armee of the South) commanded by *General der Infanterie* Felix *Graf* von Bothmer, operating on the Galician Front between Poland and the Ukraine. Bormann described the preparations:

'At the time there was no true *Jagdstaffel* assigned to the *Südarmee* on the Eastern Front, but the *Flieger-Abteilung* to which I belonged . . . was assigned two single-seat fighters, as increased Russian air activity was apparent. Most conspicuous of all was the increased number of enemy captive observation balloons. Attacks by our observation aircraft had little success; they lacked special ammunition (phosphorus) and before the big two-seaters dived down to the balloon's altitude, the thing had long since been hauled down by the Russians. Our joy was understandable when, finally, two single-seaters arrived from the Air Park at Lemberg.

'On 16 June 1917, when the *Luftschutz* [Air Defence Command] reported "three enemy captive balloons aloft", *Uffz* Carl Bücker, who flew the other single-seater, and I believed we were sufficiently equipped to attack the enemy. Shortly before take-off the roles had been assigned: Bücker was to take care of the balloon south of the Zborow-Jezierna railway line and I the one to the north. Bücker's machine, which took off before me, did not seem to be working properly, as I quickly caught up with him and soon climbed past him. At the designated point we separated. I let my bird climb peacefully to 2,000 metres and imagined that very easily, like a hawk, I would swoop down on my victim.

'Then I realized that my machine had been seen fighting the wind for some time and [my intended target] had been pulled down, and then it vanished. This dampened my eager spirits considerably; I could no longer find my target and to the south only Bücker's balloon stood there steadfastly. Minute after minute passed and the thing did not even think of going down or burning. Had Bücker's engine failed, so that he had to break off? Quickly I decided to turn southwards. With three-quarters of a tank of petrol, going at full throttle, [and] with a strong wind at my back, I headed for the balloon at a speed not previously experienced. Before even a shot had come from the Russian guns, [my] phosphorus bullets were whizzing into the target, lighted by the ribbon of smoke issuing forth. In an instant I had crossed the length of it and was climbing away. Then a quick turn! Again my machine-guns hammered away, again I had to go along the length of its grey-coloured body, which had not a thought of burning. Still closer, I attacked the old thing, which sank lower as, with feverish haste, the Russians sought to haul it down.

'Suddenly flames shot up; in a moment fire spread throughout the entire balloon, slowly the big sausage burned, [creating] a thick black cloud of smoke; somewhere in the area the tailfins drifted down, all that remained [of the balloon].

'Boundless astonishment – that was it! There was no time for long contemplations. In the course of the attack I had come down to 600 metres, offering a beautiful target to the ground defences, who had had to hold their fire in consideration of

their own balloon. In a zigzag course and with the throttle wide open, I headed west. Finally behind the protection of the Front! And now came the fervent joy of the first success and in the midst of it still the amazement at how quickly everything had happened.

'I had barely landed when I learned that Bücker had not yet returned. But in just two minutes he buzzed in and landed. "What business did you have with my balloon?" [was] Bücker's first not excessively kind question! As he told it, he had attacked the balloon from about 100 metres higher than I had. Who had set it on fire. Not even Solomon's wisdom could have decided this case.'[22]

Apparently, *Luftstreitkräfte* officials felt the credit belonged to *Uffz* Carl Bücker, for he received official recognition for this balloon as his first aerial victory. He was awarded the *Ehrenbecher* and, since the balloon had been ranging heavy artillery against the *2. kuk Armeekommando* (2nd Imperial and Royal Austro-Hungarian Army Command), Bücker also received the *kuk Tapferkeitsmedaille in Silber II. Klasse* (Austro-Hungarian Bravery Medal in Silver 2nd Class) on 31 August 1917. The presentation was made while *Uffz* Bücker was in a local field hospital, recovering from injuries suffered in a crash on 21 August. Following his balloon success, Bücker had been detached from *Fl-Abt (A) 230* to test new aircraft assigned to *Jagdfliegerstaffel Süd* (Fighter Squadron South), a new unit then being assembled in Galicia. The success of *Jagdfliegerstaffel Süd* led to the subsequent reassignment of Bücker and other *Flieger-Abteilung*-based single-seat fighter pilots in the area to the Western Front.

GUEST OF THE TOP RUSSIAN ACE

While aerial combat activity on the Eastern Front was never as extensive as in the west, German fighter aircraft were needed to counter Russian fighter squadrons that were both active and successful in defending their air space. *Uffz* Bollweg of *Fl-Abt 24* discovered this when he encountered the Eastern Front's top fighter pilot, the 17-victory ace Staff Captain Aleksandr Aleksandrovich Kosakov. Shortly after repatriation, Bollweg wrote this account:

'I took off on 18 June 1917 with *Ltn* Deter as observer in a Rumpler C Ia to determine the location of a Russian captive balloon. On the return flight we were attacked by a Nieuport single-seater over Buczacz and after the rudder was shot away we crashed 10 kilometres east of Podhajce. The

aircraft was totally wrecked. I was grazed on the leg; *Ltn* Deter was much more seriously wounded. We were surrounded immediately by about 30 Cossacks and were taken to a field hospital in Podhajce. On the second day the Russian fighter pilot Captain Kosakov sent a car and had me brought to the Russian airfield 10 kilometres north of Buczacz. He showed me all the aircraft gathered there, about six SPAD and Nieuport single-seaters. I was not interrogated. I slept in the same room with Capt Kosakov.

'At 12 midnight I got up and went to his aeroplane, pushed it out of the tent unnoticed and 100 metres away from it, to start up [the engine] there. The Nieuport was always ready for take-off. As I started out with the engine running at half-throttle, I was caught by sentries. Capt Kosakov said to me only that it would have been very nice if I had reached the German lines with his machine, but I was not to be successful.'[23]

Expecting to be punished for his escape attempt, Bollweg was relieved to note that he was not mistreated. Rather, he and *Ltn* Deter were sent to Husiatyn, where they were separated while Deter went to another hospital for treatment. They were reunited two months later and eventually went to Moscow and then along the Black Sea before they were freed by German-speaking Mennonites.

▲ **Sometimes German two-seater crews had bad luck over Russia. Russian ace Capt Ivan Smirnoff of XIX Squadron took** **this photo of Rumpler C I 4739/16 which had been forced to land behind Russian lines.**

Meanwhile, *Uffz* Wilhelm Bormann of *Fl-Abt (A) 230* continued to seek out Russian balloons. On 27 June he successfully shot down a balloon just east of a main railhead at Zborow. Two days later he scored his second victory, a balloon brought down east of Batkow. Thus, Bormann's victories, in tandem with the *Südarmee*'s advance, were successively closer to Tarnopol, a key city in the push to cut deep into southern Russia.

FINAL PUSH TO VICTORY

In fact, Bormann scored his third victory on 19 July 1917, at the launching of the German breakthrough that led to the capture of Tarnopol. He described the events:

'At 0400 hours my day began, eventful and promising. At 0300 hours artillery fire began systematically in the north, [and] at 0500 hours it began near us. At 0700 hours the first shots thundered from a 42cm mortar 3 kilometres away from my airfield. It

▲ Captured German pilot Alfred Heft (left) in front of the Morane Bullet in which Smirnoff brought him down. The aircraft bears the death's head insignia of XIX Squadron, IRAS, commanded by Aleksandr Kazakov, the top-scoring Russian ace.

groaned and gurgled through the air and a moment later a volcano erupted on the other side. It was unbelievably hazy, in addition to the suffocating vapours when the shells hit and especially the vast quantity of gas grenades. [Even though] it was quite blurry, through my field glass I recognized the silhouette of a captive balloon. I took off at about 0730 hours, but could no longer make it out from the air. I flew from there back and forth along the Front and enjoyed the indescribable view of the tremendous attack. Five to six 30.5cm shells often hit simultaneously on the *Zlota Gora* [Golden Mountain], a *Zweiundvierziger* [42cm shell] swept away six houses in Kudobince with one hit. I climbed above the dense smoke to 2,200 metres and circled the place where I presumed the balloon to be, but could not find it anywhere and flew home. Here, armed with the field glass and with no slight annoyance, I found that a second one had already been put up. I had the machine readied post-haste and at 0900 sharp took off for the second time.'[24]

Once aloft, *Uffz* Bormann found that:

'. . . this time, too, I soon lost sight of the balloons. At the Front I met three single-seat fighters of the *Staffel Wulff*, which were circling the *Zlota Gora*; I joined this carousel as the fourth aircraft. Then suddenly for a few seconds the haze parted, [and] clearly both balloons stood there. For the moment I turned my head away – I no longer wanted to see the things; indeed, for the time being I felt that the others could try their luck. Then came an emotional reversal and suddenly I knew that it was my duty to attack, but then the wall of mist closed again. I kept circling with the others and had now only one wish: that the tethered things would appear just once more!

'Then suddenly the mist got thinner, the sun shone through victoriously – both targets stood quite close to each other! Without hesitation I set out for the space between them, so that neither one would know which I would attack. At the last moment I dived on the larger balloon to the right, which was due south of an airfield. I reached it at 600 metres altitude and at 180 metres distance I fired a series of shots. Yet it did not even think of burning; I leapt over it and began the same game from the east side. While turning I could observe enemy aircraft taking off from an airfield. That meant that I had to work fast if I wanted to succeed. Again the machine-guns hammered out as much as the barrels could handle. One fell silent, [and] with the other still firing I came so close to the balloon that I could not jump over it, and so I had to pull the aeroplane nose up and let it sideslip off on one wing. I still could not observe any results. Half mad with rage I wanted to attack again, even though four aircraft were coming at me to bring me down. Then a flame erupted in one of the tailfins and with a shout of joy I turned away, back towards the Front.

'As the pack behind me hammered away with their machine-guns, a fifth [enemy aircraft] appeared right in front of me. I pulled up the fine *Haifisch* and fired off some shots from my remaining ammunition with the one operable machine-gun and at an incredible distance. He dived when he saw the ribbons of smoke, made a sweeping turn to get behind me, and that gave me the game. With the throttle wide open, the able *Haifisch* – otherwise not exactly an ideal fighter aircraft – attained considerable speed. I flew at low altitude over the Front, where there was enough activity going on, then made a low pass over my forward landing field, where due to unfavorable wind conditions I could not land (*Prinz* Leopold of Bavaria, together with *General* [Max] Hoffmann, was directing the breakthrough from a nearby observation tower) and went on further to *Fl-Abt (A) 230*'s airfield near Kniaze.

'For me the day's work was done. At the airfield I lay down in the shadow of my aeroplane for a deep – and one could well say deserved – sleep. My nerves were frazzled. But, as we later learned, the Russians had lost one of their most important balloons that day. At 0930 hours – using the observations of this balloon – the Russian batteries still intact in the south had begun to fire at our troops in the breakthrough area. At 0934 the balloon was already on fire. It was just an accident, of course, that the timing was so nice – but a happy accident!'[25]

Brusilov's final offensive did achieve some gains but was finally beaten back. In the north, the German *8. Armee* attacked Riga on 1 September and took the city two days later. Further advances helped put pressure on the Kerensky government into resigning and, on 6 November 1917 (24 October under the Gregorian calendar), Lenin and his cohorts seized power. An armistice followed and, apart from a German advance on 18 February 1918 to goad the new Soviet government into accepting peace terms, the war with Russia was virtually over. The peace treaty was signed on 3 March. Just in time for German armies on the Western Front – supported by the new low-flying *Schlachtstaffeln* (Battle Squadrons) of two-seat fighter/reconnaissance aircraft – to carry out their great spring offensive.

▼ Following the German victory at Riga in late 1917, this Grigorovich M.15 flying-boat was captured on Oesel island. Apart from a small hole below the cockpit, the aircraft appears to be in fine shape, indicating that it had been put to little recent use as the Russian military effort collapsed.

HYMN OF THE BIG BIRDS

THE EARLIER LACK of success in long-range bombing changed in 1915 with the introduction of the *Kampfflugzeug* (Battle Aircraft) series produced by the Allgemeine Elektrizitäts-Gesellschaft at Hennigsdorf near Berlin. The first model, the AEG K I brought out early in the year, was a relatively small two-bay biplane powered by two 100hp Mercedes engines. Subsequently designated a *Grossflugzeug* (Large Aircraft), the G I led to the development of the first German strategic bombers. The next model, the AEG G II powered by two 150hp Benz engines, proved able to carry a 200kg bomb load.

In 1916 the AEG G III, with its two 220hp Mercedes engines, could carry even more bombs a greater distance. Both the G II and G III were used successfully on the Western Front by the battle groups *Kampfgeschwader der Obersten Heeresleitung Nr 1* and *Nr 2*. After Romania declared war on Germany on 27 August 1916, the Central Powers launched a consolidated effort to defeat Russia's new ally and advance on her southern flank. In August *Kampfstaffeln 2, 3* and *5* of *Kagohl 1* were deployed to Romania with AEGs to support that effort. The campaign was over by year's end, with the Romanian Army effectively neutralized and German forces on the Black Sea.

Swinging southwards, the *11. Armee* under the command of *Generalfeldmarschall* August von Mackensen supported Turkish and Bulgarian efforts to defeat Serbian forces backed by British and French ground, naval and air units in nominally neutral Greece.

Ltn d Res Immanuel Braun, who completed his observer training in G-type aircraft on 5 January

▼ *Ltn* Immanuel Braun (fourth from left) and other *Kampfstaffel 3* officers in front of an AEG G III used during *Kagohl 1*'s raids along the Macedonian Front early in 1917. Braun had not yet completed qualification for his Observer's Badge so his tunic bears only an Iron Cross ribbon.

1917, was posted to *Kasta 3* of *Kagohl 1* and joined the unit in Macedonia. On 20 February 1917, five days after his arrival, *Ltn* Braun wrote to his parents:

'And now to my flying activities, which have not amounted to much so far. I have flown twice; however, only on test flights. Once we flew all the way to the front-lines. Two French aeroplanes fled when they saw our giant aircraft.

'The aircraft makes a terrible racket. The two engines together produce 500 horsepower. I sit all the way up front and am in charge. I have a machine-gun and a bombsight. The terrain here is not very good for these big machines. Three aircraft in my unit have already been heavily damaged, two so badly that they are no longer usable and each one costs 175,000 Marks! As you can see, every time we fly, hundreds of thousands of Marks are involved.'[1]

At the time, *Kagohl 1* was based at Hudova in the Vardar valley of what is now Yugoslavia. *KG 1* was some 100 kilometres north of the Greek port of Salonika (Thessaloniki), a key staging area for British and French troops in that region and, hence, a primary target for German bombers. On 27 February Immanuel Braun wrote home, describing a raid on the port carried out by the entire bombing group:

'Yesterday was a very full day, which I will never forget. At 1500 hours the *Geschwader* took off on a flight to Salonika. We had orders to bomb an army camp and an ammunition dump there. Since we had a heavy load of bombs and fuel, we had difficulty in gaining altitude. I was particularly low, only around 2,900 metres. The flight was not bad, in spite of enemy anti-aircraft fire. Those guys shot very badly.'

IN TROUBLE OVER MACEDONIA

'At about 1630 we reached Salonika. It was an indescribable sight. The large town is surrounded by big troop camps, the harbour has 60 to 70 naval vessels and large freighters, and then there is the open sea. They fired at us from all sides, land-based anti-aircraft, as well as naval artillery from the ships, and we had to zigzag like monkeys. To avoid the fire I ordered my pilot to fly out over the sea, where it was quieter. Suddenly, when I was just about to find my target, there was a big bang and the right engine stopped. An engine oil line had broken. We were about 100 kilometres from our airfield and had to fly into the wind at an altitude of only 2,800 metres. It was rather uncomfortable.

'My pilot passed me a message: "Drop bombs immediately. Must return home." I was aware of

that, as I had experienced contrary winds on earlier bombing raids. However, I did not want to drop the bombs just anywhere. Therefore, I ordered my pilot to fly towards a target that was close to our route home. It was an enemy airfield. I was quite successful, as all bombs hit the target. One aircraft was hit squarely and caught fire.

'Having dropped our bombs with a clear conscience, now we started for home, gritting our teeth. The *Geschwader* had disappeared, we were all by ourselves, and we were dropping lower and lower because the one engine was too weak by itself to carry us. Thousands of times I looked at the altimeter. We went down to 2,600 – 2,500 – 2,300 – and finally to 2,000 metres. Now, at this low altitude, we attracted fire again. I urged my pilot onwards. The exploding shells made a terrible racket, but we made it.

'When I saw a German aircraft above us at a tremendous altitude, I fired some emergency flares in order to gain his protection against enemy aircraft. But he must not have seen us. You can imagine how long the minutes seemed to be until we reached out own front-lines. Nothing is worse than having to land in enemy territory without putting up a fight.'[2]

In addition to being able to fly some distance on one engine, the AEG G III was generally regarded by German aircrews as being a very durable aircraft, better able to withstand the elements than many other aircraft of the time. *Ltn* Immanuel Braun praised the aircraft in his letter of 11 March:

'We are having unstable weather. After two days of heavy rain, now we have a strong cold wind from the north, while also having beautiful sunshine. The wind reaches velocities of up to 28 metres per second [100.8km/hr]. Thus flying becomes highly questionable. On our last flight, we encountered head winds of 24m/sec [86.4km/hr], which is quite a lot, and the aircraft shook mightily. With our *Grossflugzeuge* we can withstand a lot, since, with their weight of 45 *Zenter* [2,250kg], they are calmer in the air than the little C-type crates.'[3]

KAGOHLS REORGANIZED

While *KG 1* continued its operations on the Salonika Front, its structure was strengthened as part of the *Luftstreitkräfte* reorganization. The seven *Kagohls* were reduced to three bombing *Geschwadern* and fully equipped with G-type aircraft. *Kagohl 4*, which also had AEGs, was reduced by one *Kasta*, which went to *KG 1*. The other two-seater-equipped *Kastas* and *Kagohl* units became *Schutzstaffeln* (Protective Squadrons) and worked with the

▶To make the German bomber force more effective, *Obltn* Alfred Keller (left foreground) was ordered to develop and refine night bombing operations. Seen here talking to *Hptmn* Oswald Boelcke (en route back to France to set up his own *Jagdstaffel*), Keller faced much opposition from aircrews and had to draw on his own iron-strong willpower to achieve the night-bombing mission.

Flieger-Abteilungen. A secret *Kriegsministerium* (War Ministry) directive of 25 April 1917 informed top commanders of the evolution of the new dedicated bombing commands:

> 'The *Kampfgeschwader der Obersten Heeresleitung Nr 1* remains composed of *Kampfstaffeln Nr 2, 3* and *5*. In addition, the former *Kampfstaffel Nr 20* of *Kampfgeschwader Nr 4* will be *Kampfstaffel Nr 1* [of *KG 1*]. In due course two new *Staffeln* will be established as *Kampfstaffeln Nr 4* and *6* when personnel and equipment are available.
>
> 'A new *Kampfgeschwader der Obersten Heeresleitung (Nr 3)* will be established. To that end, the former *Kampfstaffeln 1, 4* and *6* of *Kampfgeschwader Nr 1* will be *Kampfstaffeln Nr 13, 14* and *15*. *Kampfstaffel Nr 16* will be established immediately. The establishment of *Kampfstaffeln Nr 17* and *18* will take place in due course in accordance with the availability of personnel and equipment.'[4]

Following *KG 1*'s return to the Western Front in May 1917, it exchanged its AEGs for the larger Friedrichshafen bombers. But the new *Kagohl 3* was assigned the bigger twin-engined *Grossflugzeuge* whose name became synonymous with German long-range bombers: the Gotha series. Produced by the Gothaer Waggonfabrik at Gotha, these three-bay biplanes had longer wings and fuselages and could carry half again as many bombs as the AEGs. During the subsequent aircraft bombing raids on

England, this type of aircraft became so fixed in the popular mind that virtually all German twin-engined bombers were labelled 'Gothas', no matter what their actual type.

In March 1917 Gotha G IVs began arriving at Ghistelles in Flanders, in fulfilment of *Major* Wilhelm Siegert's plans to launch bombing attacks against England, in retaliation for British raids on the German homeland during the first weeks of the war, as noted earlier in this book. With the Gotha bombers of *Kagohl 3* – also known as *das Englandgeschwader* – the German Army used aircraft to bomb England on a strategic basis, much as the German Navy had done with Zeppelin airships. German bombing personnel clearly perceived *KG 3* as an elite unit, as noted in Immanuel Braun's letter of 23 July:

> 'Finally, after three months of waiting, my greatest wish is being fulfilled. I am being transferred to the famous *Englandgeschwader*. This gives me great satisfaction, as only battle-proven officers with experience at the Front are transferred there. I will leave here tomorrow or the day after. I am tremendously envied by the others.'[5]

Kagohl 3 was commanded by *Hauptmann* Ernst Brandenburg, a regular Army officer who had served first in the trenches and then become an aviation observer. He was personally selected for

▲Easily the best-known of the German twin-engined bombers, the Gotha series was begun in 1914 when Oskar Ursinus proposed a twin-engined seaplane with a short nose and engines close inboard. A successful derivative was the Gotha G II, powered by two 220hp Mercedes engines. It gave rise to the G III (seen here), with which the bombing campaign against England was begun.

this command by the *Kommandierende General der Luftstreitkräfte*, Ernst von Hoeppner.

Ghistelles had a certain nostalgic appeal for *Major* Siegert's disciples, but *KG 3*'s primary airfields were much further inland, near Ghent. *Kastas 13* and *14* were at St Denis Westrem and *Kastas 15* and *16* were at Gontrode; later, other *Kastas* would operate from Mariakerke, Oostacker and Schelde-Windeke. An early mission over Belgium ended in disaster when, on 23 April, Gotha G IV 610/16 of *Kasta 15* was brought down over Vron by Flt-Lt L. S. Breadner of No 3 Squadron, RNAS. The crew of *Ltns* Karl Scheuren and Otto Wirth, and *Offizierstellvertreter* (Warrant Officer) Alfred Heidner were taken prisoner.[6]

At about 1700 hours on 25 May, *Hptmn* Brandenburg led 21 aircraft on *KG 3*'s first raid on England, which resulted in 4,900kg of bombs being dropped on troop encampments near Folkestone and the fortress at Dover. On the return flight *KG 3* was

attacked by RNAS seaplanes, which claim to have shot down three Gothas. *KG 3*'s losses that day were two crewmen: *Obltn d Res* Kurt Klemann (observer) and *Ltn d Res* Hans-Hennig Parschau, older brother of *Pour le Mérite* fighter ace *Ltn* Otto Parschau.[7]

On 5 June *KG 3* got closer to its real objective, London, and dropped 5,500kg of bombs on Sheerness and Shoeburyness, east of the capital.

'DAS ENGLANDGESCHWADER' OVER LONDON

Brandenburg was now ordered to lead a daylight bombing raid on London itself, a mission that had great symbolic importance to the German *OHL*, which felt that it would have a highly demoralizing effect on the British war effort. On the morning of Wednesday 13 June, Brandenburg took off with 20 Gotha G IVs. Two had to turn back and one was diverted to Margate and Harwich, but the seventeen aircraft that appeared over London dropped 4,400kg of bombs and inflicted frightful losses on the civilian population. The 162 people killed and 432 injured were the greatest casualties suffered in any single bombing attack on England during World War I. *Hptmn* Brandenburg described the raid:

'Visibility over London was exceptionally clear. With complete clarity one could recognize the Thames bridges, the railway stations, the city, even the Bank of England. Anti-aircraft fire over London was not especially strong and was badly aimed. A considerable number of enemy fighter aircraft had meanwhile nearly reached the same altitude as the *Geschwader*. In all, sixteen enemy aircraft, which were scattered, were counted. The number of enemy machines that took off [after us] was well considered to be about 30. Only one of them

actively attacked us. Flying at random and often circling, all of our aircraft dropped their bombs calmly. From the observers' reports it is emphasized that a railway station in the city, as well as a Thames bridge, probably Tower Bridge, were hit. Of all of the other bombs it can be said that the majority of them fell among the docks and city warehouses. The impact must have been strong. After the bombs had been dropped the *Geschwader* closed formation again. The [now] lightened machines flew well so that enemy aircraft gave up the pursuit at the coast. All our aircraft landed safely at the home 'field.'[9]

The secondary raid was equally successful, as (then) *Unteroffizier* Kurt Delang, a pilot, related to the author:

'While the main body of the *Geschwader* turned down the River Thames to London itself, our mission was to drop bombs on Harwich, on the east coast, far to the north of the mouth of the Thames. The attack went off without *complications*.'[10]

The one aircraft reported to have engaged the Gothas was most likely a Bristol F.2B Fighter of No 35 Squadron, RFC. An observer-gunner, Capt C. H. C. Keevil, was killed while taking on 'three Gothas straggling over Ilford.'[11] When the pilot, Capt C. W. E. Cole-Hamilton, found his gun jammed, he returned to Northolt aerodrome.[12]

Although no other British casualties were recorded, two crews from *Kasta 16* were credited with aerial victories that day: *Ltn d Res* Meyer and *Obltn* Joachim von Seydlitz-Gerstenberg, a single-seater near 'Raylight' (probably Rayleigh in Essex), and *Ltn* Schwieder and *Vzfw* Pfeiffer, a Martinsyde near London. *Offstlv* Fleischer of *Kasta 13* was also credited with a single-seater near 'Raylight'.[13]

Hptmn Brandenburg and *KG 3* returned to a heroes' welcome. The following day, the German public learned about the raid from this colourful contemporary news account:

'A *Geschwader* of our *Grossflugzeuge* reached London yesterday afternoon, dropped bombs on the fortress [*sic*] and with clear visibility observed good results of the hits. Despite strong anti-aircraft fire and several aerial combats, during which one English flier crashed into the Thames, all aircraft returned undamaged.'[14]

In point of fact, Brandenburg's force had suffered some combat damage, 'one aircraft was damaged by anti-aircraft fire, another in aerial combat,' but no losses.[15]

The raid was considered a great triumph. *General* von Hoeppner telephoned *Hptmn* Brandenburg from Berlin, offering a congratulatory message that was published for the benefit of the entire *Luftstreitkräfte*:

'The *Geschwader* has fulfilled its mission. That is the highest recognition I can accord to you and your crews. The *Geschwader* attack on London has been for years an objective of our fliers and our technology. With the execution of the attack *Kampfgeschwader 3* has provided a new basis for air attacks. I thank you and your brave crews . . . To the victorious crew of the aircraft of [*Obltn* von] Seydlitz, I convey my special recognition. Good luck in future deeds [to be carried out] under the symbolic slogan: Brandenburg over London!'[16]

▼ **Three Gotha G IVs of** *Kagohl 3* **at Nieüwmunster prior to taking off for England. Visible-** in-air identification fuselage markings are (from the left) 604/16 'K', 603/16 'MS' and 624/16.

▲For defence, the front cockpit of the Gotha had a flexible Parabellum machine-gun; the rear cockpit was similarly armed and a 'gun tunnel' was open below aft to allow the rear gunner to fire at enemy aircraft climbing from behind and below, a typical 'blind' spot.

FIRST *POUR LE MÉRITE* BOMBER COMMANDER

The day after the raid Brandenburg was summoned to the *Kaiser*'s headquarters at Kreuznach to become the first bomber commander to be awarded the *Orden Pour le Mérite*. An observer by training, Brandenburg selected one of his best pilots to fly him to Kreuznach, *Obltn* Hans-Ulrich von Trotha, a pre-war flier and an original member of the *Brieftauben-Abteilung Ostende*. They spent a long weekend with their royal host and such luminaries as *General* Erich Ludendorff.

The following Tuesday, just as von Trotha and Brandenburg took off for Ghent in an Albatros two-seater, the engine cut. The aeroplane crashed, killing von Trotha and seriously injuring Brandenburg.[17]

While Brandenburg was in hospital, on 23 June command of *Kagohl 3* was transferred to *Hptmn*

Rudolf Kleine, a highly respected leader and former *Staffelführer* with *KG 1*. He authorized eighteen Gothas to make a daylight attack on Harwich and the Royal Naval Air Station at Felixstowe on 4 July. *KG 3* caused considerable damage at Felixstowe and suffered no losses.[18]

Three days later Kleine led his first daylight raid on London, and had losses as noted:

'Twenty-two aircraft of *KG 3* dropped 4,475kg of bombs on London and the results were observed to be very effective. One aircraft of the *Geschwader* hit the port of Margate with 200kg of explosives. One *KG 3* aircraft was reported missing following an aerial combat, another crashed on landing and burned, during the course of which one officer and one *Vizefeldwebel* were killed and one officer was badly injured.'[19]

KG 3 casualties were also recorded during the daylight raid of 22 July as RFC home defence units were deployed in greater strength.

When the *Geschwader* returned on 12 August, the RFC was waiting for them. *Uffz* Kurt Delang recalled:

'Again we were assigned to bomb Harwich. When the *Geschwader* appeared at the mouth of the Thames, we were met by a large number of British

◀ Following the first successful daylight raid on London, many German luminaries visited *Kagohl 3* for a first-hand look at the new strategic bombing weapon. Here Prince Heinrich of Prussia, the *Kaiser*'s brother, is being given a cockpit tour by *Obltn* Joachim von Seydlitz-Gerstenberg, an observer credited with shooting down an RFC Home Defence fighter during the raid.

▶ Dover, England, seen from 6,000 metres over the side of a German high-altitude reconnaissance aircraft. Such photos were taken for both general intelligence and bomb-damage assessment of the effect of raids.

fighters. They followed most of *KG 3*, which turned down the Thames.

'One single-seat fighter followed us on our course along the east coast of England. This Englishman attacked our Gotha constantly from above and soon caused heavy damage to our aircraft. We were already down to 500 metres above the water when the Englishman again attacked from above. Then he flew beneath us for a long time and, off our left wing, he pulled up straight in order to gain altitude and strike again from above. I then put the Gotha into as steep a right bank as I could in order to give our machine-guns a clear field of fire. Thus, at the end of his climb, when the British single-seater had attained only modest speed, he was right in the sights of our machine-guns. Flames burst out in the single-seater and, leaving a trail of black smoke, he plunged into the North Sea.'[20]

Kurt Delang and his fellow crewmen were fortunate in being able to shake off their attacker. *Kagohl 3* suffered other casualties that day: one aircraft shot down and four crashed on landing. Delang became involved in the latter series of casualties:

'As I glided in for my landing at Gontrode, off to my right, from the north, came another Gotha, with one engine turned off. A collision seemed unavoidable. I gave both my engines the gas. The collision was avoided, but midway over the landing area our

fuel gave out. At this low altitude a banking turn was impossible. I managed to put down in a field, where the Gotha broke up completely. My observer, *Ltn* Paul Döge, and I were uninjured; the machine-gunner, *Vzfw* Paul Ruhl, suffered a broken leg when he jumped out of the Gotha just before it touched down. He thought it would burn up! He was taken to a field hospital.'[21]

DAYLIGHT BOMBING RAIDS HALTED

The German *OHL*'s desire to break British civilian morale and tie up men and material in home defence was being attained at considerable cost to *KG 3*. *Hptmn* Kleine halted daylight operations after the 22 August raid. A brief period of night-flying training followed. *KG 3*'s first night raid was launched on 3 September, when five Gothas bombed Chatham, Sheerness and Ramsgate. But night operations had perils not found in daylight missions, as Kurt Delang noted in describing his flight of 27 September 1917:

'The Gothas took off at short intervals, one after the other. Once we were in flight, a thick fog rose up. It extended across Belgium, so turning back was now impossible. Landing with full fuel tanks and bombs on board would have been suicide.

'The fog cleared over Sheerness. I went down in

order to drop bombs on the wharf area. In so doing we were spotted by numerous searchlights. I pulled up above the clouds and proceeded along in the moonlight. But, unfortunately, the elevator controls did not respond at all. Apparently, the control cable had been severed. Now it was no longer possible to keep the Gotha on an even keel, to say nothing of trying to make a landing. Without doubt the flight had to end in a crash.

'As we dipped through the clouds, again the Gotha went into a nose-dive. We dropped from 1,800 metres. I switched off the ignition for both engines so that they would cool off during the final dive. We did not know where we were. But we got lucky. The Gotha came down in Belgium, into a row of poplar trees that took the impact of the crash. *Ltn* Döge, almost without injury, ended up safely in the top of a tree; the machine-gunner, *Uffz* Jödicke, lay in the end of the fuselage with a broken arm, and the medical corpsmen found me under the wreckage. I had a slight brain concussion.

'Later, we were reunited in [Field Hospital] *Feldlazarett 396* in Erneghem, Belgium. There *Ltn* Döge said to me: "As long as I fly with you, Delang, nothing will happen to me. But if I have to fly even once with another pilot, it will look bleak!" '[22]

Kurt Delang was later posted to the bomber pilot training school at Paderborn, where he learned that *Ltn* Paul Döge did in fact perish on his next mission. Döge was part of the rising casualty list of the *Englandgeschwader*. It was clear that the Gotha bombers – and even the larger *Riesenflugzeuge* (Giant Aircraft), or R-types – were becoming increasingly vulnerable to improved Allied defensive measures, as well as British and French bombing raids over the airfields used by the German long-range bombing units.

THE BOMBERS ARE BOMBED

Ltn Immanuel Braun felt the effect of the defensive fire, as his Gotha had been badly damaged during a raid in September. But that did not stop him from participating in the mission to London on the evening of 30 September/1 October 1917. He and his pilot simply loaded up a two-seater with four 12kg bombs and followed the big birds across the Channel, and then bombed Dover. On returning to Gontrode, however, he found that 'the British had dropped a lot of bombs' there while he had been away. That evening RFC documents noted:

'No 101 Squadron (F.E.2b) carried out a raid on Gontrode airship shed and dropped two 230lb and four 20lb bombs . . . On 1 October No 55 Squadron

▲ **Knowledge of the weather was important to *Kagohl* aircrews. Here, *Ltn* Walter Georgii (right), meteorological officer of *KG 3*, is on a rooftop** station at the University of Ghent supervising the release of a weather balloon to measure winds at high altitudes before a raid on England.

(D.H.4) dropped twelve 112lb, 32 20lb and 199 1lb bombs on Gontrode airship shed. Direct hits were obtained on aeroplanes in front of the sheds, and a fire was started near the large shed.'[23]

Despite these incursions, *KG 3* continued to carry out attacks on England, as well as joining other *Kagohls* in striking targets within the immediate area. *Geschwaderkommandeur* (Group Commander) Rudolf Kleine, who had meanwhile received the *Orden Pour le Mérite* on 4 October, led such a mission on the afternoon of 12 December. The Gothas were flying at 2,500 metres when they were intercepted at about 1415 hours by a Flight of Nieuport 27s from No 1 Squadron, RFC. In his combat report, Capt W. W. Rogers wrote:

'Just after climbing through the clouds I saw two formations (nine and eight) of Gothas coming west [at] about 7,500 feet. I climbed up with the patrol

▲ Night flights over England, thanks to the cover of darkness, permitted the aircraft to fly lower and they could therefore carry more bombs. The Gotha G V being loaded here already has two 100kg bombs attached to the fuselage and the groundcrew are adding five 50kg bombs.

▶ Preparing a Gotha G V for a high-altitude flight, ground crewmen of *KG 3* pour liquid oxygen into special containers to vaporize the chemical as an aid to breathing. Valves on the side of each container regulated the flow of oxygen into rubber bladders. To use the oxygen, the aircrew sucked on a breathing tube attached to the regulator valve.

and observed one EA turn back east, so [I] attacked it, firing 3/4 drum at 30 to 20 yards range. EA burst into flames, fell to pieces and crashed north of Frelinghem.'[24]

The entire crew perished: *Hptmn* Kleine, *Ltn* Werner Bülowius (observer), *Ltn* Günther von der Nahmer (pilot) and *Gefr* Max Weber (air-gunner). They were given a heroes' funeral, presided over by *Hptmn* Brandenburg, who cut short his convalescent leave to resume command of the *Geschwader*.

KAGOHLS REORGANIZED AGAIN

To counter the threat posed by America's entry into the war, *General* Ludendorff strongly urged expanded aerial bombing capacity on the Western Front. *KG 3*'s operations over England and, in the latter part of 1917, *KG 4*'s assistance on the Italian Front were prime examples of the use of aerial bombing. *Kogenluft*, however, favoured increasing the number of *Jagdstaffeln* to provide air cover for the valuable aerial reconnaissance provided by the *Flieger-Abteilungen*. The immediate answer was another reorganization of the *Kagohls*, increasing the number of *Geschwader* by decreasing the number of *Staffeln* within each from six to three; the sole exception was *KG 3*, which kept its strength at six *Kampfstaffeln*.[25]

Thus, on 18 December 1917, the *Kriegsministerium* announced an '*Umwandlung*' (transformation) of the *Kampfgeschwader der OHL* into six *Bombengeschwader der OHL*.[26] Abbreviated *Bogohl*, the units were joined by a seventh and, from the Bavarian forces, an eighth *Geschwader*. Ultimately, the new *Bombengeschwader* were composed as follows:

Bogohl 1:	*Bostas 1–3*
Bogohl 2:	*Bostas 10–12*
Bogohl 3:	*Bostas 13–18*
Bogohl 4:	*Bostas 19–21*
Bogohl 5:	*Bostas 4–6*
Bogohl 6:	*Bostas 7–9*
Bogohl 7:	*Bostas 22–24*
Bogohl 8b:	*Bostas 25–27*

The third major *Grossflugzeug* was produced by the Flugzeugbau Friedrichshafen on Lake Constance in southern Germany. Founded by Ferdinand *Graf* von Zeppelin, the firm produced a range of naval aircraft, as well as the much-used bomber aircraft often mistaken for Gothas. Just slightly smaller in size than the Gotha series, the Friedrichshafen

bombers carried the same bomb load (500kg) at slightly greater speed.

MORE NIGHT BOMBERS

Former *Obltn* Oskar Kuppinger, who assumed command of *Kasta 3* of *KG 1* in June 1917, recalled the Friedrichshafen bombers:

'Called "FdH" for short, the aircraft had three bays of struts and "pusher" type engines located inboard near the fuselage. Since the propellers were at the aft part of the engine nacelles, when the aircraft was in flight no small object – not even a pencil – was allowed to fly backwards from the cockpit, which was at the leading edge of the wings. Such flying objects would invariably cause the propeller to split apart. Hence, the spent cartridges of the observer's machine-gun were caught in a pouch attached to his gun.

▼An observer-gunner in the '*Kanzel*' of a Gotha G V kept the oxygen tube in his mouth as a precaution against oxygen starvation as the aircraft climbed to high altitude.

Just behind the gunner is the pilot's rear-view mirror which enabled him to see the rear gunner without changing position.

'In addition to the observer's machine-gun, the rear *Fliegerschütze* [air-gunner] had two machine-guns to attend to: one was ring-mounted and movable, as in a C-type aircraft, and the other fired towards the rear from below. To work the latter gun, the *Fliegerschütze* had to lie on the floorboard of the aircraft and open a hatch to allow the machine-gun a field of fire. A *Motorbedienungsmann* [engine service man] sat near the pilot during the flight to observe the various pressure gauges and the radiator temperature.

'The regular 50kg bombs were attached to the underside of the aircraft, level with the bottom of the bottom wings . . . Some aircraft had the capacity to carry one 300kg bomb. Normally, each aircraft carried a total of 500kg of bombs. The observer always loaded up his *'Kanzel'* [pulpit] in the front of the aircraft with additional 10kg bombs, which were dropped over the side by hand.'[27]

Pre-war flier *Hptmn* Alfred Keller, who began developing night operations when he converted *Feldflieger-Abteilung 40* into a night-operating unit in 1916, had been *Kommandeur* of *KG 1* since the spring of 1917. After bringing the unit from Macedonia to Flanders, he helped to shape and refine German strategic bombing, particularly at night. In correspondence with the author Keller wrote:

'Since the defences there were too strong for daytime operations of formations of large aircraft, I had to convert the *Geschwader* to night flying. Consequently I received new aeroplanes, twin-engined Friedrichshafens, which we painted all black. Converting the *Geschwader* to night operations was a difficult task for me because the aircrews had a strong aversion to night flying and they had no experience at it. A large proportion of the pilots asked to be transferred to fighter or other aviation units. I was forced to change considerably

the personnel make-up of the *Geschwader*. Then came the break-in period to train the crews for night flights against the enemy. But, as the old saying goes: "Practice makes perfect." Soon I could report to the *OHL* that the *Geschwader* was ready to go.'[28]

Oskar Kuppinger remembered Keller as 'a man of iron will in carrying out the flights that were ordered by the *OHL*. He did not pass up any mission that was at all possible for the *Geschwader* to undertake. *Hptmn* Keller was always the first one in his aircraft and the first to take off.'[29]

On 4 December 1917 *Hptmn* Alfred Keller was presented with the *Orden Pour le Mérite*. Oskar Kuppinger recalled that even high honours did not deter the *Geschwaderkommandeur* from his main purpose:

'When *Hptmn* Keller received the *Pour le Mérite*, all the crews of *Bogohl 1* thought "tonight it will be quiet". That evening in the railway cars that served as our *Kasino* there was a half-bottle of German *Sekt* at every place at the dinner table. Since the *Führer* of *Bombenstaffel 2*, *Obltn Freiherr* Marschall von Bieberstein, was the squadron leader with the most time in service, he had to make the general remarks of congratulations to *Hptmn* Keller on

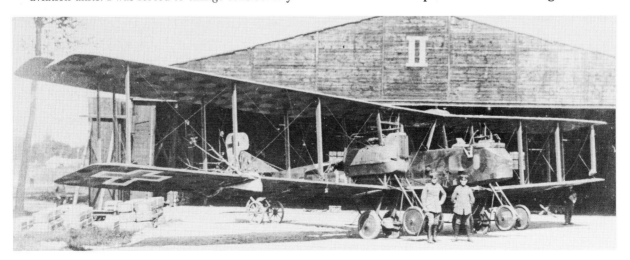

▼ *Ltn d Res* Adolf Tochtermann (left) and *Ltn d Res* Immanuel Braun had a narrow escape in their Gotha G V. While taking off on a night mission with *Bogohl 3* on 30 May 1918, the aircraft struck two poplar trees and three telephone poles. The Gotha continued to fly and Tochtermann managed to bring it back to Gontrode for a safe landing. Evidence of the night's misadventure can be seen in the poplar tree debris still in the struts of the starboard wing.

◀ For use against special targets the AEG G IV could be armed with two 300kg bombs. Heavy single bombs were generally released in close proximity so as to not upset the balance of the aircraft.

behalf of all crews of the entire *Geschwader*. He said to me, "I cannot make a speech while I am sober". We urged him to empty the half-bottles of *Sekt* that had been set out. He drank two or three, which we refilled immediately, and then delivered his stirring speech perfectly.

'After the meal, *Hptmn* Keller pushed aside the curtain of his window, looked out at the night sky for a while, then reached for the telephone and called the airfield to order the aircraft to be prepared for take-off immediately. This directive had an extremely sobering effect on all the people at the party. After the flight, a few of us got together to toast Keller's award with a bottle of *Sekt*, but, of course, by that time the earlier high spirits had disappeared.'[30]

BOMBING PARIS AT NIGHT

In January *Bogohl 1* changed airfields from Ghistelles, Belgium, on the *4. Armee* Front south to Etreux, France, on the *2. Armee* Front, the latter location being closer to the next major bombing objective – Paris. Oskar Kuppinger recalled:

'On the night of 30/31 January the first raid from Etreux to Paris took place in retaliation for British and French bombing attacks on "open" cities along the Rhine. My pilot, *Vzfw* Julius Tillmanns, and I went up in a DFW C-type aircraft to fly a reconnaissance mission while big clouds moved through the night sky. Meanwhile, the FdH aircraft stood loaded and ready to take off from our airfield. If my reconnaissance proved that a flight over Paris was possible, then I was ordered to fire white and green flares many times; I was to fire red flares only if it appeared to be impossible.'[31]

Within five minutes after take-off Kuppinger determined that a flight over Paris was easily

possible. He fired the prescribed flares and urged Tillmanns on towards Paris. Over the city Kuppinger dropped some 10kg bombs and several hundred yellow leaflets, explaining the reason for the raid in German and French. French anti-aircraft fire opened up on the DFW, but did not come close to it. The raid was successful and all the *BG 1* aircraft returned to Etreux.

Shortly afterwards *Obltn* Kuppinger was transferred to the *Geschwaderschule* (Bombing Squadron School) at Paderborn in eastern Germany. There his experience helped to shape the training of future *Bogohl* aircrews, but he missed the first massive, multi-*Geschwader* raids on Paris led by *Hptmn* Keller.

At about the same time *Ltn d Res* John Knauer reported from the Paderborn school to *Bosta 23* of *Bogohl 7*. Operating from an airfield just east of Valenciennes, *Bogohl 7* flew AEG G IV aircraft, which offered many improvements over the G IIIs used by the *Kagohls*. The G IV was fitted with two 260hp Mercedes engines and could carry 700kg of bombs (vs. 500kg in the G III). Knauer recalled:

'We did not learn the objective of any evening's mission until the briefing just before take-off. At that time the *Geschwaderkommandeur* would review the target and supply us with such information as advance airfields where we could land if we had engine trouble or some other problem. We were kept in comparative ignorance about other *Bogohls*, their locations and their objectives. This was done so that if we were captured, we would really have nothing to tell the enemy interrogators. We did know, however, that we often worked in conjunc-

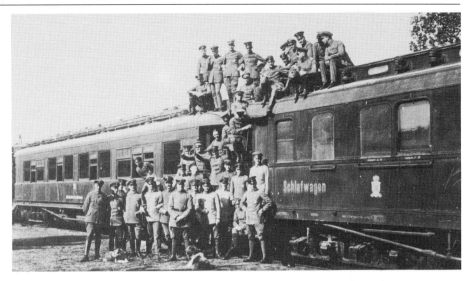

▶ The bomber units travelled in style. Here, officers of *Kagohl 1* used two of their sleeping-cars as the background for an informal portrait at Ascq railway station, 10 kilometres east of Lille, in June 1917. *Geschwader-Kommandeur* Alfred Keller is in the centre of the front row.

tion with *Bogohl 1* commanded by *Hptmn* Alfred Keller.

'While we were being briefed for the night's mission, our faithful mechanics were getting our aircraft ready. The chief mechanic, a man for whom we all had high regard because his knowledge and ability kept us in the air and alive, made the final check of each machine. Then we pilots and aircrewmen arrived and prepared for take-off. We started out in short intervals of about one minute apart, one machine after the other rolling down to the flight line. The *Startoffizier* [Operations Officer] quickly gave each aircraft a last-minute inspection with his flashlight and then waved us on.

'We generally left at dusk, while the sky was still red in the west, and this presented an eerie sight from the ground as each of the big bombers rolled along the ground and then into the air with its great load of fuel and bombs. Our planes must have looked like some great prehistoric birds, struggling to get airborne against the red twilight of the primeval world.

'Bearing such a heavy load, our bombers rose very, very slowly. You couldn't force them to climb; you had to rely on a favourable wind and the steady rhythm of the engines. With a full load of bombs we were never able to climb any higher than 2,000 metres or so. But the big question was how high we would be when we crossed the lines. When the wind was strong or the weather was bad, we could scarcely make 1,300 metres, which was rather low, for the mass of searchlights could get you. Once one searchlight found you, a dozen more quickly got on to you and illuminated the aircraft for the gunners on the ground. Every anti-aircraft battery in the area would open up on such a target, making life very difficult for the aircrew. The noise of the engines would be overwhelmed by the louder noise of explosions all around. If you were fortu-

nate to fly through such a barrage, the very least that would happen is that your aircraft would have many small holes, which would need to be patched during the next 24 hours so that the machine would be ready for the next night's mission.'[32]

Just as night-flying home defence squadrons in Britain had managed to curtail air raids across the Channel, the Allied air arms in France developed night fighters to counter the threat arising from *Hptmn* Alfred Keller's co-ordinated raids. John Knauer remembered:

'The enemy night fighter squadrons learned that we started at dusk, so that was the time they looked for us. Once it became dark, they would have trouble finding us. One night, just after we left Valenciennes, we must have been sighted by a night fighter of one of the opposing squadrons (it was impossible to tell the nationality of the aircraft; all we could really see were the tracer trails of the phosphorus machine-gun bullets). I first became aware of this when my gunner began firing into the darkness . . . A few minutes after he fired, he fell back into his compartment, wounded by the enemy night fighter. The observer took his place at the machine-gun and we continued our mission. Fortunately, the night fighter broke off contact. The other machine-gun – in the *Kanzel* or forward compartment – was unmanned and I certainly could not leave the pilot's position to fire it.'[33]

As the German Army prepared for its Spring 1918 offensive, support in various forms was received from the *Luftstreitkräfte*. The *Bombengeschwaders* hit both front-line and rear area targets not directly related to the several Fronts; the latter as a means of distracting Allied armies and forcing

▲ Friedrichshafen G III 162/17 of *Kagohl 2* being prepared for a night bombing mission. The Friedrichshafen's 78ft wingspan was a foot longer than the Gotha's and its 42ft fuselage was 2ft longer than the Gotha G V; both bombers used two Mercedes 260hp engines.

them to defend rear areas more heavily. Knauer again:

'*Bogohl 7* took part in the raids on Paris led by *Hptmn* Keller on the nights of 8/9 and 11/12 March 1918. Keller was the overall commander of *Bogohls 1, 2, 5* and *7* for these operations. There were many targets to be hit – ours was the Sevran munitions factory – but these flights were just part of our routine duties. About the same time we made a night raid on railway lines in support of our ground troops in the area and that was one of the few times we actually worked with the army.'[34]

RAIDS DURING THE MARCH OFFENSIVE

At the outset of the German offensive *Bogohl 7* was moved from Valenciennes south-west to Peronne. The new airfield was still on the *2. Armee* Front, but much nearer the lines and thus closer to Paris and nearby strategic targets. On 22 March, the day after the offensive began, *Bogohl 7* received a new *Geschwaderkommandeur*, Hermann Köhl, who had been a *Staffelführer* during *BG 4*'s successful tour of duty on the Italian Front and who had long experience in single- and twin-engined aircraft. Köhl was promoted to *Hauptmann* the day he assumed command of *BG 7*.

Hptmn Köhl was a very active bombing commander; he undertook missions of his own or led his flights into battle against heavily defended targets such as the munitions dump at Blargies. He completed his 800th flight while with *BG 7* and was proposed for the *Orden Pour le Mérite*. As recorded in his memoirs, Köhl regarded the occasion with some misgivings:

'Everyone was gathered around to congratulate us. That night I did not take off, but instead drank a half-bottle of *Sekt* with [my pilot Franz] Schlenstedt. I had the feeling that now I was due for the *Pour le Mérite*, which I would have received a year ago if I had not made an unauthorized flight to Paris.

'But I was uneasy about this thought. For us fliers the *Pour le Mérite* was thought to be a bad luck award. Almost all those who received it were soon on the casualty list or the register of the dead, and one did not need to be at all superstitious, as it had no supernatural basis. Whoever received this highest wartime decoration as an officer of lower rank had to have already accomplished all sorts of things; whoever received it did not go home, but stayed out there at the Front and fulfilled his duty, only now the right way, until the day came when fate drew a thick line and added up the sum. It was not any different for me and I thank God that I did not meet my death.

'With this not very pleasant thought, I fell into a deep sleep out of which I was awakened the next morning by a message of acknowledgment from the *Kommandeur der Flieger* [of the *2. Armee*]. Great enthusiasm reigned throughout the *Geschwader*. I was privileged to hand my able pilot, *Vzfw* Schlenstedt, his promotion to officer rank. The same evening I received the news that I would be presented the *Pour le Mérite* by the Army.'[35]

Later that evening, 21 May 1918, Köhl and Schlenstedt flew in an AEG two-seater to reconnoitre Paris. A second aircraft, with *Staffelführer* Falke aboard, accompanied them. Dropping flares periodically, they could make out the targets to be hit by the big bombers. But the flares attracted attention and soon French anti-aircraft fire opened up. Köhl's aircraft was hit and began to lose altitude. Falke's machine disappeared as Schlenstedt and Köhl went lower and lower. They landed in a meadow described by Köhl as 'somewhere between Paris and the Front'.

The landing was uneventful and they managed to burn the aircraft before setting off in the direction of the front-line, some 45 kilometres away. They were intercepted by French troops en route and taken prisoner.

Back at *Bogohl 7* there was great hope that the newly honoured *Kommandeur* and his pilot would manage to return. Indeed, hopes were buoyed by the experience of a *BG 7* crew just a few days earlier. It was reported in the *Nachrichtenblatt*:

'An AEG aircraft [of *BG 7*] that took off on a bombing flight on the night of 16/17 May was forced by anti-aircraft fire to make an emergency landing south-east of Longueau–Amiens. The crew – *Ltn d Res* Prüssner, pilot; *Ltn d Res* Margull, observer;

and an *Unteroffizier* air-gunner – set fire to the machine and ran east in the direction of the burning city of Villers-Bretonneux. The *Unteroffizier* got lost, but both the officers, using English names and speaking English phrases, succeeded in slipping through three British reserve positions and the heavily occupied forward line, after which they hid in a dug-out, then on to a German listening post.'[36]

Hermann Köhl and Franz Schlenstedt were not so lucky. Initial escape attempts proved fruitless, but both men finally reached Switzerland in 1919 and were repatriated from there.

Just before Köhl's capture, another monumental event took place. On the night of 19/20 May 1918, the *Englandgeschwader* made its last flight over the Channel. A massive formation of 28 Gothas and three *Riesenflugzeuge* struck London. One Gotha was forced to land in England and five others were shot down. According to a German authority, 'the pressure of events in France led to the cessation of raids on England, and the bombing squadrons were

▼ During a tour of the Front in 1917, *Kaiser* Wilhelm II visited *Kagohl 2* and inspected their Friedrichshafen G III bombers. Note the 'lucky' horseshoe attached to the front of the aircraft the monarch is reviewing.

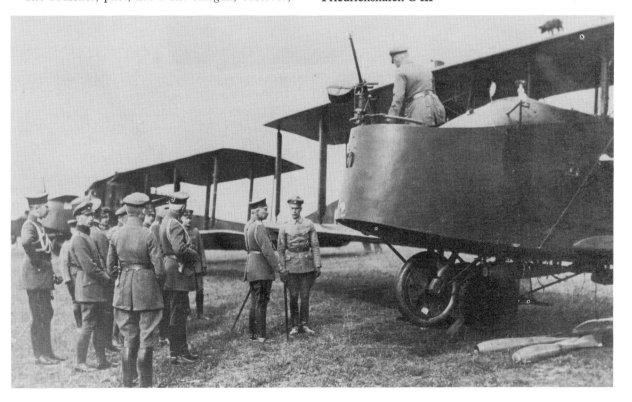

◄ In addition to two internal bomb racks, each holding five 12kg bombs, larger ordnance could be carried beneath the Friedrichshafen's fuselage and released in flight.

◄ For use against ground forces, Friedrichshafens could be fitted with a special rack for smaller (12.5kg) bombs.

exclusively engaged, from May onwards, on the Western Front.'[37]

Ending the multi-aircraft raids on London also meant a shift in emphasis away from Paris. The *OHL* turned its attention to targets that were more related to the battlefronts. In late May *Obltn* Oskar Kuppinger left the *Geschwaderschule* for the *18. Armee* Front to take command of Hermann Köhl's old *Staffel*, *Bosta 19* of *Bogohl 4*. The unit flew a different type of aircraft, but the hazards of night operations remained the same, as he described:

'*Bogohl 4* was equipped with AEG G IV bombers, which were more manoeuvrable than the Friedrichshafen G IIIs I had flown in while in *Bogohl 1*. The normal bombload for the AEG was about 700kg.

'During *Bosta 19*'s first mission under my command, a tragic event took place. Twin brothers in separate aircraft were killed on the same night, at different points in the same mission. Following a raid on Compiègne on the night of 11/12 June, *Ltn*

▶ AEG G IV 1126/16 was captured and evaluated by the French. The colours of the large hexagonal lozenge camouflage fabric were also applied to the engine nacelles and, in this case, a shark's mouth was painted on the bottom front of the observer's cockpit.

Hans Witte and his crew from *Bosta 19* came diving in at low altitude and crashed while attempting to land on a fog-shrouded airfield at Danizy. Those killed with *Ltn* Witte were his pilot, *Uffz* Karl Müller, and *Fliegerschütze* Willi Schwalm. Meanwhile, *Ltn* Manfred Witte, an observer with *Bosta 21* and the twin brother of the officer in my *Staffel*, perished somewhere in the vicinity of Compiègne. According to later reports, his aircraft crashed behind enemy lines. We buried our three casualties in a cemetery in Ham on 13 June. Funeral music was provided by musicians from the *Königin Elisabeth Garde Grenadier-Regiment Nr 3*.

'As my old pilot, [newly promoted] *Ltn* Julius Tillmanns, had also been stationed on the home front and not yet been assigned back to a front-line unit, I selected another pilot, *Ltn* Eberhard Grude.

'The *Bogohls* had been ordered to send single aircraft on missions over Paris to agitate the defence forces there. So it was that *Ltn* Grude and I flew to Paris on the night of 28/29 June with 680kg of bombs. The French were ready for us. A few times the searchlight had our machine in its cone of light, but we evaded this undesired illumination by making sharp turns. Enemy night fighters frequently spotted us in the searchlight's beams, but were unable to hit us. During the flight back, searchlights pursued us all the way back to Compiègne.'[38]

Oskar Kuppinger's personal war diary shows that *Bosta 19* was in action continually during the

▲ The Friedrichshafen bombers, often mistaken for Gothas, were very active along the Channel coast. Here, a special flight led by *Obltn* Oskar Kuppinger, *Führer* of *Kasta 3* of *Kagohl 1*, patrolled over the water, looking for enemy warships to bomb. A captured British machine-gun was fitted to the top wing to 'dissuade' any potential attackers from above.

month of July, flying 23 sorties, in many cases several per night. The entire *Geschwader* dropped over 1,000,000kg of bombs that *month*.[39]

The month of August was even busier; *Bosta 19* flew 28 sorties as part of the struggle to hold back the relentless Allied advance. Both *BG 1* and *BG 4* were operating in the *18. Armee* sector and scored significant hits. They felt their adversaries' sting as well, as noted in a *Kofl 18. Armee* report:

'The *Bombengeschwaders* penetrated the enemy's defences during the early days of the battle east of Ham and they bombed primarily the railway stations. Concentrated in large formations at medium and low altitudes and flying with strong protection by single-seaters, later in the day they attacked both front and rear areas. At night there was a break in the darkness due to the brightness caused by the [enemy] bombing attack on St Quentin. An ammunition dump of *Bogohl 4*, with about a hundred 50kg bombs, exploded. Rail traffic in the area was not noticeably disturbed. The enemy night attack squadron was protected by the unfavourable night conditions. Hence, roads and railway lines were closely tended with searchlights during the raid.'[40]

The slow but steady retreat along the Front hampered resupply efforts. Thus, in September, *Bosta 19* flew only fourteen sorties as the *Geschwader* began to run low on supplies and equipment. As if that were not enough, Oskar Kuppinger recalled a particularly unnerving experience during the conclusion of a flight in early September:

'The airfield was brightly illuminated by our searchlight truck and *Ltn* Grude was just about to

set our AEG down when the aircraft shook with a great jolt. Suddenly it had lost all forward air speed. Grude immediately increased engine power and pulled up and circled the airfield.

'He landed a few minutes later without further trouble. During an inspection of the aircraft after we had landed, we found in the tail a 50kg bomb that had broken into three pieces. While dropping bombs over the target, the front and rear fastening devices on the bomb had not released simultaneously. Hence, the bomb had not dropped and, instead, had hung on like a battering ram below the aircraft during the return flight. On landing, it tore through the floor of the machine and broke apart. We never determined why it had not exploded. After that it became standard procedure for the air-gunner to look through the lower rear gun tunnel following every drop to make sure all the bombs were gone.'[41]

A short time later *Obltn* Kuppinger was ordered back to Germany for six days. When he returned to *BG 4*, he was:

'. . . met by two officers of my *Staffel* who gave me the sad news that three AEG aircraft had not returned from their night flights [between 15 and 20 September]. Among the missing aircrewmen was *Ltn* Julius Tillmanns, who had finally returned to the Front in August as a member of *Bombenstaffel 19*. During my absence he flew with another observer and his aircraft was attacked by enemy night fighters and forced to land. Tillmanns and his observer, *Ltn* Gerlach, were unhurt and were taken prisoner; their air-gunner, *Gefr* Kurth, was killed during the air fight. The other two aircraft that failed to return in that short period were shot down and destroyed; all six aircrewmen were killed.

◀ After the war the civil airline *Deutsche Luft-Reederei* took advantage of the AEG G V's useful load (2,700kg) and converted a former warbird into a transport for passengers, mail and other cargo. DLR established one of the world's first scheduled airmail services. The passengers, clad in wartime observers' flying suits and helmets, were provided with a pre-flight glass of *Schnapps* to keep them warm during the open-cockpit flight.

▶In November 1919 when the German railway was hit by strikes and coal shortages, *Deutsche Luft-Reederei* used this converted Friedrichshafen G IIIa to provide primary mail delivery between major cities.

'The lost aircraft were easier replaced than the missing aircrews. Thus, we had three new aircraft without crews. Our mechanics always had these additional aircraft ready for take-off during preparations for our missions in case one of our regular machines would not start.

'During five or six night flights in September and October, our bombs were fitted with delayed-action fuses set to detonate the bombs 30 seconds after impact. This was necessary because, to hit smaller targets, we had to fly very low, at 50 metres or less, and the heavy aircraft needed the 30-second delay to clear the blast area of their own bombs.

'Our last flight was undertaken on 8 October 1918. During that night, *Ltn* Grude and I got away six times to bomb encampments from St Quentin to Amiens. After that, *Bogohl 4* made a gradual retreat through Belgium and back to Germany.

'As the days and weeks passed we waited for orders to take off – but they never came. What did happen was a massive outbreak of influenza. Many members of the German Army fell victim to this malady during the final days of the war and after the Armistice. In my *Staffel* alone we lost three or four men to influenza.

'After the announcement of the Armistice on 11 November 1918, members of my *Staffel* destroyed all serviceable equipment and burned all unnecessary documents. The petrol was drained from the aircraft and was collected for use [as motor vehicle fuel] during the march homeward. The aircraft engines and the rigging on the wings were all rendered useless by shots from our weapons before we set out on the trip back to our homeland.'[42]

TWILIGHT OF THE BOMBERS

Oskar Kuppinger's experiences at war's end were similar to members of other *Bogohls*. In *BG 3*, for example, *Ltn* Immanuel Braun's lingering bout of influenza kept him off flying status for the last two months of the war. At the end of October he wrote home:

'As far as the general situation is concerned, we can only grit our teeth. Poor Germany. I had always imagined that, after all this fighting, the return home would be different.'[43]

Bogohl 7, which lost 37 aircraft when Handley Page O/100 bombers of No 207 Squadron, RAF, bombed Saultain airfield on the night of 23 September, dispersed its personnel to other units. *Ltn* John Knauer went to the *Geschwaderschule* at Paderborn, where there was little turmoil when the war ended,

'. . . but that was largely due to the fact that there was little military organization left. No orders were given, so none were disobeyed. After the Armistice, we were asked to fly several aircraft to Strasbourg for delivery to the Entente, but no one volunteered to do this, so the aircraft stayed at Paderborn and were eventually destroyed in huge bonfires. Then we just went home.'[44]

The destruction of the German *Grossflugzeuge* was extensive, but not complete. Despite the efforts of well-meaning Germans to keep their aircraft from fulfilling anyone else's strategic bombing efforts, a number of G-type machines survived and were used for constructive purposes. Converted Friedrichshafen G IIIs were used by Germany's first civil airline, *Deutsche Luft-Reederei* (German Air Charter Company), to transport passengers. In the decades following World War I, a long list of former *Bombenflieger* flew the civil successors to the AEGs, Friedrichshafens and Gothas on peaceful missions, opening up air routes around the world.

5

SEA HAWKS

IMPERIAL GERMANY, being a relatively new state, was late in emerging as a naval power and late in developing an effective fixed-wing aviation component. The pre-war naval aviation emphasis was on lighter-than-air craft, air*ships* to be commanded, crewed and deployed in the manner of other naval vessels. For reasons of economy, the *Reichs-Marine-Amt* (Admiralty) ordered existing landplanes to be fitted with floats to create a token force of seaplanes. Thus great internal obstacles had to be overcome in order to develop the units that became such an important part of German military aviation in World War I.

Kapitänleutnant zur See (Lieutenant-Commander) Johannes Moll, who qualified for *Deutscher Luftfahrer-Verband* (German Air Travellers Association) licence No 699 on 20 March 1914 and later became head of the Aviation Department in the *RMA*, noted:

'Seaplane flying before the war was the stepchild of the Navy, which relied on airships for reconnaissance at sea in co-operation with the Fleet and expected practically nothing from aeroplanes. Seaplanes, if not just playthings, were at most thought of as sports objects and were not granted appropriate personnel, material and money. All naval aviation was combined into the *Marine-Flieger-Abteilung* [Navy Flying Section], with headquarters in Putzig near Danzig and which was under the command of the *Reichs-Marine-Amt* and which, except for the *Flugstation* [Air Station at] Putzig, was subordinate to *Seeflugstationen* [Seaplane Stations] at Kiel, Heligoland and Wilhelmshaven. The total strength of personnel before the war came to about 200 people, so that only Putzig and Kiel were at full strength. Heligoland and Wilhelmshaven were only in operation and functional during times of Fleet manoeuvres. About 20 pilots, without exception all young naval officers, had been fully trained before the war; there were no observers. It was assumed that on mobilization young officers would be ordered from the Fleet and they could be relied on to assume observers' duties without special training.'[1]

On that unenlightened basis, Moll stated:

'During the first weeks of the war there were only six aircraft in Heligoland to operate with the High Seas Fleet and only three serviceable aircraft for observation work over the approaches to the Baltic.'[2]

Britain, France and Russia (using mainly French-built aircraft) had an early lead in deploying aircraft for over-water use, but the Germans had the operational advantage of better sited air stations. Once aircraft production was increased to meet the needs of the growing number of naval aviators and observers in training after the outbreak of war, German naval fliers became an important presence wherever they operated.

NAVAL AIR BASES EXPANDED

To strengthen the naval aviation presence in the North Sea between Germany and Britain, the *Flugstation* at Heligoland, outermost of the islands off the Frisian coast, was joined by two other air stations: a primary facility at Borkum, commissioned on 1 August 1914 under the command of *Kptnltn z S* Otto Bertram, who received *DLV* licence No 123 on 9 October 1911; and a subordinate facility at Nordeney, commissioned on 29 August under *Oberleutnant zur See* (Lieutenant) Reinhold Otte, who had received *DLV* licence No 543 eleven months earlier. Initially the North Sea air stations' missions were reconnaissance and attacking submarines within the limits of their capabilities, but the inadequacy of their capabilities soon became clear. On 28 August eight British cruisers made a raid in the Heligoland Bight with relative ease and were not hampered by the station's two serviceable aircraft, which had to fly at 20 metres' altitude due to bad visibility that day.[3]

In addition to lack of adequate aircraft to meet the great naval threat from Britain, the first German naval air units had communications and co-ordination problems. The latter were to be solved by placing the North Sea air stations under the *II. Seeflieger-Abteilung* established in Wilhelmshaven in October, but lack of wireless-telegraphy equipment in the aircraft prevented the new command from receiving instant sightings of enemy activity in the area and making the appropriate co-ordinated response.

The vulnerability of important areas within Germany (and the concomitant inability of German Army and Navy units to provide proper defence) was made evident by these raids early in the war:

22 September 1914, raid by Royal Naval Air Service aircraft on airship sheds at Düsseldorf and Cologne.

8 October, RNAS raid on Düsseldorf resulting in the destruction of the Zeppelin-built airship *Z9*.

21 November, RNAS 120-mile raid from Belfort, France, to the Zeppelin sheds at Friedrichshafen carried out by four RNAS Avro 504 aircraft and causing severe damage.

As the Zeppelins had not yet proved their usefulness, as British aircraft were operating from continental bases in Ostende and Dunkirk, and as the Army's offensive unit, the *Brieftauben-Abteilung Ostende*, was not yet in position, it was clear to the *RMA* that rapid development of its own extra-territorial force was imperative.

FIRST DEFENCE AT ZEEBRUGGE

Consequently, men and material of the first *Front-Seeflugstation* left Wilhelmshaven on 4 December 1914. The station consisted of three aviation officers, one warrant officer, 55 men and two 120hp-engined Friedrichshafen FF 29 seaplanes (Nos 203 and 204).[4] Two days later they arrived at their destination: the bleak breakwater at Zeebrugge, on Belgium's North Sea coast. The railway station hall on the Zeebrugge Mole was immediately converted into a seaplane hangar. One wall was removed and replaced by a large sliding door. The officers were housed in the Palace Hotel at the foot of the Mole and the mechanics were billeted in nearby homes.

Under the command of *Obltn z S* Friedrich von Arnauld de la Perrière, station-based aircraft reconnoitred the Channel area, as well as the coasts of Britain, France and Holland. The unit also worked with German air and surface craft in the area, and co-operated with coastal artillery.

The land-based *I. Marine-Feldflieger-Abteilung* left for Flanders on 20 December and went first to Snaeskerke and then to Mariakerke; it was joined in that region on 20 February 1915 by the *II. MFA*; both were responsible for artillery co-operation and aerial reconnaissance over the *land* areas under naval control.[5]

FIRST NAVAL AIR RAID ON ENGLAND

These seaplane and landplane units were unable to prevent the 24 and 25 December RNAS raids on Nordholz and Cuxhaven, respectively. But these heavier-than-air units initiated the German bombing campaign. On 21 December 1914 a lone aircraft appeared over Dover, dropped two bombs into the water near the Admiralty Pier and then flew off.

▼The beach at Zeebrugge where a major German naval base was established. In the background is the Grand Hotel, where officers were billeted; in the foreground are tracks for the railway station hall, which was converted into a seaplane hangar.

Dover was visited three days later by a high-flying naval aircraft, which dropped a bomb near the Castle, causing some broken glass. On Christmas Day 1914 a German seaplane flew up the Thames to Erith, on the outskirts of London, and dropped two bombs, which exploded harmlessly near Cliffe station; the seaplane dodged anti-aircraft fire and shook off three pursuing British aircraft.

A Zeebrugge-based seaplane made a daytime raid over Braintree, Coggeshall and Colchester in Essex on 21 February 1915. Five days later three seaplanes set out for Britain; two attacked the SS *Cordoba* without success, the other failed to return to Zeebrugge. The following day a British tug docked at Lowestoft with two German naval aviators aboard, *Kptnltn z S* Stephan Prandzynski and *Fähnrich zur See* (Midshipman) Heyen. Their aircraft had gone into the sea on the way over and they survived a night of rough water and snowstorms only by clinging to the wreckage of their aircraft.[6]

AIRSHIP RAID ON ENGLAND

On 20 March four German aircraft were spotted heading for the Downs and, although one dropped several bombs near a steamer, no damage was caused. A single machine flew over Kingsdown on 16 April and dropped bombs which exploded in open fields; again, no damage resulted. The night attack by the Army airship *LZ38* on 29 April 1915 marked the first military airship raid on Britain. Commanded by *Hauptmann* Erich Linnarz, the airship dropped 26 bombs on a run from Ipswich to Bury St Edmunds and three high-explosive and 40

▲ The breakwater provided a calmer sea state for Hansa-Brandenburg W 12s and other seaplanes at the Zeebrugge Mole.

incendiary bombs on the latter town before heading out to sea again.[7]

Linnarz and *LZ38* returned several times, as did other Army and Navy airships. German naval aircraft generally confined their activities to attacks on British shipping off Dover, although on 13 September a seaplane appeared over Cliftonville and dropped ten bombs, killing two civilians and wounding four.

The Zeebrugge *Front-Seeflugstation* continued to develop. Better facilities were built, including a central workshop at nearby Lisseveghe. *Chef-Ingenieur der Reserve Dr-Ing* Stein took command of the workshop on 15 May and converted a school building into a first-rate support facility which did everything from assembling new aircraft brought in by rail to overhauling and repairing existing aircraft at the Flanders seaplane station.

Development of the station and support of its mission was undertaken by all hands, including the station commander, von Arnauld de la Perrière, who continued to fly combat missions. On 17 December 1915, however, he and his observer, *Leutnant zur See* Virchon, made a forced landing in Friedrichshafen FF 33E No 473 near Nieuport and were captured by the French. *Obltn z S* von Arnauld de la Perrière was succeeded by *Kptnltn* Walther Faber, another pre-war flier (*DLV* licence No 390 on 5 May 1913).[8] On 6 January 1916 Faber was relieved by *Kptnltn* Bernhard von Tschirschky und Boegendorff (*DLV* licence No 698 on 17 March 1914).

LAND-BASED NAVAL AIRCRAFT

Meanwhile, land-based German naval aircraft in Flanders were beginning to make their mark. These operations were recorded by Fritz Stiefvatter, a 27-year-old construction engineer, who joined the Navy in 1914 and requested pilot training. Posted to the *I. Marine-Feldflieger-Abteilung*, Stiefvatter noted his duties in a diary excerpt included in his 4 November 1915 weekly letter to his fiancée:[9]

'We fly towards the front-lines twice; the second time I see two Frenchmen rushing towards us. One a Farman and one a smaller Morane. The big one turns away, while the little one approaches me. Now it's time to leave. I head down to our territory. Then I see that yet another machine also runs away, even though those guys had machine-guns on board while we had only a pocket knife.'

Life as a naval two-seater reconnaissance pilot is described in other letters:

9 November 1915: 'During a patrol flight on Thursday evening [4 November] saw quite by chance how the British were opening a sluice and trying to flood our positions. I brought it to my observer's attention and, when we reported it later, we learned that this report was extremely important. Perhaps we had saved the lives of some of our comrades.'

15 November 1915: 'Hurrah, it's raining. Therefore I don't have to fly the machine. And so I will tell you the story of "Long Max". Surely, you have read in the newspapers that Dunkirk has been fired upon by a long-range gun. People talk about a giant gun of the newest type. Actually, it is a 38cm naval gun. A cannon. When the first shot fell, the French were as astounded as could be. They sent up all their seaplanes to look for the German Fleet. Of course, they found nothing. All they found were their own landplanes; the poor fellows had nothing to laugh about. Finally, after a day-long search, one of them came back with the proud report: Ahoy, I have it, the cursed battery of the *Boches*. It is southeast of Dixmude, north of the great highway, right next to a small wood. The British brought up 21cm and 15cm batteries, trained them on the target precisely as it was on the map and, in the dark of night, started an artillery assault on the poor "Long Max". And so it was settled. The people of Dunkirk slept quietly again.

'The day after, at 8:00 in the morning, there was a frightful crash. Oh, what's the matter? One side of a church fell away. The damned *Boches* must have another heavy gun. Again the fliers went chasing out. As they searched, a new shot hit Dunkirk at 12 o'clock and then again in the evening. Now all the artillery observers were on a sharp look-out. They were supposed to watch for a suspiciously big muzzle flash. After a long search they came back here again. Curses, it must be the "Long Max" again. Therefore the creature was still alive. Again he was covered up. But the Max kept firing. Now French artillery officers noticed that when they got a bearing on the muzzle flash of the "Long Max", it always came from a place other than where the fliers reported. Next there was a great crash on the other side. Now the position of the

▶ The Friedrichshafen FF 33E was one of the mainstays of German naval aviation. Equipped with a wireless-telegraphy set, it could range far over the sea and report ship traffic and other useful intelligence.

monster had to be photographed. The statements of the fliers had been correct. But the shots came from nearby. Thereupon the poor "Long Max" was demolished with [the help of] aerial observation. It took 500 hits and then the battery had to be evacuated.'

17 November 1915: 'I went over to the airfield and made a test flight with my new machine. It ran extremely well. In level flight at 150 kilometres [per hour].'

20 November 1915: 'At 3:00 in the afternoon I had to go up with [*Leutnant*] Leffler to look for enemy batteries. At 700 metres altitude the cloud layer was thick west of the Mole at Nieuport and over enemy territory and so we searched for big guns through the thin spots here. Beneath us the clouds flitted by, with only an occasional hole to look through. Above us was bright blue sky. I fly along contentedly, looking for an enemy flier here and there against the sky, but there is none to be discovered. I am quite pleased that it is Saturday and try everything possible with my machine; there – ping! – about 30 metres ahead of me is a milky-white cloudlet. It twists around like a corkscrew. Near the machine there is one. Oho! Now another. The ribbons have me neatly between them. About 30 or 40 cloudlets surround me and I jiggle the machine to the left, tip it on one wing, let them slip by to the right and go into a turn. The cloudlets tear at me and follow, but I must not turn away, as the battery must be discovered.

'After a long, long quarter of an hour, we find the enemy batteries and can only laugh at the Englishmen; for, at a speed of 200 kilometres per hour and in a steep dive, we are soon out of the danger zone. We land after a long, flat glide.'

At the end of February 1916 *Vizeflugmeister* (Aviation Chief Petty Officer) Fritz Stiefvatter

returned home for well-deserved leave. He left his family and young wife with the good news that he had been recommended for promotion to *Leutnant zur See* and proposed for the *Eisernes Kreuz I. Klasse*.

On Sunday morning, 12 March 1916, while on a flight over Mariakerke, near Ostende, Fritz Stiefvatter's aircraft was attacked by British fighters. He and his observer, *Steuermann* (Helmsman's Mate) Jost, a seasoned veteran of a year's service with the *I. MFA*, shot down one of the attackers. Then another came out of the mist unnoticed and got in a burst of fire which hit *Vzflgmtr* Stiefvatter in the left temple. The pilot's last act was to steer the machine away from the attacker and towards German lines. With that slim margin of safety and despite being wounded in the thigh, the observer managed to gain control of the aircraft and bring it down to a safe landing. An engineering company working nearby rushed over and removed the two crewmen. By then, Fritz Stiefvatter was dead.

At 1600 hours on 15 March the entire complement of the *I. MFA* attended Fritz Stiefvatter's funeral in Ostende and accompanied the flower-covered coffin to the train that would take it home. One of Stiefvatter's former observers, *Ltn z S* Leffler, and his mechanic accompanied the coffin back to Germany for burial under the high lime trees of the naval pilot's town cemetery.

AIR FIGHTS OVER THE SEA

German naval air units also encountered stiff resistance and incurred losses during their raids on Britain. In response to German seaplane attacks

along the Kentish coast in January and February 1916, No 5 Wing, RNAS, was formed at Dover under Squadron-Commander Spenser D. A. Grey. The unit moved to Coudekerke aerodrome, near Dunkirk, in early March to carry out bombing missions against the German airfield at Houttave, between Ostende and Bruges, and the seaplane base at Zeebrugge.

Even the Royal Flying Corps had a hand in stopping the German air assault following a six-seaplane attack on Dover, Ramsgate, Deal and Margate on the afternoon of Sunday, 19 March. The *RFC Communiqué* reported:

'2nd Lt R. Collis and Flt-Lt Emery (FE), while flying over the channel at 8,000 feet, saw a hostile machine . . . making for Deal. They flew up channel and met this hostile aeroplane on its return. Lt Collis was then at 8,000 feet and the hostile machine at 4,000 feet. Planing down with engine throttled back until within 150 yards, the observer opened fire immediately behind. The hostile machine did not return the fire and made no attempt to manoeuvre out of range. After a drum had been expended, the enemy was observed to plunge down towards the sea with a steep right-hand bank and with irregular puffs of smoke coming from the engine.'[10]

The station war diary noted that *Ltns z S* Hans Rolshoven and von Frankenburg were forced down in Friedrichshafen FE 33F No 537. They managed to restart the engine, however, and returned to Zeebrugge; indeed, they flew the same aircraft on subsequent missions.[11] Another account notes that, shortly afterwards:

◀ As part of the interdiction process, German seaplane crews, such as those aboard this Friedrichshafen FF 33E (No 694), often landed and questioned merchant ship crews in the English Channel and North Sea. On many occasions, aircrews seized enemy or neutral ships carrying contraband and transmitted for assistance from neighbouring surface craft.

'Flight-Commander R. J. Bone, from the Westgate naval air station, chased one of the seaplanes in his Nieuport scout and shot it down into the minefield off the Goodwins.'[12]

During this action, the German seaplanes were a mixed bag of Friedrichshafen FF 33Bs, 'Es and 'Fs and a Hansa-Brandenburg NW and Gotha UWD. German naval records show none of these aircraft lost as a result of the 19 March 1916 action. The only casualty listed is a slight wound suffered by the new *Front-Seeflugstation* commander, *Kptnltn* von Tschirschky und Boegendorff, who flew as the observer in Hansa-Brandenburg NW No 521. The German side of the encounter with Flight-Commander Bone was told by von Tschirschky's pilot, *Oberleutnant der Reserve der Marine-Artillerie* (Reserve Lieutenant in the Naval Artillery) Friedrich Christiansen, leader of the flight:

'During the flight back, still 10 kilometres inland, we were attacked from behind and out of the sun by a small, agile British land-based single-seat fighter and we were so taken by surprise that the opponent was able to get within 20 metres to give us his first greeting with a stream of machine-gun fire. A hailstorm of hits on our aircraft. The radiator line was shot away and a valve-rocker on one engine cylinder was destroyed. In addition, *Kptnltn* von Tschirschky was shot in the shoulder and grazed on the head, and therefore could no longer use his Mauser automatic rifle – at the time seaplanes did not yet have machine-guns.'[13]

Christiansen twisted and turned his big seaplane and noted nervously that one of the floats had been hit by a shell (which turned out to be a dud). The engine began to malfunction and hot water from the radiator streamed into the pilot's face and obscured his view. He took the big two-seater lower and lower, just a few metres over the tops of houses in Deal, in the hope of shaking off his pursuer. Fl-Cdr Bone hung on doggedly.

Five kilometres off the coast, Christiansen managed to set down in a fog bank, safe from the Nieuport – and unaware that he was in a minefield. The punctured float soon took on water and pulled the seaplane into a list until a bottom wing touched the water. But the aircraft remained afloat and, despite his own thigh and hand wounds, Christiansen kept the craft moving. He repaired the radiator line and refilled the cooler with sea water. By hiding in the fog he eluded nearby ships and made his way across the Channel. Christiansen later observed:

'The flight out lasted two hours, the return flight took seven hours. No wonder that those back at the base had already given up hope for us.'[14]

Friedrich Christiansen – popularly known as 'Krischan' – was not a young man when he entered aviation. Born on 12 December 1879 in Wyk on the North Sea island of Föhr, he started by following the family tradition of service in the merchant marine. He completed a year's compulsory military service in 1902 and then went back to sea. Returning to his home port of Hamburg in the spring of 1914, Christiansen attended an aviation meeting at Fuhlsbüttel and decided on the spot to learn how to fly. At the age of 34, he passed his pilot's examination on 27 March 1914 and received *DLV* licence No 707. He took part in flying competitions throughout the summer and, when called up to serve at the outbreak of war, he went directly into naval aviation.

One of his former observers, *Dr* Fritz Stormer, wrote to the author that Christiansen first:

'. . . was assigned to the seaplane station at List auf Sylt. He was promoted to *Leutnant*, but did not belong to the unrestricted line officers' corps, all of whom had the words 'zur See' after their titles of rank. They were also the only group to wear the naval officers' *Dolch* [dirk] initiated by the Czar of Russia, while all other naval officers – those from naval artillery, medical corps, engineer corps and naval infantry – wore the long sabre.

'In any event, "Krischan" soon became renowned for his splendid leadership abilities and successes, and he was promoted to *Oberleutnant*. On 12 December 1917, when he was presented with the *Orden Pour le Mérite* and also became a *Kapitänleutnant*, we all wanted to see him promoted into the seagoing naval officers' group. But

"Krischan" declined and wore the uniform and long sabre of the naval artillery, which in the eyes of the Navy was not "zur See".'[15]

SUBMARINE AND SEAPLANE RESCUES

Friedrich Christiansen certainly earned the honour of being the first German naval pilot to receive the *Orden Pour le Mérite*. He was involved in aerial action from the beginning of the war and always displayed great courage, daring and leadership. During a flight in November 1916, he and his observer, *Monteur* Zeh, stayed aloft so long that they were cut off from Zeebrugge by a sudden North Sea storm. Christiansen landed on the water and spent nine hours in rough seas and darkness, trying to coax his badly damaged seaplane back to base. Suddenly, the German submarine *UB10* surfaced nearby and the skipper, *Obltn z S* Amberger, 'invited' Christiansen and Zeh to return to port with him.

During a subsequent low-level mission – ranging coastal artillery against British destroyers heading for Zeebrugge – engine trouble forced Christiansen and *Fähnrich z S* Exner down on the open sea. They were saved by the appearance of *UB1*, which blew up the crippled seaplane and then dived to safety with the crew.

Christiansen was flying with *Vizeflugmeister* Maukisch during a naval and air battle between Ostende and the mouth of the Thames on 5 July 1917. After the German torpedo-boat *S20* took a devastating hit, the naval pilot landed nearby and

▼German naval air crews made regular contact with friendly submarines, turning over rescued sailors and delivering important despatches.

▶ Sturdy floats on the Friedrichshafen FF 33 provide a bridge for an observer to make his way to a submarine. Note that a sailor has placed a small cushion between the boat and the float to prevent the latter being damaged.

▼ The observer of this Hansa-Brandenburg W 12 climbed out on to the starboard wing to compensate for damage to the left float and so allow the seaplane to taxi back to base.

he and his observer pulled three surviving crewmen out of the water. With one man sharing the observer's cockpit and the other two on the floats, the seaplane headed into the wind for take-off.

But the next scene must have cut at Christiansen's sailor's heart. He recalled:

'Scarcely had we tied the first two to the floats when more than 20 men swam towards us in order to cling to the aircraft as it rolled furiously in the groundswell. But that had to be prevented, for the rescue of the pitiful comrades lay in the quickest flight home.

'The machine was already overloaded. Machine-guns, ammunition, a hundred litres of petrol and other equipment went overboard. But now the engine did not want to start and a number of those ringing us in the water succeeded in hanging on to the floats. Only with brute force were these poor people condemned to death. It was a hard decision, but it had to be!

'At last the engine started. During the take-off run out of the area of those wretched comrades facing death, one of them tightly grasped the underside of a float. Despite that, we made the take-off – defenceless, totally handicapped, an easy prey for any enemy. Our decline would have sealed the fate of all survivors. The impressions at take-off and the abandonment of the unfortunate ones were terrible and unforgettable. A beastly shrill cry from the 60 hoarse human throats filled the air. Those engulfed were unable to grasp that in our take-off lay the only hope for the others.

'"*Du Fliegerhund* ["You flier dog"], not taking us with you, leaving us here in the drink!" That was the last thing ringing in our ears as we took off.'[16]

Following the aircraft's quick return to Zeebrugge, Christiansen himself led twelve seaplanes and four torpedo-boats on a night rescue mission to the scene of the action. A 2½-hour search led to the recovery of 25 survivors and 38 bodies. Christiansen was awarded the *Rettungsmedaille* (Life-Saving Medal), a high honour that recognized his selfless devotion to seamen in peril.

SEAPLANE BOMBERS OVER THE BALTIC

In the Baltic, German naval units found the Imperial Russian Navy to be a less formidable opponent than the British and French. Indeed, the worst enemies were often the elements of nature. *Generalingenieur der Luftwaffe a D* (Engineer General of the Air Force, Retired) Wolfram Eisenlohr was a naval aviation observer in World War I. In May 1917 he was assigned to the *Seeflugstation* at Windau, on the coast north of East Prussia (and today the Latvian city of Ventspils). Seaplane squadrons at Windau, nearby Lieben and Arngernsee were then charged with observation and photo-reconnaissance in and around the Gulf of Riga, particularly the offshore islands of Oesel, Moon and Dägo. The anticipated German offensive was aimed at Reval (now Tallinn, capital of Estonia) and Petersburg (now Leningrad) and these islands would be involved. The station at Windau deployed three large twin-engined Friedrichshafen FF 41A seaplanes for these and other operations in the area. The former observer remembered:

'At that time we were still sending reports back to base by using carrier pigeons; as we had no radio on board, we carried a cage with carrier pigeons. As soon as we had an important report to send, I wrote it on a scrap of paper and placed it into a small metal canister fastened to one of the pigeon's legs. With a powerful swing, the pigeon would be thrown out of the aircraft. Generally, it took to the air very quickly and began the homeward-bound flight. Indeed, most of the pigeons made it back. At the time I was the unit's *Brieftauben-Offizier* (Carrier Pigeon Officer) and so pigeons that did not meet the requirements for service met with a sad fate: they "travelled" to the cook's pot.'[17]

Ideally a *Seeflugstation* would have an inlet to provide relatively calm seas for taking off and landing. Windau was at the mouth of the River Windau, right on the Baltic Sea. *General* Eisenlohr recalled the effect of the station's location and other factors:

'Our daily flying time averaged one or two hours. When we flew depended first of all on the weather. One needed good visibility to make a reconnaissance flight. On the other hand, bombing flights were carried out during relatively bad weather. Of course, the condition of the sea also played a part, as we had to take off and land on [open] water. The two-seat Friedrichshafen reconnaissance aircraft in which I flew could endure a sea state of 3 to 4. For the relatively smaller seaplane fighters, such a sea state was too high. Even for us, though, in too strong a sea condition there was the danger that, while taking off or landing, the floats would be torn

▼ *Leutnant zur See der Reserve* Wolfram Eisenlohr's dress uniform bore both Iron Crosses and his Naval Pilot's Badge. He was one of six brothers serving in World War I, three in the Army, three in the Navy.

off and, without question, the aircraft would nose over.

'During bombing attacks we flew at altitudes of 2,000 to 3,000 metres. While laying mines, we flew down quite close to the surface of the water; we flew at altitudes of 6 to 8 metres. To maintain this low altitude over the water, we used a sort of *Schleppantenna* [trailing aerial]. When the tip of the aerial touched the water, a small light went on in the pilot's cockpit, so that he could be sure that he was not flying too high over the water.

'Reconnaissance flights were normally carried out alone; that also held for minelaying flights, which were carried out mainly at night to avoid enemy defensive fire.

'During bombing flights, however, we flew mostly in threes and many times in larger groups. When we first made bombing flights, we carried small 5kg bombs; they were such small things that they could be dropped by hand comfortably. Later we had 10kg bombs which, likewise, were very simple in their operation, but with which one could hardly aim at a ship with good accuracy. Finally, in 1917, we received 60kg bombs.'[18]

SIGHTED WARSHIP, SANK SAME

It was with this type of ordnance that (then) *Ltn z S* Wolfram Eisenlohr secured a place in history as being the first German to sink an enemy surface warship with a bomb dropped from the air.

On the afternoon of 22 August 1917, Eisenlohr and his pilot, *Flugobermaat* (Aviation Petty Officer) Gruber were on patrol in their Friedrichshafen FF 41A during the German offensive against Riga, the Baltic port city and capital of Latvia, supported on the right flank by advances through Lithuania. Just off the south-east coast of Oesel Island, Eisenlohr saw two Russian destroyers at anchor. Recognizing

a major target and eager to preserve the element of surprise, he directed Gruber to return to Windau immediately. There *Ltn* Eisenlohr reported his discovery to the station commander, *Kptnltn* Mans, who then organized an early evening raid.

Three Friedrichshafens left Windau just before dusk. As they approached Oesel, Eisenlohr saw the two ships still lying at anchor. He described the raid this way:

'In the nose of our aircraft there was a big open "balcony" where the observer sat. As we neared the target, the pilot, who sat behind me, could no longer see the object of our attack [his view being obstructed by the bottom wings]. Thus my duty as observer was to signal to him to drop the bombs at the right time.

'I had the advantage of being able to follow very well the course of the bombs dropped by the two aircraft ahead of ours. Before us lay two Russian destroyers. The observer of the preceding aircraft dropped four bombs on each one. I followed the course of the falling bombs and saw that each one hit closer and closer to the ship, but that the last one detonated about 10 metres ahead of it. I concluded that if I were to drop all eight bombs one right after the other, the probability of a hit would be much greater. My fifth bomb was actually a hit. It struck *Stroini* in a sensitive spot and caused it to sink. By good fortune, the water in that part of the Baltic Sea was not very deep, so the destroyer did not sink completely. Rather, it settled in, with part of the superstructure towering out of the water. Thus, it was possible to rescue the crew.'[19]

▼After being hit by Eisenlohr's bombs, the 350-tonne *Stroini* settled into the mud. It was not completely sunk, but further German naval air efforts hampered salvage attempts.

The Russians attempted to salvage the 350-tonne *Stroini*, but their efforts were repelled by German aerial attacks, causing further damage and loss of life. Ultimately the destroyer was abandoned and Baltic storms completed the destruction begun by Eisenlohr and Gruber.

For his role in the sinking of *Stroini, Ltn z S* Eisenlohr was awarded the *Ehrenpreis* (Trophy of Honour). Often presented to victorious combat pilots who stopped and seized vessels on the high seas, the distinction also honoured other meritorious acts.

Wolfram Eisenlohr also participated in another naval aviation 'first': the destruction of a warship by aircraft-laid mine. As he noted:

'With the help of Friedrichshafen torpedo aircraft, [on 7 September 1917], we were able to lay 750kg sea mines. I was the first one on the German side to drop them. About a month after laying this mine barrier [26 September], the Russian destroyer *Okhotnik* hit one of the mines and sank. This time, too, the entire crew could have been rescued. However, it was especially tragic that – as this incident was just before the Russian Revolution –

▶ The naval *Ehrenpreis* presented to *Ltn* Eisenlohr following his successful attack on *Stroini*. The legend reads: 'To the victor in aerial combat, 22 August 1917.'

◀ **Friedrichshafen FF 41A**
of the type used by
Ltn **Eisenlohr and**

Flugobermaat **Gruber to**
bomb the Russian
destroyer *Stroini*.

the men prevented their officers from climbing into the lifeboats, and so they went down with the ship.'[20]

The outbreak of the revolution weeks later led to the virtual collapse of hostilities in the Baltic. Consequently many aircrews were reassigned. In the case of Wolfram Eisenlohr it was to command the Observers' School in Wiek auf Rügen and then to become Adjutant to the *I. Seeflieger-Abteilung* commanded by *Kptnltn* Mehnert. He later became a pilot and rose to general officer rank in the *Luftwaffe* before retiring in 1944.

MORE AIR UNITS FOR FLANDERS

As part of the reallocation of naval aviation resources, *Marine-Feldflieger-Abteilung III* was removed from the Russian Front and disbanded. Personnel and equipment were absorbed by the two Belgian-based *MFAs*. That event was but one of several developments that would make the Flanders facilities critically important to German success on the Western Front.

Overseeing the entire effort was *Kommando des Luftfahrtwesens des Marine Korps* (Aviation Command of the Naval Corps) led by *Kapitän zur See* Stubenrauch and with headquarters at the important naval and submarine base at Bruges. Reporting to Stubenrauch, a regular Navy captain, were two *Gruppenkommandeure* (Group Commanders), one for seaplane operations and one for landplane

operations. Seaplane operations were, logically, concentrated at the coastal bases at Zeebrugge and Ostende. Landplane operations, including the *MFAs, Marine-Jagdstaffeln* (Naval Fighter Squadrons), and *Küstenstaffeln* (Coastal Protection Squadrons), were at Houttave, Nieuwmünster, Uytkerke, Stalhille and other inland bases and often worked with the *4. Armee*, which was in northern Flanders and whose air units were close by.

On 15 September 1917 *Obltn d R d M A* Friedrich Christiansen was given command of the Zeebrugge seaplane station, by then known as *Seeflugstation Flandern I*.

A sister unit at Ostende, *Seeflugstation Flandern II*, was established on 11 March 1917 and commanded by *Kptnltn* Bücker. *Seeflugstation Flandern III* was established at Nieuwmünster on 1 October 1917 under the command of *Ltn z S* Hans Rolshoven and, despite its name, provided *land*-based fighters, reconnaissance and bombing aircraft to assist the other two stations. All three units were under *Kptnltn* von Tschirschky und Boegendorff, who had been promoted *Gruppenkommandeur der Seeflieger*, based in Zeebrugge. Former observer *Dr* Fritz Stormer recalled:

'The Zeebrugge seaplane station was charged with overseeing the area known as "Hoofden", the expanse of water up the Dutch coast to Scheveningen, from there across the English Channel to Yarmouth, up the British coast to the River Thames and back across to Zeebrugge. The Ostende seaplane station was responsible for the mouth of the Thames to Margate and across the Channel to Ostende. These stations also had control in their

▶ The change of command at *Seeflugstation Flandern I* on 15 September 1917 was hosted by *Kptnltn z S* von Tschirschky (second from the left), who was succeeded by *Obltn d R d M A* Friedrich Christiansen (second from the right). Seen crouching between them is *Obltn z S* Erich Killinger, who became the station's Adjutant.

◀ A Curtiss flying-boat of the RNAS on fire and sinking after an encounter with aircraft from the Zeebrugge naval air station.

areas of all of our ship traffic, submarines, boom defence nets, minefields, navigational buoys, etc., as well as the responsibility of reporting all changes in position of enemy destroyers, minesweepers and submarines. Of course, they also attacked from the air enemy blockade-runners and aviation units.'

SEAPLANE DEFENSIVE TACTICS

'Opposing the enemy seaplane units in our area [Dr Stormer recalled] was comparatively easy, as our Hansa-Brandenburg aircraft were superior to the British flying-boats in terms of speed, manoeuvrability and armament . . . On the other hand, the drag of our twin floats put us at a serious disadvantage if we were ambushed by British or French land-based fighters. Our best defence was to fly in tight formation, close to the water. Our two-seat reconnaissance aircraft were each equipped with a ring-mounted machine-gun for the observer, so by using this formation the combined firepower of five aircraft could be brought to bear on an opponent.

'Generally the *Staffel* flew in a wedge-shaped formation, with the *Staffel-Kapitän* [Flight Leader] in the leading aircraft. Behind him and to the right was the Photo Officer and Deputy Commander of the unit. During an attack by fighters coming in from above and behind, the aircraft under attack went even lower so that a sloping "V" was formed and all machine-guns had an unobstructed field of fire. It was a lesson learned through hard experience that made land-based enemy fighters respect our formations, gliding along close to the surface, which gave a slight advantage against the classic attack from above and behind. Perhaps this explains why enemy forces inflicted only light casualties on our naval observation aircraft.'[21]

TRACKING ENEMY AIRCRAFT AT SEA

A combined operation of the three Flanders units, led principally by Friedrich Christiansen in Hansa-Brandenburg W 12 seaplane No 1183, was described by *Gruppenkommandeur* von Tschirschky in a report summarizing the events of 15 February 1918:

'At daybreak flying was possible, although it was very hazy, partially misty even to the west. The attack on the Channel appeared as if it would be successful, for by 0800 all boats were assembled at full strength. More precise information could not be ascertained; in particular, requirements for support or reconnaissance could not be accommodated.

'Consequently, at 0930 I ordered the take-off of the first flight of the *C-Staffel* [from *See II*] and the *Sicherungsgruppe* [Protection Flight from *See III*] with the order to locate the [enemy] blockade-runners, to determine their strength, and to make continuous reports. Simultaneously I had *See I*, the *Holland-Staffel*, take off with the order to fly back and forth over the blockade zone from the Dutch coast to Ymuiden at about 30 nautical miles off the coast and, as opportune, to observe commercial shipping traffic and attack with bombs.

'At 1000 both *C-Staffeln* of *See I* took off with this instruction: *Staffel I* flies over the eastern steam-powered North Hinder lightship *Yarmouth*, the *II. Staffel* over the Westhinder Sunk lightship *Shipwash*. Both *Staffeln* to rendezvous as possible between *Shipwash* and *Yarmouth* and deny [the enemy] control of the sea lanes from Orfordness – North Hinder to Westhinder – Zeebrugge.

'Shortly before the leading aircraft of the *II. C-Staffel* was launched, we received the report based on an intercepted enemy radio transmission that somewhere in area 059 Beta an enemy aircraft had made a forced landing. As quick action was necessary to bring the machine under our control, I waived the order of co-operation between both *Staffeln* and ordered the *II. C-Staffel* (commanded by *Ltn d Res* Becht) to look for the forced-down aeroplane and, so far as possible, to bring back the crew immediately.

'All missions were greatly hindered by the at times very unfavourable weather. The aircraft from *See II*, which were already in the air when the enemy transmission was intercepted, were in 058 B [and] had located blockade-runners consisting of one monitor and nine destroyers. They were continuously observed and reported by wireless telegraph.

'The *II. C-Staffel* of *See I* meanwhile searched for the forced-down enemy aircraft in quadrants 059 B and 060 B, but located nothing, as the blockade-runners likewise had already searched for the missing machine; it could not be determined

whether it had been picked up as, due to the low cloud cover, it was impossible to fly low over the enemy ships. The *Staffel* came back, reported the results and between 1150 and 1330 [hours], carried out an attack in the sea area 011 and 012 B. There were sighted two British cruisers and some other vessels, which were not precisely identified in the haze. It is assumed that this represented the southern convoy escort. Due to ever-decreasing visibility, this flight had to be broken off.

'The *I. C-Staffel*, under the command of *Obltn d R* Christiansen, encountered during the execution of their mission in [area] 120 Alfa a large number of warships escorting a Holland to England convoy that was protected by two big Curtiss flying-boats.

▼Sea map used by Zeebrugge aircrews to identify activities within their area of operations. Co-ordinates from this map are referenced in *Gruppenkommandeur* von Tschirschky's report quoted in the text.

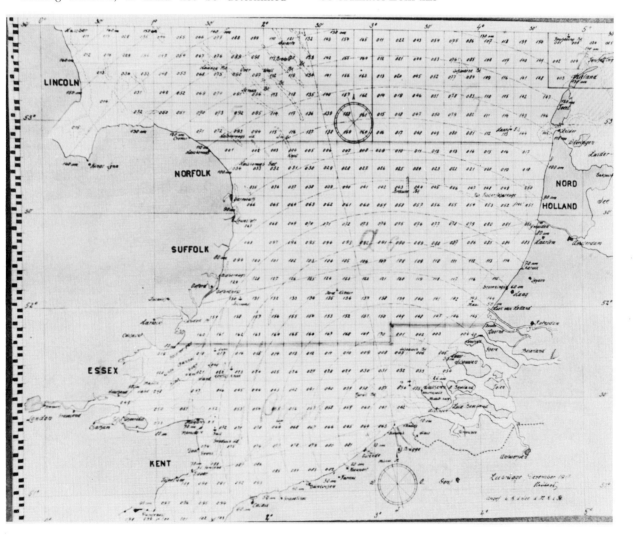

The flying-boats were approximately 2,000 metres away from each other. The one closest to it was immediately attacked by the *Staffel*. During a dogged pursuit the flying-boat was sent down in flames. In the water three crewmen hung on to the wreckage. The second flying-boat in no way assisted the one under attack, but, on the contrary, tried to escape to the north-west. The leading aircraft 1183 [a Hansa-Brandenburg W 12] and the whole *Staffel* immediately went in pursuit of it; continuously from then until over the port of Lowestoft, No 1183 came within approximately 1,200 metres. At a distance of 800 metres the second flying-boat was sprayed repeatedly with 500 rounds. Results could no longer be determined as British ships and coastal batteries went into action. The other *Staffel* aircraft, low on fuel, had to break off.

'Both enemy flying-boats, during the battle, carried some big bombs, apparently depth-charges for use against submarines . . .

'The *Holland-Staffel*, consisting of three FF 220 Ps C H F T aircraft [Friedrichshafen FF 49C, with 220hp Benz engines, one machine-gun and a radio transmitter and receiver] which for attack against anticipated escort craft were each armed with six 10kg bombs, had not seen the convoy due to the prevailing poor visibility. Fighter flights of the *Seefrontstaffel* [equipped with single-seat seaplanes] had to break off early due to lack of visibility. Long-range reconnaissance over the Channel could not be carried out for the same reason.'[22]

FIRST US NAVAL AIR CASUALTY

RNAS records of this encounter show that two Curtiss H.12B flying-boats (N4338 and N4339) left Felixstowe at 0845 hours on 15 February 1918. Four RNAS crewmen were in one and three RNAS members and a US Navy pilot, Ensign Albert D. Sturtevant, in the other. During the encounter with the *I. C-Staffel*, one Curtiss 'boat was shot down, leading to the deaths of the crew, including Sturtevant, who thus became the first US naval aviation casualty of World War I.

The crew of the first aircraft claimed that both flying-boats had been attacked by 'ten Hun seaplanes, fast little single-seaters'[23] which separated the two British machines and shot down one. To do otherwise, of course, would have inferred that Sturtevant and his crewmates had been deserted by the other Curtiss crew. It should be noted, however, that a normal German seaplane sortie consisted of three to five two-seat aircraft.

Performance of the German seaplane units improved when the trusty Hansa-Brandenburg W 12

biplanes were replaced by W 29 monoplanes, which offered a clearer view and were faster and more manoeuvrable than the W 12s. But even brand-new aircraft can have problems, as former *I. C-Staffel* observer *Dr* Fritz Stormer remembered when he and a pilot were ordered to ferry a new Hansa-Brandenburg W 29 back from Warnemünde in May 1918:

'We flew over to Kiel, where the aircraft was examined once again. Then we went over the Kaiser Wilhelm Canal and on to Nordeney to refuel. From there we accompanied a *Staffel* to Texel [the Dutch island], where we were required to make special arrangements to fly past the Hook of Holland, without, of course, violating Dutch neutrality, and then on to Zeebrugge.

'Just before we got to Texel, my engine began to act up. When it continued to run roughly, I signalled the rest of the formation that we would be

turning back. The engine held out only until we got to the small island of Rottumeroog and then it stopped altogether and we had to land in a strong north-west wind and in choppy seas. Everything went all right, but in the course of this erratic landing we found ourselves driven over to the Dutch coast with a relatively new type of aircraft. As the Dutch were not too well disposed towards us and, despite their official neutrality, were strongly sympathetic to the British, in no case could the aircraft be allowed to fall into their hands completely undamaged.

'The *Staffel* that I was accompanying radioed Borkum for help in the form of a three-bay Friedrichshafen seaplane, which landed near us with its engine running. Unfortunately, in the turbulent sea the towline did not function according to plan and the line fell into the water during every attempt to link the two craft. I undressed, inflated my life-jacket and jumped into the water. As I had to swim in choppy water and against a strong current, I soon used up my strength and had to be pulled aboard the Friedrichshafen. My pilot was also ordered to jump into the water and swim over to the rescue aircraft.

'Meanwhile, we had drifted so close to the coast that we could easily make out the Dutchmen on the shore waiting to meet us. When my pilot came aboard, I manned the machine-gun at the front of the big twin-engined rescue aircraft. Even though we were within the 3-mile limit of Dutch jurisdiction, I directed a stream of incendiary and tracer fire at the fuel tank of my beautiful new machine, which contained my uniform and other utensils, but which had to be set afire to prevent it from being seized. Although I was firing in the direction of the open sea, now I was committing a hostile act

▼A Hansa-Brandenburg W 29, wearing late wartime markings, seen approaching Zeebrugge on one of its final missions in the area.

that the Dutchmen did not like, as they apparently assumed that they were going to take possession of the aircraft we had to abandon. They opened fire on us immediately, shooting as long as we remained idling in the water. But their shots fell short and we were able to take off. Thus, I returned to Borkum dressed in little more than a life-jacket.'[24]

As a contrast to [then] *Ltn* Stormer's encounter with the neutral Dutch, RAF historian H. A. Jones noted the degree of civility exercised among the belligerents:

'On the 6th of June [1918] another flying-boat from Felixstowe was shot down by five German pilots, but the British crew, including the commanding officer of the Felixstowe air station, Lieutenant-Colonel E. D. M. Robertson, were taken from the wreckage, after clinging to it for eight hours, by "Large America" [Curtiss H.12] flying-boats sent out specially to find them. The Zeebrugge pilots were not only aggressive fighters, but they usually revealed themselves to be good sportsmen. They might, on this occasion, have continued their attacks on the flying-boat after it was wrecked but, instead, one of the German pilots had landed alongside the British craft and had pointed in the direction of the shore, presumably to encourage a hope that help would be forthcoming.'[25]

Activity along the Flanders coast intensified, as both sides sought to gain control of the waterways. Zeebrugge, at the seaward end of the canal German submarines used to reach their pens at Bruges, was a favourite British target. While land-based German fighter aircraft of the three *Marine-Jagdstaffeln* in Flanders attempted to ward off Allied bombers, the seaplane units addressed the offshore threat, both above and below the water.

SINKING A SUBMARINE

'It was almost routine with us [*Dr* Fritz Stormer recalled] that whenever "Krischan" took off, something would happen. Thus, on grey overcast mornings, always flying with the sun at his back, he succeeded in reaching the English coast and finding maritime traffic there. He would then surprise the enemy and attain some great success, such as on 6 July 1918, when he attacked the British submarine *C25*.

'When he surfaced, the submarine skipper must have been completely surprised by the German aeroplanes overhead, as it seemed that he never thought to stop travelling on the surface and dive to safety beneath the waves. Either that or, during the first burst of machine-gun fire, his diving planes must have been shot away.

'During our attack, one of the submarine crewmen came out into the conning tower with a machine-gun and attempted to ward us off. Since the submarine was now going full speed ahead, that reinforced the thought that the boat had been rendered unable to dive when the five Hansa-Brandenburgs first opened fire. As we later learned first-hand during a test on the docks at Bruges, the *SMK* [*Stahlmantelgeschosse* = steel-jacketed] bullets could penetrate the smooth pressurized hull of a submarine.

'When our *Staffel* sent back a wireless message relating our success, aircraft of the *II. C-Staffel* took off loaded with 5kg and 10kg bombs. They found the British submarine being towed by a sister boat, *E51*. As soon as the leading submarine spotted the second wave of our aircraft, the towline was severed immediately and the undamaged submarine made a crash dive beneath the water. Now the *II. C-Staffel* went after the stricken *C25* with machine-gun fire and bombs, and also scored a number of hits on it. We were satisfied that the boat had been put out of action.'[26]

Despite hard-fought actions on their part, the German naval fliers of Flanders were driven from their bases during the Allied advance along the Western Front. On the stormy evening of 29 September 1918, *Ltn* Fritz Stormer was visiting a friend aboard a torpedo-boat tied up at the Mole when he was instructed to go ashore immediately. All boats put to sea and did not return for several hours. The next morning air station commander Christiansen informed all officers that the successful British tank attack had broken the German lines at Cambrai and, consequently, evacuation and consolidation of naval forces was necessary.

RETREAT

'On 1 October [*Dr* Stormer again] personnel and equipment from the naval station at Ostende arrived at Zeebrugge on the first leg of their evacuation. All the baggage was shipped by barge to Antwerp, while the people streamed into Zeebrugge, where we all had a splendid time. There were many special provisions brought in by all the submarines, so we had our choice of the best wines, chocolate, cognac and liqueurs.

'Soon, however, the order came for us to evacuate. As I had long been trying to transfer to landplane operations, I was pleased to be ordered to *See FI*, then at Zeebrugge. My new unit did not stay there long, however. In short order, the military installations at the Zeebrugge Mole were blown up . . . and we then began an orderly retreat.'[27]

During a lull in the British advance, *See III* headed westward again, occupying an airfield at Ekloo, east of Bruges. Fritz Stormer's new duties:

'. . . consisted of reporting daily the slow but certain advance of enemy units. Apparently enemy anti-aircraft units were with or just behind the leading elements of the enemy advance, as they fired at us as soon as we crossed the lines. We observed no enemy fighter squadrons and at this time we were not attacked in the air. From Ekloo we were transferred to Maldeghem, near Antwerp, where I soon became one of the many people in our unit confined to bed by the devastating influenza then sweeping Europe.'[28]

While Stormer was recuperating from the flu, naval mutinies in Germany led to the establishment of communist-style revolutionary organizations throughout the Army and Navy. He recalled:

'We were ordered by our headquarters to hold elections among our troops for seats on a Workers' and Soldiers' Council. This came after many aviation units requested authorization to bomb and strafe the mutinous naval units in Kiel to restore discipline among troops in our homeland. At first, our station commander, some *Staffel-Kapitäne* and a *Feldwebel* were elected to the Council. Although it had not been influenced by our officers, the result of the election was not recognized by our *General-kommando* [Corps Headquarters] and the election had to be held again, this time with the provision that no officers could be elected to the Council.'

By the time the armistice was signed, on 11 November, many of the would-be revolutionaries had stolen or destroyed much of the naval air units' equipment. One new and inexperienced two-seater crew tried to fly back to Germany but became disorientated and landed behind Allied lines, where they were taken prisoner and not repatriated for some time. By the end of the month, Fritz Stormer and many other members of *See III* made their way back to the naval aviation headquarters detachment at the Johannisthal airfield outside Berlin where, with little fanfare, they were released from active duty.

Fritz Stormer later became a dentist and, after being called up for *Luftwaffe* service in World War II, held staff positions and was discharged with the rank of *Major der Reserve*. His old boss, Friedrich Christiansen, went on to a civil aviation career, highlighted by service as captain of the world's largest flying-boat, the Dornier Do X. A General in World War II, Christiansen was for a time Military Governor of Holland. After the war he retired to his family home in Wyk auf Föhr, overlooking the sealanes that had once been the battleground for the Imperial German Navy's 'sea hawks'.

▼Albatros D III (with the rounded rudder of the D V) of the *Seefront-Staffel* at Nieuwmünster. This unit was later redesignated the *4. Marine-Jagdstaffel*.

6
THE OTHER RED BARON

CERTAINLY the most celebrated German pilot of World War I was *Rittmeister* (Cavalry Captain) Manfred *Freiherr* von Richthofen. In two-and-a-half years of fighting, his 80 aerial victories made him the 'ace of aces' of all nations and his 'trademark' of flying all-red aeroplanes – a colour he felt reflected martial valour – combined to weave the stuff of which legends are made. And, in that era of so-called 'knights of the air', add the fact that he was a member of the lesser nobility, honoured with more than twenty high awards by emperors and heads of other royal houses, and an image of immense proportions emerges: 'The Red Baron'.

Almost lost in the shadow of this propagandist's dream was his younger brother, Lothar *Freiherr* von Richthofen. Lothar's tally of 'only' 40 aerial victories, scored during 77 days at the Front, earned him but a handful of awards. In fact, flying in the same squadron and in red aircraft made distinctive by splashes of the yellow used by his old Dragoon regiment, Lothar von Richthofen was a noted fighter pilot in his own right and much more than 'the other red baron'.

The Richthofen family had been prominent in the eastern European province of Silesia for generations. Indeed, the family name comes from the German words *Richt Hofen* – 'court of judgment'. For supporting Prussian monarch Frederick the Great in seizing Silesia from Austria, in 1741 the family was elevated to baronial ranks and male members were granted the hereditary title of *Freiherr*. Long associated with statecraft, the family began its military heritage with Albrecht *Freiherr* von Richthofen, father of the two fighter aces. Albrecht was in fact on active service in the Regular Army when they were born in Breslau (now Wroclaw, Poland), Manfred on 2 May 1892 and Lothar on 27 September 1894.

While Manfred was raised in the military tradition and began his training at the Cadet School at Wahlstatt at the age of 11, Lothar remained in the public school system in Breslau. Only after matri-

culating at the local *Gymnasium* (high school) did Lothar apply for military service. He was inspired by Manfred, since 1912 a *Leutnant* in the elite light cavalry *Uhlanen-Regiment Nr 1 'Kaiser Alexander III'*, and signed up as an officer candidate in *Dragoner-Regiment Nr 4 'Von Bredow'*, also a mounted unit. Lothar was commissioned and at the outbreak of war sent to the War School in Danzig. But anxious to see action – as described in his brother's letters from the Russian Front – Lothar left the War School and rejoined his regiment en route to Belgium.

Lothar's unit spent a brief time in Belgium and France before being sent to the Eastern Front for the winter months. In the east, Lothar first encountered the obstacles of frustration that sent so many cavalrymen into the *Fliegertruppe*. One winter night he was sent out to reconnoitre the Russian lines east of the River Warthe (now Warta) in Poland, but found that all the bridges were down. He swam the icy waters to gather intelligence on the other side, and never forgot his land-bound limitations. Small wonder, therefore, that when Manfred left the Uhlans in June 1915 to begin training as an aviation observer, Lothar knew that his own time with the Dragoons would not be long.

OBSERVER OVER THE LINES
At Manfred's suggestion, Lothar began training as an observer the following summer and by year's end was flying with *Kampfstaffel 23* over Verdun and on the Somme Front. There Lothar enjoyed a range of activities denied him in service on the ground. With his pilot, *Leutnant* Kreutzmann, Lothar could fly far over enemy lines to gather the intelligence information needed by the generals. Most of all, he enjoyed the challenge of night bombing. Daylight bombing raids were carried out at high altitude in order to elude the fierce anti-aircraft fire that protected ammunition dumps and other important targets. But at night Kreutzmann had to take the aeroplane closer to the ground, so that the targets could be identified and, at low

own airfield. Kreutzmann had the uneasy feeling that he was heading into French-held territory and might not have enough fuel to return to his own lines. He had no choice but to land and hope to get his bearings on the ground.

Luckily, Kreutzmann found a clearing and made a perfect landing. Lothar looked around and said that he thought they were behind French lines. The aircraft could easily be flown out again, but first Lothar wanted to capitalize on the situation: hearing what he thought to be French voices approaching, he proposed to sneak through the mist, capture a French soldier and take him back in the aircraft. Lothar's great plan fizzled out when the voices turned out to be those of German soldiers on a routine patrol within their own lines.

BROTHERLY COMPETITION

There was competition between the brothers and by this time Lothar was feeling eclipsed by Manfred's mounting successes as a fighter pilot. Selected by the great ace *Hauptmann* Oswald Boelcke, Manfred was clearly one of the rising stars of *Jagdstaffel 2* on the *1. Armee* Front, not far from where Lothar was enjoying his less glamorous nocturnal adventures.

Good observers were much in demand, however, and Lothar was released from *Kasta 23* only after considerable delays. Indeed, his initial flight training had to be carried out during his spare time. It took Lothar six months to qualify as a pilot, a joyous event noted by Manfred in his letter home of 28 December 1916:

'Papa and Lothar were with me on Christmas Day. It was a memorable holiday. There is more fun to such a Christmas in the field than you at home would think.

'Our celebrations consisted of a Christmas tree and an excellent dinner. On the next day, Lothar went up alone for the first time, an event equalled only by the first victory.'[1]

The brothers celebrated New Year's Day together at *Jasta 2*'s airfield at Lagnicourt. On 3 January 1917 Lothar was still there and watched with envy from the ground as Manfred brought down his 16th victory in a fight almost directly over the airfield. That event surely strengthened Lothar's desire to become a *Jagdflieger*.

Normally Lothar's new status as a pilot would have meant only a change of assignment within his present two-seater squadron. Eventually, with luck and persistence, he might have been transferred to

▲Brotherly co-operation is the picture that wartime propagandists painted of Manfred von Richthofen (left) and his younger brother, Lothar. By the time this photo was published in a popular postcard series, both brothers had received the *Orden Pour le Mérite* and were accomplished fighter pilots. But a strong sibling rivalry compelled Manfred to criticize the efforts of Lothar, whose approach to aerial combat was more emotional than his brother's and got him into some hazardous situations.

altitude, Lothar had a better view of the results of his work. He liked nothing better than to leave a blazing target, with the full fury of French ground gunners directed at him. On many occasions *Leutnants* von Richthofen and Kreutzmann flew two and three raids before the early glow of dawn spoiled their element of surprise.

At the end of one raid, the cloak of night almost proved to be their undoing. A thick mist covered the ground and made it impossible to find landmarks that would enable them to get back to their the *Jagdstaffel-Schule*. But Manfred's growing influence changed that. By the time Manfred assumed command of *Jasta 11* on 20 January 1917 (having received the *Orden Pour le Mérite* on 12 January), he was Germany's highest-scoring fighter ace and could easily request the small favour of having his brother posted to the same unit. In that way, the personalized training Manfred had received from his mentor Boelcke could be transferred to Lothar.

LOTHAR THE FIGHTER PILOT

The brothers had about two weeks to work together with the effective Albatros D II fighters then based at Douai; ever the even-handed commander, Manfred von Richthofen gave no more time to his brother than to any other newcomer to his unit. Manfred's letter of 26 March 1917 assesses Lothar's initial combat performance, but not without noting his own superior achievements:

'Yesterday I brought down my 31st and the day before my 30th. Three days ago I received my promotion to *Oberleutnant* and have thus gained a full half-year [seniority over officers in his cadet class]. My *Jagdstaffel* is shaping up well. It really gives me great pleasure.

'Lothar had his first aerial encounter yesterday. He was satisfied with it because he hit his adversary who, in our parlance, "stank", leaving a black,

smelly trail [of oil and fuel] behind him. He did not go down, of course – that would have been too much luck. Lothar is very conscientious and will do well.'[2]

Three days later Lothar's courage and tenacity paid off. At about 1700 hours, he was in a flight that came upon an F.E.2b which had crossed over the German lines south of Lens. Lothar dived on it. While his Albatros was clearly faster and more manoeuvrable than the 'Fee' (nickname of the F.E.2b), the two-seat pusher biplane of No 25 Squadron, RFC, did have a flexible Lewis machine-gun in the front cockpit and a second Lewis gun on a telescopic mounting to enable the observer to fire backwards over the top wing. Indeed, a 'Fee' from this squadron had been responsible for the 1916 demise of Max Immelmann. In this instance, observer 2nd Lt A. G. Severs used both guns effectively to fend off Lothar von Richthofen. But Lothar persisted, finally found a 'blind' spot and got in a burst of fire that disabled the engine and mortally wounded the observer. F.E.2b 7715 came down in no man's land, where the pilot, 2nd Lt Norman L. Knight, was taken prisoner and his observer transported to a field hospital, where he died of his wounds.

Back at Douai, the other pilots of *Jasta 11* lauded the victorious Lothar for scoring the unit's only

victory that day. Manfred, however, was not alto-gether pleased with his brother's performance. He felt that Lothar was daring to the point of reckless-ness and did not employ the careful methodology needed to make the best use of their airborne gun platform. Manfred considered Lothar to be a 'shooter,' not a skilled hunter as he was.[3]

'BLOODY APRIL' AND A DOUBLE KILL

Lothar, determined to prove himself, shot down two enemy aircraft on 11 April. On a morning patrol, shortly after 0900 hours, Lothar, *Leutnants* Kurt Wolff and Karl-Emil Schäfer, and *Vizefeldwebel* Sebastian Festner attacked four Bristol F.2B Fighters of No 48 Squadron, RFC, over Gavrelle, east of Arras. Over Mouville Farm, south of Arras, Lothar brought down A3323 crewed by 2nd Lts George N. Brockhurst and C. B. Boughton, both taken prisoner; and Wolff was credited with A3338, Capt David M. Tidmarsh and 2nd Lt C. B. Holland, both POW. German sources credit Schäfer with A3318, 2nd Lts Robert E. Adeney and L. G. Lovell, both killed in action, and acknowledge Festner's claim of an F.2B, although there is no correspond-ing No 48 Squadron loss for the latter. At 1250 hours, Lothar and Schäfer were credited with shooting down a pair of Sopwith two-seaters south

and east of Arras (but, again, no RFC losses match the claims).

Two days later, Lothar scored another double victory during a fight with R.E.8s of No 59 Squad-ron and F.E.2b's of No 25 Squadron over Vitry, south-west of Douai, in which Manfred achieved his 41st victory, Wolff his tenth, and Festner his ninth. Again, Manfred was critical of his brother's style of airfighting:

'When he shot down his fourth and fifth adversaries [on 13 April] I had an opportunity to observe him. We attacked a flight. I was the first [to single out an adversary]. My opponent was soon despatched. I looked around and saw that my brother sat behind a British machine from which flames shot out and which then exploded. Near this Englishman flew a second. He [Lothar] did nothing else to the first, who had not yet gone down and was still in the air. He turned his machine-gun on the next one and immediately shot at him even though he had barely finished with the other. This one also fell after a short fight.

'At home [Douai] he asked quite proudly: "How many have you shot down?" I said quite modestly: "One". He turned his back to me and said: "I got two," whereupon I sent him up to the lines to check. He had to determine the fellows' names, etc. Late in the afternoon he came back after having found only one.

'Consequently, the enquiry was difficult, as it

◀ The Royal Aircraft Factory F.E.2b was a strong opponent when Lothar von Richthofen began flying with *Jasta 11*. Indeed, his brother Manfred was later wounded in a fight with a 'Fee' and his friend Karl Emil Schäfer was killed in a fight with one.

▶ Lothar von Richthofen learned how to outmanoeuvre the F.E.2b. His first confirmed aerial victory was a 'Fee' shot down over Vimy on 28 March 1917. His 17th victory was also an F.E.2b, brought down over Gavrelle on 1 May 1917. It may have been the machine seen here, 4968 of No 18 Squadron, RFC, which fell that day.

usually is with such shooters. It was not until a day later that the troops reported where the other lay and confirmed what we had all seen.'[4]

SAVED BY SCHÄFER

On the morning of 25 April 1917 Lothar's impetuosity almost cost him his life. Ranging far over British lines, he attracted the attention of 2nd Lt Charles V. Darnell and 2/AM G. Pawley in F.E.2b A837 of No 25 Squadron and the chase was on. Lothar prudently withdrew and was not worried when Gunner Pawley used his forward gun during the initial pursuit.

'In the greatest hope [Lothar late wrote] I said to myself: Just wait, when they get close all their bullets will be used up and their guns will jam. Then suddenly I felt a hit in my machine! A main control wire was shot through. As a result, I could no longer make sharp turns for fear that the wings would not stay together. Now, even without the Englishman on my neck, I would really have to crash.'

The 'Fee' came closer and Lothar could hear the clatter of its machine-guns and see the grey smoke trails of incendiary bullets streaming past his Albatros. He waited for the inevitable.

'But what did I see there?' he wrote of his deliverance. 'The British aircraft was ablaze, and behind him flew [Karl-Emil Schäfer in] a German machine! Thank God! I would have bet that within the next half minute I would have been shot down or that the wings would have fallen off. Arriving back home, I merely gave Schäfer my hand and invited him that night to have a bottle of champagne. It was good that one could at least do that.'[5]

Schäfer's 23rd victory, achieved over Bailleul at 1045 hours (German time), was noted in the RFC combat casualty register as follows: 'About 9–35 am [British time] machine was shot down by HA and fell in flames between Willerval and Bailleul. Pilot and observer [sic] killed.'

In spite of Manfred's criticism, Lothar put up a star performance during what is now called 'Bloody April,' the month that British military aviation lost one-third of its force. From his double score on 11 April through a double on 30 April, Lothar von Richthofen accounted for 14 confirmed aerial victories. It was not the equal of Manfred's 21 kills that month, but quite respectable for a new *Jagdflieger*.

Lothar's most unusual aerial victory – and not just for that month – must surely have been his

13th; scored shortly after noon on 29 April. Manfred and Lothar von Richthofen had taken off after being alerted that a flight of SPAD S.VII fighters had crossed the lines. The French-built SPADs of No 19 Squadron were a better match for *Jasta 11*'s Albatros D IIIs than the slow, under-powered British aircraft that suffered such terrible losses that month. And the leader of the SPAD flight, Major H. D. Harvey-Kelly, DSC, was no newcomer, having piloted the first British military aircraft to arrive in France after the outbreak of war in 1914.

The British fighters initiated the attack over Izel, west of Douai, but lost the advantage as the encounter headed southwards toward Sailley. Within a short time Manfred killed 2nd Lt Richard Applin in SPAD B1573 and Wolff fired the fatal shots into Major Harvey-Kelly's aircraft, A6681. The younger von Richthofen forced Lt W. N. Hamilton in SPAD A6753 to land after an encounter that reinforced Manfred's contention that Lothar was no 'hunter'.

After having pursued Hamilton for fifteen minutes in a series of descending curves, Lothar expended his full ammunition supply of 1,000 bullets. It was only as he closed in for the kill that he discovered that he was out of ammuniton. As Lothar described it:

'Finally, I think of a rather desperate measure: shall I knock off his rudder with the help of my propeller? Then he is done for, but with me it would be the same.

'Another theory: If I turn off the engine the moment I touch him with my aircraft, what then? At this moment, my Englishman turns and looks in a horrified way at me. Then he stops his engine and goes down, landing somewhere near our third line. I can see his engine still running on the ground.'[6]

Not to be cheated of the fruits of victory, Lothar made a series of low, menacing passes over the SPAD, enough to dissuade Hamilton from any thought of destroying the aircraft. In fact, Hamilton later reported that his fuel tank had been hit and was empty by the time he landed; therefore, he was unable to set fire to his machine. He was uninjured and taken away by German infantrymen.

PERFORMING FOR 'PAPA'

Major Albrecht von Richthofen was visiting Douai at the time and had in fact watched his sons bring down the SPADs. He was at the hangars when the red Albatros's returned. Like a schoolboy, eager to

▶ Taller than his brother, Lothar von Richthofen always stood out in a crowd. Lothar (XX) and Manfred (X) are seen here at a parachute demonstration in 1917. At that time fighter pilots did not have parachutes and the brothers' comments helped determine that the life-saving devices could be adapted to small fighter aircraft.

▶ A typical scene at *Jasta 11*: Manfred von Richthofen (left) leading the way out to the flight line while Lothar walks a pace or two behind.

boast of his achievement, Lothar was the first out of his aeroplane and went straight up to his father, saluted smartly and reported proudly: '*Guten Tag, Papa,* I have just shot down an Englishman.'

Moments later, a calmer, more self-confident Manfred greeted the *Major* with: '*Guten Tag,* Papa, I have just shot down an Englishman.' Manfred later wrote:

'The old gentleman was happy, one could see that. He is not one of those fathers who worries about his sons; on the contrary, I believe that at the very least he would have liked it best if he could have sat in a machine and fired away [with us].'[7]

Later that day the bearded head of the family had more reason to be proud. During an afternoon flight Manfred shot down his 50th enemy aircraft at 1655 hours. And on an evening patrol the eldest son scored victories 51 and 52. In conjunction with the latter engagement, at 1950 hours Lothar von Richthofen shot down a B.E.2e of No 12 Squadron, RFC, his 14th victory. But his achievement was overlooked at the celebration dinner that night. All eyes were on Manfred, who was interrupted long enough to take a telephone call from *6. Armee* Headquarters. He was read the text of a congratulatory telegram from *Kaiser* Wilhelm.

Up early the next morning and eager to 'have an Englishman for breakfast', as *Hauptmann* Boelcke used to say, Lothar attacked a B.E.2e of No 16 Squadron, RFC, flying between Vimy and Viller-wall; at 0715 he sent it down in flames near Mericourt. The crew, 2nd Lts N. A. Lawrence and G. R. Y. Stout, were dead when troops arrived at the scene of the crash.

Manfred was not flying that day and so Lothar continued his hunt unrestrained by the pressure of having to keep up with his brother. Within half an hour he was pursuing a 'Vickers' heading for Douai, a favourite target for British bombers. The aircraft, most likely an F.E.2d of No 57 Squadron, was brought down over Izel. With victories 15 and 16 confirmed, Lothar von Richthofen returned with satisfaction to his airfield.

The next day, 1 May, Manfred went on leave, as ordered by the High Command. Aware of the benefits of keeping the Richthofen name associated with combat success, the *Kaiser* himself is credited with giving *Jagdstaffel 11* a new name: *Jagdstaffel Richthofen*. Accordingly, the High Command arranged for Lothar to be named acting *Staffel-Führer* in Manfred's absence, even though other squadron members were senior in rank and had higher victory scores. Lothar did not disappoint his superiors or fail to impress his comrades. That evening he shot down an F.E.2b of No 25 Squadron, RFC, near Gavrelle.

Five days later Lothar shot down Armstrong Whitworth F.K.8 A9999 of No 2 Squadron, RFC, south of Givenchy. The 'Big Ack,' as the F.K.8 was called, was known to be a slow but sturdy reconnaissance aircraft, capable of putting up a solid defence. Lothar persevered, however, and added victory No 18 to his list.

LOTHAR VERSUS ALBERT BALL

Even while on leave Manfred posed problems for Lothar. The massive publicity given to Germany's greatest living fighter ace while back in his Fatherland would surely have come to the attention of Allied intelligence. Accordingly, Manfred's absence from Douai was a good time for the RFC to settle old scores from 'Bloody April'. As RAF historian H. A. Jones noted:

> 'In an endeavour to catch the German aeroplanes during their periods of greatest activity, patrols by eighteen fighters of the 9th Wing were ordered to be in the neighbourhood of the German aerodrome

at Douai in the morning and in the evening of 7 May. One of these patrols in the evening had severe fighting. The aeroplanes chiefly involved were ten S.E.5s of No 56 Squadron. Of six SPADs of No 19 Squadron, which were patrolling in conjunction with the S.E.5s, only one joined in the fighting, which was confused by rain and poor visibility, and took place through layers of cloud. The remaining SPAD pilots lost touch with one another and saw nothing of the combats.'[8]

During that rainy evening of 7 May 1917 one of the most controversial aerial combats of World War I took place. RFC fighter ace Captain Albert Ball, DSO, (posthumously awarded the Victoria Cross) and *Leutnant* Lothar *Freiherr* von Richthofen had a one-to-one encounter. It was probably the most noted German-British air fight since the 23 November 1916 battle when then highest-scoring British ace Major Lanoe George Hawker, VC, DSO, was shot down and killed by Manfred von Richthofen.

Albert Ball, whom the Germans called 'the British Richthofen', was not quite 21 years old, but he was the British Army's first triple recipient of the DSO and an extraordinarily talented combat pilot, the victor in 44 aerial battles. During the confusion brought on by the bad weather that evening, Ball and Capt C. M. Crowe had become separated and then were able to link up over Fresnoy at about 2000 hours British time (2100 hours German time). The remainder of the flight is summarized by H. A. Jones:

> 'After a time Captain Ball was seen to fire two Very lights, following which he dived on a single red fighter near Loos. Captain Crowe dived also and a SPAD of No 19 Squadron joined in. All three British pilots attacked the enemy single-seater in turn and then Ball and the German pilot disappeared, still fighting, into a cloud bank. Captain Crowe followed, but when he came through the clouds he could see nothing of either the British or German aeroplanes. He therefore returned.'[9]

Capt Ball was pursuing Lothar von Richthofen, who had become separated from his three *Staffel-Kameraden*: *Ltns* Eberhard Mohnicke, Georg Simon and Wilhelm Allmenröder. Allmenröder rejoined Lothar just in time to witness the fight, which he described in a letter:

> 'We were flying patrol from south to north over the trenches at an altitude of about 2,000 metres, and I was searching for enemy fighters, looking up and down. Suddenly, in a north-easterly direction, about 100 metres above us, I spotted four enemy

biplanes, which, turning left, tried to come in behind us. They were led by a fighter with long pennants attached to the wings . . . Naturally, I wanted to improve my position by gaining altitude and clearing my tail. I began a flat, slow climbing turn to the left, always looking behind me, but when I had flown a complete circle, I found that I could not see any other aeroplane in the sky.

'I looked around and saw, about 200 metres below me, Lothar in a wild, circling dogfight with a British fighter. Both opponents circled around below me, but neither had a chance to shoot. As I was higher, I would have had a chance to fire, but I had a feeling that I had better not interfere. Apart from this, I could not understand where the other enemy aircraft had gone, and I was afraid they might return.

'Below me, each opponent tried to improve his position by [making] wide left turns; however, no one gained an advantage and not a shot was fired. Meanwhile, it became darker and darker. Off to the north-east, Douai was barely visible, and a dense haze was forming over the ground. Five to eight minutes passed. The sun had just gone down. Suddenly, as if both had received an order, the two left the circle and flew straight away – Lothar to the south, his opponent to the north.

'I thought that they wanted to stop the fight because of the darkness, but then both turned and rushed at each other as if they intended to ram. Lothar dipped under the other and then both turned and rushed again at each other, only a few shots being fired. At the third frontal attack, Lothar

came from the south and his opponent from the north. I waited. The machine-guns peppered again. This time, Lothar's opponent did not give way sideways, but dived down to the ground. I had wanted to see where the aircraft crashed, but I became anxious because Lothar also went down in a rather steep turn and disappeared in the mist.

'I flew back to our airfield to order a search to be made for Lothar. As I jumped out of my machine, it was almost night. I was immediately informed that Lothar had made an emergency landing because his engine had been hit. He himself was not injured.'[10]

A German doctor verified that Lothar's opponent, Capt Ball, perished from crash injuries, even though his S.E.5 had sustained several hits. There are several versions of who 'got' who in this encounter and they are muddied by Lothar's initial contention that he shot down a 'triplane' that day. Earlier he had shot down a Nieuport over Gavrelle and probably did see Sopwith Triplanes of No 8 Squadron, Royal Naval Air Service. But the evidence makes it clear that Lothar von Richthofen and Albert Ball were the combatants in the low-level aerial duel over the villages of Seclin and Annoeullin. The latter location was the site of Capt Ball's funeral with full military honours.

This event was, of course, just what the German High Command wanted to hear. Even though it is likely that Ball and von Richthofen caused each

▶ As a member of *Jasta 11*, Lothar von Richthofen always had access to the latest and best aircraft, such as this Fokker tri-plane. After the Albatros fighters went into a period of decline, due to unexplained structural failures in the air, Anthony Fokker regained his lost position with the Dr I triplane, which served in many units until very late in the war.

other to go down, Lothar was widely hailed as the victor over the pilot who was then Britain's highest-scoring fighter ace. A German message dropped over British lines informed:

'RFC Captain Ball was brought down in a fight in the air on the May 7, 1917, by a pilot of the same order as himself. He was buried at Annoeulen.'[11]

Immediate parallels were drawn with Manfred's encounter with Major Hawker; not only could Lothar *not* escape Manfred's shadow, he was being shaped by it.

On 9 May, the day of Ball's funeral, Lothar scored his 21st victory, a Bristol F.2B fighter brought down along the road from Roeux to Gavrelle. The next day he was in a fight with two Sopwith Scouts, probably from No 66 Squadron, and shot one down between Sailly and Vitry. On the afternoon of the 11th, Lothar von Richthofen and Wilhelm Allmenröder brought down a pair of Bristol Fighters of No 48 Squadron near Izel.

Lothar was superstitious. When he left his Dragoon regiment for *Kasta 23*, he took his riding crop along on bombing missions as a talisman. In *Jasta 11*, however, the long stick did not fit easily into the tight cockpit of an Albatros fighter. Yet he was reluctant to give it up, especially after learning that noted ace *Ltn* Kurt Wintgens was shot down and killed during the one flight in which he failed to carry a similar riding stick. Only the substitution of a pair of Manfred's old fur gloves made Lothar feel secure enough to leave the riding crop on the ground. The gloves accompanied Lothar as he scored his first ten aerial victories. After that, he received a new Albatros D III and had gained enough confidence to leave the by-now tattered gloves behind. But he did not entirely lose his superstitious bent, including an aversion to the number 13. The events of 13 May 1917 only reinforced his fears.

UNLUCKY 13: FIRST CRASH

On that Sunday, Lothar and *Ltn* Karl Allmenröder, brother of the pilot with whom the acting *Staffel-Führer* had scored his 23rd victory, were flying over British lines at 1130 hours when they spotted a lone B.E.2 two-seater below them. Lothar signalled his intention to prevent the reconnaissance aircraft from reaching German lines and went after it. The B.E.2 pilot went lower and lower hoping that British anti-aircraft guns would hit his pursuer. Despite

that danger, Lothar closed in and opened fire. The two-seater went down near Arleux.

A light haze obscured the entire area and Lothar stayed low, looking for a landmark. As he groped his way along, ground batteries opened fire on him. Suddenly he felt intense pain in his left hip and was horrified to see a large bloodstain along the leg of his flying suit.

Despite the wound, Lothar managed to guide the aircraft along until the firing stopped and he found that he was over German lines. He headed for a clear spot and put the machine down. When he regained consciousness, he was in a hospital in Douai.

Manfred was enjoying his hunting vacation in the forests near Freiburg im Breisgau when he was informed of his brother's mishap. After learning the circumstances of the incident and ascertaining that Lothar was not grievously injured, Manfred's only comment in a letter home was: 'Lothar has been playing the fool again.'[12]

Lothar's wounds were serious enough, however, to keep him out of action for five months. The only consolation was that, on the day after he went into hospital, he was awarded the *Orden Pour le Mérite* – only four months after Manfred had received the same distinction. Lothar was succeeded as *Staffel-Führer* by *Ltn* Karl Allmenröder, who held the post only until 15 June, when Manfred cut short his leave and returned to lead *Jasta 11* in the face of steadily growing success by the unit's RFC opponents. Ten days later Manfred was named *Kommandeur* of the newly created *Jagdgeschwader Nr 1* composed of *Jagdstaffeln 4, 6, 10* and *11*. Back at the Front, Manfred wrote home:

'I visited Lothar [in hospital] and arrived just in time to see him before his removal. He looked tanned and very well, stretched out full length on a divan. He was fully dressed and wore the *Pour le Mérite* around his neck. He is able to walk and ride a horse again, but must have a good long rest.'[13]

MANFRED WOUNDED

Then, on 6 July, Manfred was wounded during a fight with F.E.2d's of No 20 Squadron. He lost consciousness for a brief period but managed to bring his Albatros D V down near Wervicq. The ace was taken to *Feldlazarett 76* (St Nicholas' Hospital) in Courtrai, where it was found that a bullet had grazed the left side of his head. The period of both Richthofen brothers being absent from the Front ended on 25 July, when Manfred returned to the *Jagdgeschwader*'s airfield at Marckebeeke. But he never really got over his wound and endured recurring headaches until his death.

After Lothar's return, on 25 September 1917, he was given command of *Jasta 11*, then on the *4. Armee* Front. He was however able to do little flying. Thinking a new machine might give him renewed confidence, Lothar joined Manfred on 30 October in a test flight of newly arrived Fokker Dr I triplanes. Lothar soon experienced engine trouble and began losing altitude over Zilverberg. He made a perfect landing. This time it was Manfred who, in his haste to aid his brother, did not keep a cool head; he landed too fast and totally wrecked Fokker Dr I 114/17. Both brothers were uninjured.

Lothar's first victory in a triplane – and his first as full-time *Staffel-Führer* – was scored on 9 November 1917. At 1030 hours he shot down a Bristol Fighter over British-held territory north-west of Zonnebeke. He and Manfred each shot down a Bristol Fighter at 1400 hours on 23 November during a fight just west of Seranvillers; it was Manfred's 62nd victory and Lothar's 26th and his last for the year. On 30 November Lothar flew with Manfred and *Ltn* Siegfried Gussmann in an attack on S.E.5s of No 56 Squadron flying over the area between Moeuvres and Bourlon Forest. Manfred and Gussmann each accounted for an S.E.5.

The brothers and their father spent a second Christmas together at the Front, after which Manfred and Lothar were called home on leave, Manfred for a general rest, Lothar to attend to an inflammation of the middle ear. As part of their light duties, they were sent to witness the Russo-German peace negotiations at Brest-Litovsk. But the brothers were warriors, not politicians, and their barely hidden boredom with the peacemaking process resulted in their being invited to Bialo-wicza, once the hunting preserve of the Russian Czars. Even in the woods the competition continued and Lothar did not consider the hunt a success until he, too, had bagged a red stag.

On 20 January 1918 the Richthofen brothers returned to Berlin, where they were feted at every turn. The gaiety of nightlife in the capital was an arena in which Lothar could outshine his brother. Half a head taller than Manfred, Lothar was the more gregarious of the two; indeed, a ready smile and a piercing gaze were among the charms that drew women to him. Lothar is said rarely to have

declined feminine companionship. In contrast, Manfred was painfully shy around women and revealed little about the one steady contact he is known to have had; he was more comfortable in the company of senior officers whose influence would be useful in obtaining more experienced pilots and new and better aircraft for his *Jagdgeschwader*.

At the end of the brothers' leave Manfred returned to the Front alone. In a letter dated 11 February 1918, he explained to his mother, with a prophetic note about his own fate:

'I am sorry that I was kept in Berlin so long that I could not come to Schweidnitz to say goodbye. It would have been so pleasant, and I was looking forward to it.

'Now I think I will not come back to Germany for a long, long time.

'Keep Lothar with you as long as possible. He is rather negligent with his ears and does nothing to cure them. He misses nothing here. Tell him from me that he should not leave before the first of March. Should things become more lively here, I will advise him by wire.'[14]

Five days later Lothar was back at *Jasta 11*'s airfield at Avesnes le Sec, north-east of Cambrai. The winter weather was unfavourble – largely rain and low cloud, strong wind at altitude and fog on the ground – but plans for the coming spring offensive were being discussed and Lothar felt a *Staffel-Führer* should be with his unit.

In March British air activity in Flanders in-creased as more and more aircraft were ordered over the lines to look for troop and matériel concentrations. The conclusion of the Russo-German peace treaty meant that many more German divisions were coming to the Western Front and Allied planners needed to know which of their areas to strengthen in anticipation of the offensive.

At midday on 11 March enemy air activity over the German *2. Armee* Front was especially heavy and Lothar von Richthofen led a flight out to interrupt the British intelligence-gathering process. Just after 1300 hours he saw a Bristol F.2B of No 48 Squadron, an old adversary of *Jasta 11*. Following a short fight, Lothar sent the two-seat Bristol Fighter down near Fresnoy le Petit. It was his 27th victory.

The following day Lothar and Manfred, together with *Ltn* Werner Steinhäuser, had a very successful encounter with a formation of F.2Bs from No 62 Squadron, RFC. During the ensuing fight, Manfred achieved his 64th victory, Steinhäuser scored his fourth, and Lothar shot down two, his 28th and 29th victories. It was like old times, with Manfred as *Geschwader-Kommandeur* in the lead and Lothar at his side. Lothar later recalled:

'Arriving at the Front, we saw about ten Englishmen heading for our lines at high altitude . . . As soon as we reached their altitude, 5,500 metres, we proceeded to attack. As always, my brother was on them first; he attacked one and forced him to go down. The Englishman tried to get rid of his opponent by diving and turning. My brother stayed behind him. With more hits he then forced him [the F.2B pilot] to land the crate near our airfield.

'I had merely been an observer at the beginning of this fight and had seen that my brother had only the one opponent. In such cases one does not need help. Therefore I looked around for a victim of my own. To that end there was one especially suited for me about 100 metres below, beneath the British squadron. I attacked him.'[15]

Once again Lothar showed himself to be a 'shooter'. He got far ahead of his comrades and was quickly surrounded by other Bristol Fighters. Continuing to dive for another 100 metres, Lothar noted that only one British aircraft followed him down. As if at a signal, the F.2B and the Fokker triplane levelled off, circled around and charged head-on at each other with a combined airspeed of 400 kilometres per hour. Armed with only two forward-firing machine-guns, Lothar had to make a decisive shot on the first pass or risk being hit by the Bristol's rear-seat gunner as the two fighters passed each other:

'We rushed towards each other shooting. At the last moment I noticed I had hit him. A blazing aircraft whizzed by me. I pulled my machine around and made such a sharp turn that I was three-quarters on my back. A sea of fire in the form of the Englishman whistled right by me. The observer stood up and stared into the flames. Completely ablaze, the British machine made another turn. Both crewmen jumped out along the way [they would have had no parachutes]. The rest of the machine fluttered in the air.'[16]

Lothar returned to the general mêlée going on and shot down a second Bristol Fighter, wounding both crewmen.

UNLUCKY 13: LOTHAR DOWN AGAIN
The following day, Wednesday, 13 March 1918, the brothers made their last combat flight together.

During the course of a morning fight with Sopwith Camels and Bristol Fighters, Lothar's aversion to the number 13 proved, once again, to be well founded. He later wrote:

'Our squadron flew to the Front under the leadership of my brother. We had scarcely arrived at the Front when we met a swarm of Englishmen. Everyone chose an opponent and attacked him, and so did I. I attacked my opponent in a dive. Then I heard a loud crash within my machine! It was hit. Only too late I noticed what was wrong. My Fokker triplane suddenly became a biplane. It is a horrible feeling to be minus one wing at 4,000 metres. I quickly broke away from my Englishman. He was really quite stupid and did not follow me. Nothing could have been easier than to shoot me down in this condition. With both remaining wings I could still bring it into a normal glide, but only straight ahead, as the rudder no longer functioned.'[17]

It is not clear who put Lothar von Richthofen out of action. Manfred was in command of a *Jagdgeschwader* of more than 30 aircraft, Fokker triplanes and Albatros D Vs. On this occasion eleven of the previous day's opponents, Bristol Fighters of No 62 Squadron, were patrolling a line from Cambrai to Le Cateau in support of an attack on Denain by D.H.4 two-seat day bombers from Nos 25 and 27 Squadrons, while two Flights of Sopwith Camels of No 73 Squadron were on the line from Cambrai to Villers to Outreaux.

JG I lost only one triplane in the engagement, Lothar's aircraft, but the *RFC War Diary* for 13 March recorded two versions of the event:

'Capt A. H. Orlebar, No 73 Squadron, dived on a Fokker triplane, opening fire at close range. The EA instantly nose-dived, its top plane coming off . . . Capt G. F. Hughes and Capt H. Claye, No 62 Squadron, in a general engagement between his patrol and a very large formation of EA Scouts, shot down one EA triplane, which was confirmed by other members of the patrol to have crashed. He then attacked one of three triplanes which were diving on his tail. This EA went down vertically; the top plane was seen falling away in pieces.'[18]

In an extraordinary display of piloting skill, Lothar brought his crippled aircraft down to 500 metres and, using his limited controls, moved towards a flat landing spot. Suddenly a high-tension wire loomed directly in front of him. There was neither time nor room to manoeuvre and, with columns of men marching on either side of the pole, Lothar had no choice but to go straight into the

▲Following his crash on 13 March 1918, Lothar von Richthofen was sent to the Aaper Wald clinic in Düsseldorf. He was the clinic's most illustrious guest and, as he progressed, he was asked to pose for a group photo with other patients and members of the medical staff.

'The blood he spat out did not come from any internal injuries. He had merely swallowed some during his fall. He is in the hospital in Cambrai and hopes to be back at the Front within a fortnight. His only regret is not to be able to be with us at the present moment.'[19]

Manfred's assessment of Lothar's injuries was over-optimistic. Lothar's facial injuries were so serious that he was sent back to Germany, to the Aaper Wald clinic in Düsseldorf, for further treatment. After that, a long period of home rest was prescribed for the 23-year-old fighter pilot and victor in 29 aerial combats.

Thus, Lothar was not at the Front when the Germans' great spring offensive was launched on 21 March. And he was not there on 21 April 1918, when his illustrious brother was shot down and killed during a fight with Sopwith Camels of No 209 Squadron of the recently created Royal Air Force.

Manfred fell within British lines and was given a funeral with full military honours befitting his rank and stature. His memory was honoured by the *Luftstreitkräfte* on 20 May, when *JG 1* was redesignated *Jagdgeschwader Freiherr von Richthofen Nr I*.

Meanwhile, Lothar was filled with rage and guilt:

'At first I didn't believe it, but the reports in the newspapers were so detailed – it must be true.

'I lay in a clinic in Düsseldorf and did not help my brother! How often had we both saved each other's lives – on his last flight I had let him down.

'My parents, all my relatives and friends pestered me about not going back. Yet I had taken an oath of revenge and I had to fulfil it no matter what the cost. Everyone conspired against me. The Commanding General of the *Luftstreitkräfte* offered me a very nice adjutant's billet at Headquarters. My doctors didn't want to let me out; they wrote I was not "fit for duty". But before that became known, I had to get to the Front, otherwise I would not be allowed to go back to my *Jagdstaffel*.'[20]

After enduring many long bureaucratic battles, Lothar showed his usual impetuosity and simply checked himself out of the clinic. He telephoned the Air Chief of Staff's office in Berlin and requested to be returned to his unit. Obviously, no one would refuse a Richthofen and he was soon on his way.

When Lothar got to France, however, he encountered the Commanding General of the *Luftstreitkräfte*, *General* Ernst von Hoeppner, and the *Feldflugchef*, *Oberstleutnant* Hermann von der Lieth-Thomsen, on a tour of rear area air facilities. They sat the young *Leutnant* down and used all their

wire. He awoke in a field hospital and later recalled:

'My head is bound up and I cannot touch it. Aha! Now it dawns on me: I wanted to land and make a turn! In the attempt to turn I crashed and lost consciousness. I had been hit only in the head and legs. My hands were still on the control stick. As my comrades said later, they had taken my crash for a death dive.'

Ten days later Manfred wrote home:

'You will have received my telegram advising you of Lothar's fall. Thanks be to God, he is doing nicely. I visit him daily. Please, Mother, don't worry about anything. He is really doing quite well.

'His nose has already healed, only the jaw is still bad, but he will keep his teeth. Above his right eye he has a rather large hole, but the eye itself has not been damaged. Several blood vessels burst under his right knee and in the left calf.

persuasive powers to get him to return to Germany. Lothar politely declined their arguments and blandishments. At the end of the session he was allowed to return to the Front.

During Lothar's convalescence, command of *Jasta 11* had been held on a temporary basis by four different pilots, including the rising star of the *Luftstreitkräfte, Leutnant der Reserve* Ernst Udet. On Lothar's return to *Jasta 11*, based at Monthoussard Ferme on the 7. *Armee* Front, on 19 July, he resumed his position as full-time *Staffel-Führer*. On the 25th, he demonstrated his old talents by shooting down a Sopwith Camel. That success, Lothar's 30th, also was recorded as the *Jagdgeschwader*'s 500th victory.

The following day *Oberleutnant* Hermann Göring, who had risen to command the *Jagdgeschwader*, went on leave. In his absence, Lothar was appointed acting *Kommandeur. Obltn* Erich Rüdiger von Wedel, a promising young ace, assumed temporary command of *Jasta 11*.

The next few days were relatively quiet and on 30 July the *Jagdgeschwader* changed airfields, pulling back to Puissieux-Ferme, north-east of Laon. While the move was another signal of gradual German withdrawal, it did not dampen the spirits of the men under Lothar von Richthofen's command.

On 1 August the *Jagdgeschwader* logged eleven victories. Two of them were Lothar's and identified by him as American-piloted and French-piloted SPAD S.XIIIs. He had little regard for his American opponent, apparently one of the six losses suffered

that day by the 27th Aero Squadron, USAS. Lothar wrote:

> 'The American was just a beginner. There were four of them and three of us. I was somewhat higher than the American. In a moment I was near him, fired about 50 shots and the enemy aeroplane fell out of control. A gentleman who flew with me also thought that he would like to shoot down the American. He recognized the enemy just as he saw me behind him and then the Yankee fell. A quick grasp of the situation means life for a *Jagdflieger*. Thus, the American did not notice me at all and really had a beautiful death.'[21]

At 0420 hours (British time) on 8 August 1918, the Amiens Offensive was launched. Under cover of thick ground mist and massive artillery support, British forces regained important positions in France and the German Army suffered its greatest defeat since the beginning of the war. The offensive concentrated on the German 2. *Armee* Front, but the effect was felt up and down the line. *Jagdgeschwader Freiherr von Richthofen Nr I* was sent from the 7. *Armee* Front it usually patrolled up to the 2. *Armee* area; an interim airfield at Peronne was assigned to the Wing.

During afternoon and evening patrols, the *Jagdgeschwader* accounted for the destruction of fourteen RAF aircraft and suffered no losses. For the first time in his career, Lothar von Richthofen shot down three enemy aircraft in one day, a Sopwith Camel and two S.E.5s. His companion, *Ltn* Erich Loewenhardt, commander of *Jasta 10*, also shot down three that day. Lothar later wrote:

◀ On returning to active service, Lothar began flying the Fokker D VII. As in the past, the family patriarch, *Major* Albrecht von Richthofen (right), was invited to see his son 'perform' with the new aircraft. The Fokker D VII was a superior fighter and one of a handful of weapons specifically denied to the Germans under the 1919 Treaty of Versailles.

'The next day Loewenhardt and I each shot down two Englishmen. It was nice to fly with Loewenhardt, almost the way it was with Manfred, if only to compare a little. We had got to know each other well in a short time and we had a splendid understanding of each other in the air. I was happy to have found someone again since Manfred on whom I could rely. Loewenhardt expressed a similar view about me.'[22]

LOEWENHARDT KILLED

On 10 August *Jastas 10* and *11* formed a combined Flight of twelve aircraft, mostly newcomers on their first flight over the lines. Loewenhardt led in his bright yellow Fokker D VII while Lothar was close by in his red Fokker. At noon the Germans avoided a flight of S.E.5s, but shortly afterwards spotted a lone fighter trailing behind. Loewenhardt led the fledglings in a dive to provide close instruction in how to surprise the enemy as he scored his 54th aerial victory. Lothar described the scene:

'Right behind the Englishman was Loewenhardt in his bright yellow machine. I saw immediately that one of the others was unnecessarily close [to Loewenhardt]. But four or five of them did not see that; instead they flew right behind Loewenhardt, apparently to share in the fight. How often was it said that only one man could do the shooting. One had to be ready to attack in case that man's guns should jam and he had to turn away. Suddenly I see that the Englishman is trailing a ribbon of smoke behind him and diving steeply. At about the same moment, what's this! Loewenhardt is no longer flying behind the falling Englishman; instead there is a wild confusion of thousands of splinters.

Immediately I make a steep dive to see what is really wrong. It is immediately clear – Loewenhardt has been rammed!'[23]

In the next instant Lothar saw one man in a parachute. A look at the man's big fur gloves confirmed that it was not Loewenhardt. *Ltn* Richard Wentz, the pilot who collided with Loewenhardt, later confirmed the ace's death.

The following days were full of ominous symbols. The course of the war required a change of airfields the day after Loewenhardt's death. Even a successful pairing with Ernst Udet – in which they each shot down a D.H.4 – did little to raise Lothar's spirits. Another airfield move on 12 August accompanied Lothar's double victory, his 39th and 40th. The first of the two Sopwith Camels he shot down was piloted by Capt J. K. Summers of No 209 Squadron, the unit with which Manfred had had his last air fight. And the following day, Tuesday, was the *13th* of August.

UNLUCKY 13: LOTHAR'S THIRD CRASH

'I just wanted to fly, to dispel the last misgivings about the 13th [he wrote]. If it were another day, perhaps I would not have started out at all, for I had had to endure three different urgent car trips. But, no, today the spell of the 13th must be broken.'[24]

Flying a Fokker D VII out of Bernes on the *2. Armee* Front, Lothar had few aircraft with him due to heavy casualties of the preceding days. Indeed, near the Front he linked up with flights from *Jagdgeschwader 3 (Jastas 2, 26, 27* and *36)* led by

▶ **Lothar von Richthofen was racked with guilt over Manfred's death, thinking he might have done something to prevent it. Later Lothar formed a close friendship with *Obltn* Erich Loewenhardt (right), *Staffel-Führer* of *Jasta 10*. Lothar was present when Loewenhardt, a 53-victory ace, collided with one of his own aircraft and subsequently died.**

Hauptmann Bruno Loerzer and *Jagdgruppe 9 (Jastas 9 and 10)* led by *Obltn* Robert Greim.

Soon Lothar spotted a two-seater and dived towards it, firing away. When he looked round to see which of his comrades joined him for the chase, Lothar was startled to see that he was being pursued by six British fighters. Just as he began to pull away, he felt a terrible pain in his right leg. He had to use both hands to pull the wounded leg off the rudder bar so that he could steer the aircraft. While he wore a parachute, Lothar found himself getting so weak that he knew he did not have the strength to jump out of the machine. Consequently, he rode it down to a small flat area among the shell holes of the earlier Somme Front battles.

Lothar's combat flying days were over, but not his aviation career. After the war he married *Gräfin* (Countess) Doris von Keyserling, the daughter of a former privy counsellor to *Kaiser* Wilhelm II. They had a daughter, but the marriage did not last. Lothar became a farm manager and, finding that too tame, took a position in industry. But when the commercial air service *Deutsche Luft-Reederei* began flying routes within Europe, Lothar von Richthofen joined the company as a pilot.

He flew the Hamburg to Berlin route, carrying mail and passengers in 'civilianized' former bombers with seats in the former crew positions and reconnaissance aircraft with similar accommodation where the observer used to sit. Bad weather was now Lothar's principal enemy in the sky, so he was unprepared for the events of 4 July 1922. On his final approach to Johannisthal airfield, the cradle of German aviation, the engine of his converted LVG C VI two-seater failed. Lothar looked for a flat spot to land, no doubt relieved that it was only the 4th of the month and not the 13th. His passengers, American film actress Fern Andra and her manager, braced themselves. Then the plane hit a high-tension wire and crashed, seriously injuring the passengers and killing Lothar von Richthofen.

The nation mourned the loss of the second Richthofen brother to fall from the skies. The body of *Oberleutnant a D* Lothar *Freiherr* von Richthofen was returned to the family home in Schweidnitz and buried in the family grave alongside that of his father, *Major a D* Albrecht *Freiherr* von Richthofen, who died just after the war.

It was first thought that, when Manfred's body was eventually brought home from France, the brothers would be reunited in Schweidnitz. But even in death Manfred von Richthofen received preferential treatment. In November 1925 his remains were accorded one of the largest state funerals in German history, attended by eight knights of the *Orden Pour le Mérite* as pall-bearers and other German and Allied airmen. Manfred's burial took place in the *Invalidenfriedhof*, the cemetery reserved for Germany's greatest heroes, in Berlin. City officials in what is now Swidnica, Poland, do not even acknowledge the final resting place of the other 'Red Baron'.

◄ A crash was Lothar's fate as well. After the war while piloting a converted LVG C VI, he crashed in bad weather. The two passengers survived, but Lothar von Richthofen was killed. At his funeral the memorial tribute of the Association of German Fighter Pilots accorded Lothar the equal status he had long sought: 'Now the brothers, upon whom all Germany once looked with pride, are united in Valhalla.'

7
AIRMEN ON A TETHER

WHEN ONE THINKS of captive observation balloons, carried aloft by highly explosive hydrogen gas and linked to the ground by only a steel cable and a telephone line, the balloon's vulnerability to the elements and enemy aircraft comes readily to mind. Such a scene was the 26 June 1916 incident described by *Ltn* Sturm of *Feld-Luftschiffer-Abteilung 27*:

'I heard the sound of the engine and suddenly saw the [enemy] flier as he dived on the balloon at about 300 metres away from a north-easterly direction. During the ascent I had already fastened the parachute harness and hung the release line over the side. When I saw the flier coming at the balloon, immediately I scrambled over the side of the basket and jumped at the moment of the explosion. The parachute opened smoothly. At first I found myself so close to the burning balloon envelope that I was in danger of having the parachute catch fire. Shortly after the opening of the parachute, I heard machine-gun fire flying by me, directed by the pilot at the parachute. This observation was also made from the ground. The parachute descent lasted about two minutes. I landed smoothly and uninjured.'[1]

While hostile aircraft always presented a great danger, the balloons were difficult targets and they compensated for their vulnerability by being useful in local-area aerial reconnaissance and ranging artillery. Before the advent of heavier-than-air craft, captive balloons were the air arm of military units and Germany became a leader in balloon development with the introduction in 1896 of the *Drachen-Fesselballon* (Kite Captive Balloon) developed by *Major* August von Parseval and *Hauptmann* Hans Bartsch von Sigsfeld. The *Drachen's* long body and one stabilizing fin gave it distinct advantages over the spherical balloons used by other nations.

Balloon development was not well utilized during pre-war manoeuvres and therefore little understood by field commanders at the outbreak of war. As *General* von Hoeppner noted:

'During the mobilization the suggestion was made in various quarters that [balloons] not be included at all as their use in the field promised no success. The Chief of the General Staff [*General* von Moltke] did not share this view. Ordered to mobilize were: eight *Feld-Luftschiffer-Abteilungen* [Field Airship Sections], one for each *Armee*, and 17 *Festungs-Luftschiffertruppen* [Fortress Airship Forces].'[2]

Before the war there had been one Prussian and one Bavarian *Luftschiffer-Bataillon* (Airship Battalion). From these were formed eight Prussian and two Bavarian *FLAs*, each of which, including a *Gaskolonne* (gas crew), was made up of ten officers, 270 men, 194 horses, 35 vehicles and one balloon; each could carry a second balloon but only with impaired mobility.[3]

The balloons were cumbersome and often difficult to handle, especially in bad weather. The weight came from the envelope (outer covering) which was made of cotton and impregnated with rubber for durability. The first *Drachens* held 600 cubic metres of hydrogen, which was supposed to bring them up to 800 metres altitude; in fact, rarely were they able to ascend over 500 metres. To gain altitude by reducing weight, the relatively heavy wicker basket provided for the observer was discarded by some units and the observers sat in a 'saddle' arrangement attached to the balloon by lines and connected to the ground by the main cables.[4] Within that precarious arrangement and a constant rocking that made many *FLA* officers 'seasick', the observers used binoculars to view activity behind enemy lines, mostly troop and traffic movements. At a time when aircraft could not communicate with ground stations, balloon observers had the distinct advantage of two-way telephones to provide immediate information about ground activity or to work with artillery batteries to zero-in on targets.

BALLOON USE GROWS

At the beginning of 1915 the *FLAs* received larger balloons. With 800m3 and 1,000m3 capacities, they

were supposed to be capable of ascents to 1,000 and 1,200 metres and be more stable in the stronger winds found at higher altitudes. That year the *FLAs* were also given greater mobility. Initially the balloons were raised by a hand winch and lowered by hitching a team of horses to the winch. As a unit needed some 1,500 metres of clear space for the horses to draw its balloon to the ground, it created a visible presence easily spotted by enemy photographic reconnaissance and was limited to operating only in areas with suitable accommodation for the horses. Some enterprising *FLA* commanders used captured engines to make powered winches, but in the spring of 1915 the *Inspektion der Luftschifftruppen* (Inspectorate of the Airship Force, abbreviated *Iluft*) began to provide petrol-engined Protz power winders.[5]

The limited help provided to the ground units by aircraft in 1915 prompted *Iluft* to make several improvements in *FLA* operations. Observers were given improved binoculars and cameras to enhance their reconnaissance abilities. When enemy aircraft took greater notice of balloons, observers were provided with improved parachutes (at a time when aircraft crews had none); attempts by balloon

▲ At the beginning of the war the *Feldluftschiffer-Abteilungen* took to the field with 600m³ balloons which could be moved by the LFA's ground crew. It was felt that the unique shape of the Parseval-Sigsfeld *Drachen* balloons required no national markings. Indeed, the configuration gave rise to the nickname '*Nulle*' (testicle).

observers to shoot down attacking aircraft made no sense, so they were encouraged to jump from the balloon at the first sign of trouble. The new Paulus parachutes were packed in a sack attached to the basket and the observer simply buckled into a harness and stepped over the side, after which the 'chute deployed on a static line and he floated to the ground. Fully deployed, the 'chute covered 46.5 square metres and was made of silk impregnated with a fire-proofing chemical.[6]

With these improvements and attempting to fill the intelligence gap left by aircraft, balloons experienced tremendous growth in 1915. In January of that year there was a total of nine balloons on the Western Front, including those already assigned to the *Festungs-Luftschiffertruppen*.[7] By year's end there were 40 *FLAs*, fielding more than 80 balloons on the same Front.[8]

In the spring of 1916, at the outset of the Battle of Verdun, the *AOK 5. Armee*, commanded by *Kronprinz* (Crown Prince) Wilhelm, created a new command structure to co-ordinate balloon communications. A *Ballonzentral* (Balloon Central Staff) worked with the *Armee-Oberkommando* (Army Headquarters), spreading out the balloons to serve ground units all along the Front; it also presented collected information about the attacks to the *General-Kommandos* (Corps Headquarters).[9] American aviation historian John R. Cuneo noted:

> 'For the first time in history there were a large number of captive balloons in one small sector. This branch of the [air] service had grown rapidly in 1915 . . . [and by 1916 the *FLAs* each] had two and, some three, balloons. Although primarily used for artillery observation, there was some expectation that they would help the commands to follow the progress of the attack.'[10]

German General Staff Chief Erich von Falkenhayn planned to draw French forces into a ruinous battle to defend Verdun, a city sacred in French memory for the valiant stand made there in the Franco-Prussian War of 1870–1871. The proposed great triumph, nominally led by the *Kaiser*'s heir apparent, made great use of aviation. The extensive balloon network was protected by the *Sperreflüge* of nearby air units. As previously noted in this book, however, C-type and even E-type aircraft had little success in defending balloons and in keeping improved French and British aircraft from raiding areas behind German lines. Furthermore, French tenacity and the opening of new hostilities on the Somme Front combined to defeat von Falkenhayn's great plan. On 29 August he was dismissed and replaced as Chief of the General Staff by *Generalfeldmarschall* Paul von Hindenburg and his able assistant *General* Erich Ludendorff.

ALLIED BALLOONS CAPTURED

Meanwhile, on 5 May 1916, the German balloon service reaped an intelligence bonanza when high winds along the front caused numerous French balloons to tear loose and drift over the lines into German hands. German balloons were also affected, as recalled by former observer Karl Kuster:

> 'A terrific wind broke without warning over the Front. It tore loose every balloon on the Front . . . When my balloon broke free, it broke at the balloon attachment and all the ⅜in [11mm] steel cable restraining it fell to the earth. The balloon and I took off upwards into this black storm cloud. Until

▶ **This captured Russian kite balloon, almost identical to the Parseval-Sigsfeld design, was used by the *3. Garde-Infanterie-Regiment* at Tarnopol in 1916.**

that moment, the wind had been howling and roaring and pulling at the balloon with monstrous hands, but the moment I was free, I rode [out] this storm in absolute silence. I can't really tell how high I went, but I do remember that the altimeters we carried were pegged at 2,000 metres and I went beyond that. Our balloons at that time, with all their gear, could only get up to about 1,000 metres.

'I had received no training in how to handle a free balloon and there was a technique to this. About all we had been told was how to handle the valve lines. We had one to "valve the gas out slowly" and the other was what we called a "rip cord", which dumped half the gas to prevent the balloon from going back up during a landing. I hung in there on the valves and finally . . . we hit our maximum altitude.'[11]

When the balloon began to descend, other inadequacies of captive balloon operations became apparent to *Ltn* Kuster. The gas remaining in the balloon became compressed and lost its ability to lift. Kuster should have been able to throw ballast overboard, but, as he noted, he had none:

'We felt about [ballast] like we did about our parachutes at this point in the war. We didn't carry them because we wanted to get up as high as we could and they were just dead weight . . . So it was with the sand. I was supposed to have five bags of ballast, but all I had was a battery box for my telephone and a big map board. I proceeded to

▲ *Feldluftschiffer-Abteilung* 7 began applying national markings to its balloons in early 1916. But as balloon losses rose at a dramatic rate later that year, the practice was halted temporarily.

throw everything I had overboard, in a vain attempt to slow my fall . . . The balloon and I had started to go down and the air started to howl again in an upwards direction. All the loose lines were fluttering upwards. We were falling too fast. All of a sudden, the balloon [envelope] turned nearly inside out, forming almost a parachute. I had dumped so much of my gas that it was nearly empty and I firmly believe that this saved my life. I came down out of the clouds without the slightest idea of where I was, but I remember that I was met by a most generous fire from every soldier who had a rifle. They didn't know whether I was French, German or English and there were balloons coming down all over. At that time we carried no national markings on the balloons. Later, of course, the Allies put on their cockades and we put on our crosses.'[12]

Ltn Kuster's balloon landed with such force that he was knocked unconscious. The balloon continued to travel along the ground and dragged the observer's basket across a field and into nearby woods. There he was extricated by German troops and taken to a field hospital for treatment of a fractured ankle.

▲ *FLA 7 Drachen* aloft during the Battle of the Somme in 1916. The solitary duty of the observer is apparent.

The prevailing west wind not only carried *Ltn* Kuster and other German balloon observers to safety within their own lines, it also delivered French balloons into enemy hands. One contemporary German account noted:

'A great number of French captive balloons were torn loose by the sudden storm yesterday evening and were carried over our lines; more than fifteen have been recovered so far.'[13]

FRENCH BALLOONS COPIED

The captured balloons were described by John Cuneo as being a superior design of 'the type made by Captain Caquot of the French balloon service, which was smaller than the German kite balloons, yet because of its design was sturdier and able to ascend higher'. Soon the Germans introduced an 'Ae' type ($850m^3$), which was 'an improved copy of the Caquot model. Because of the shortage of rubber its envelope was at first only partly made of rubber and later of entirely unsatisfactory substitutes. In other ways, it was as good as or better than the Allied types.'[14]

The improved balloon came none too soon, as Allied attacks against German balloons increased noticeably at the beginning of the Battle of the Somme. *Hptmn* Stottmeister, an *FLA* commander, later wrote:

'On the first day of the attack [1 July 1916] the enemy undertook a surprise air attack against all the balloons in order to wipe out all these troublesome aerial reconnaissance devices with one blow. He was successful in setting fire to six balloons in the air and a number of observation officers were killed. The effect on the field airship troops was at first depressing because, as a result of the enemy superiority, the attacks were repeated immediately as soon as they saw one balloon [aloft].'[15]

Two days later an assessment of the attacks and the remedial action needed was noted in a communiqué issued by the *Chef des Feldflugwesens*, *Oberstleutnant* Hermann von der Lieth-Thomsen:

'The overwhelming majority of attacks have occurred by taking advantage of cloud cover. Most reports speak of a sudden and surprising assault by the [enemy] pilot coming from out of the cloud layer. In so doing, not only are the attackers not discovered in time, in many cases, but they are able to avoid being fired upon.

'Without exception a group of [enemy] aircraft simultaneously carried out attacks against several balloons. About a third of the attacks were successful. The times of day of the attacks were quite varied; they played no special role.'[16]

▲The greatest danger to balloons in 1916, both on the Verdun Front and on the Somme, was the fast single-seat enemy fighter equipped with incendiary rockets. Designed by *Lieutenant* Y. P. G. Le Prieur of the French Navy, the eight rockets were fired simultaneously by an electric switch. The Nieuport 11 seen here was a particularly effective balloon-buster.

◀To keep attacking enemy aircraft away from the balloons, some *FLAs* launched big kites, such as those seen here, up to the same altitude as the *Drachens*.

◀The anti-aircraft kites were as much a hazard to the *Drachens* as they were to enemy fighters. The balloon observer in this photo was no doubt concerned that the kites near him would become entangled in his lines or puncture his balloon.

Thomsen noted that some attackers fired rockets at distances ranging from 50 to 200 metres. Others dropped 'a bomb-like incendiary device (lead casing, 30cm long, 10cm wide) with a phosphorus charge inside. These bombs, equipped with a delayed-action fuse, were dropped at a great height over the balloon and on exploding produced a big, whitish cloud, from which fiery cones spewed forth in a symmetrical spray.'[17]

In his communiqué, which went to Aviation Staff Officers (*Stofl*) in all *Armees*, the *Feldflugchef* candidly evaluated the current inadequate state of balloon defences and indicated changes to be implemented immediately:

'Firing at the attacking fliers with *Fliegerabwehr-Kanonen* [anti-aircraft guns] remains unsuccessful. The [previously noted] first manner of attack, under the cover of clouds, has contributed to [the situation]. There have been occasions when machine-guns that were ready to fire at attackers already spotted, failed to act at the moment they intended to open fire. They did not respond at the decisive moment. It is recommended that they ensure their ability to fire by firing test shots at the right time.

'Defence by firing from within the balloon basket has occurred in two cases. Both were unsuccessful. In one case the balloon crew fired from the basket without noticing that the balloon was already on fire; they lost valuable time in saving themselves with a parachute jump. In most cases firing from the basket was impossible because the attacker was hidden from sight by the balloon itself – that is, by the stabilizing fin. Our own fliers were not always in place for [balloon] defence at the right time. Even in the future this will not always be possible. Assigning a flier to each individual balloon as protective aircraft (which has been suggested repeatedly) is not feasible. The available pilot strength is not sufficient to allow that; they are required for other important missions. Providing *Sperre- und Jagdflugdienst* [barrier and fighter aviation] of the type that is currently allowed for balloon protection must suffice.

'It has been recommended that throughout the captive balloon service a special [form of] balloon protection be installed around each balloon launching area. However, it should be noted: Box kites have been tested often and thoroughly as protective devices against attacks by enemy fliers, especially to protect airship bases. Nowhere have the experiences been satisfactory. Launching and keeping the kites up require certain wind velocities. Numerous special personnel are required to operate them . . . When the distance between the individual kites is not very great, soon the wires become entangled

when [the kites] sway in the air [and] the whole system crashes. Above all, I draw attention to the danger posed by numerous kite cables to fliers on our Front.'[18]

Thomsen reiterated that, once an attack began, the best defence for the observers was to leave the balloon and the best hope for saving the balloon was to haul it down quickly and try to ward off a continued attack with intensive ground fire.

BALLOONS BECOME MORE IMPORTANT

While launching extensive air attacks against German balloons, the Allies made widespread use of their own balloons. Some 30 balloons appeared on the Somme Front alone and they effectively directed heavy artillery fire against German troop and artillery positions.[19] Balloons suddenly took on a new importance and to counter this threat, *General der Infanterie* Max von Gallwitz, commander of *Armeegruppe Gallwitz* on the 2. *Armee* Front, and the *Feldflugchef* (Thomsen) proposed to the *OHL* the formation of a 'very strong balloon operation under a well-qualified officer':

'Gradually 18 *Feld-Luftschiffer-Abteilungen* with 50 balloons, more than half of the field airship troops on the Western Front, were sent to the Somme.

'A position analagous to the *Stabsoffizier der Flieger* [*Stofl*] in the *AOK*s was created for a staff officer for balloons in the *Armeegruppe* [*Gallwitz*]. He organized the communication system along the lines of that used at Verdun; a *Ballonzentral* was established at every *AOK* and advanced as far forward at the Front as possible; the telephone linkages did not go directly [to the *Zentrale*], but via the *Abteilung* staffs.'[20]

The success of the new system made it all the more imperative for Allied fighter pilots to go after German balloons. It must have been a chagrined *Hptmn* von Hatten, commander of *FLA 2*, who reported the loss of Balloon No 3 to a rocket-carrying Nieuport biplane on the evening of 14 September 1916. Due to poor visibility, the balloon was unmanned and aloft at only 250 metres altitude when the attack began at 1945 hours. *Hptmn* von Hatten reported:

'The [enemy] pilot came gliding in swiftly from the direction of the Front, pulled away to the right at about the same altitude as the balloon and, despite brisk fire from *Flak* units and machine-guns, attacked (with the north wind) from the direction of the stabilizing fin. As in earlier attacks, two bundles of five incendiary rockets were fired from launching tubes installed on the lower wings, about 150 metres over the balloon. After about 30 seconds they ignited the gas and the balloon crashed in flames.

'Shortly before the attack a German formation of seven aircraft flew over the balloon and were in the area. The enemy machine, which immediately climbed away swiftly, had an encounter with the German formation some distance away and, after some shooting, went off in a southerly direction without being pursued.'[21]

Balloon historian *Hptmn* Stottmeister noted that, during the Battle of the Somme, among the units that performed exceptionally well were Prussian *FLA 7* and Bavarian *FLA 7*:

'In many places it was not possible to get any closer than 7 kilometres from the Front, because through haphazard laying of telephone lines by the opposing troops, the countryside looked like a big maze of wires into which the balloons could not go. Also there were many difficulties still to be overcome between troops and balloons; there were still divisions that had not yet worked with a balloon and which first had to learn to give them appropriate assignments.'[22]

Ltn d Res Dr Peter Rieper, who joined Prussian *FLA 7* in mid-1915, was with the unit when it was assigned to Metz-en-Couture on the *1. Armee* Front in September 1916. Despite the development of 'Ae' type balloons by Germany, Rieper's unit used *Drachen* balloons until 1917. Recalling the autumn 1916 campaign, he wrote:

'The Somme was hell . . . We were shot at by machine-guns and shells, but, thanks to being a small target, we were hard to hit. It was all the worse when we were down [on the ground]. It rumbled and crashed all around, the earth burned, fountains of mud and dirt poured on to us on the short way to the dug-outs. Marchais, Noyon, Equancourt . . . the area was desolate, a flat countryside without trees and shrubs. With the ground boggy, the protective trenches and dug-outs could be made only somewhat stable, and it rained continuously . . .

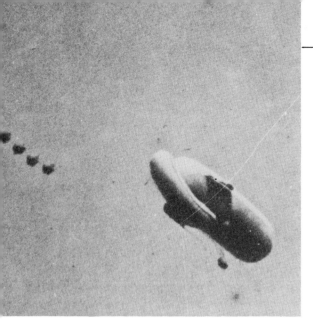

▲When ground units near balloons in the *1. Armee* sector complained that reports were slow in reaching them, a new system of communication was tried in January 1917. Visual communication was established with large red and black spheres that the observer sent down along part of his tether line. The four spheres attached to the *Drachen* in the photo warned ground troops of an imminent enemy attack; the same signal used for artillery units indicated that a barrage was needed in the designated sector. It was hard to tell which colours were being used and whether the message was for infantry or artillery; hence, the system was discarded in favour of a signal lamp of such intensity that it was visible during bright sunlight.

◀ *Ballonzug 16* used an abandoned clay pit near Crevecoeur in June 1917 to conceal this 850m³ 'Ae' type balloon. This view shows to good advantage the left and right stabilizing fins (partially deflated here) which distinguished the 'Ae' from the earlier Parseval *Drachen* design.

'Moreover, the view was mostly bad. The autumn storms drove the balloons here and there; whoever was not "seaworthy" had a hard life. I could bear it . . . During a storm with strong turbulence (wind velocity of 10 to 11m/sec [36 to 39km/hr]) which made aerial observation somewhat impossible, I succeeded in staying in the air with seven [other] *Drachens* for over three hours and, indeed, mostly at an altitude of 700 to 770 metres. That had not been previously or since achieved with manned *Drachens* . . . Despite the gales, the observation basket hung calmly as long as the *Drachen* was more or less intact, because the movement one way was compensated by the [basket's] movement the other way.'[23]

By autumn 1916 the new dedicated fighter units – *Jagdstaffeln* – were in place and offered better protection to German balloons. *FLA 7* was within the operational area of the new Albatros fighters of *Jagdstaffel 2*, commanded by *Hptmn* Oswald Boelcke, and on 1 October Peter Rieper had a chance to see the great ace in action against a B.E.2c:

'He shot down his 30th aircraft near Equancourt; the debris landed 25 metres away from our ground station. Fortunately, he was able to make an emergency landing at Fins, near our balloon hangar, and that was appropriately celebrated.'[24]

BALLOONS REORGANIZED AFTER SOMME BATTLE

The Battle of the Somme was the turning point for the development of balloon observation. Experience showed that balloons were much better suited for short-range observation, in close co-operation with ground units. During the winter of 1916–17, the *Feld-Luftschiffer-Truppe* underwent a further reorganization and expansion to facilitate co-operation with ground forces. In fact, *Infanterie-Ballone* (Infantry Balloons) were established specifically to work with ground troops. The Western Front command structure was arranged so that seven *Ballonzentrale* would be responsible for 53 *Feld-Luftschiffer-Abteilungen*, under which were a total of 128 *Ballonzüge* (Balloon Trains).[25] Bavarian *Ballonzüge* continued to maintain their regional identity and numerical designations (even when they were the same as those of nearby Prussian units), but often were integrated within Prussian *FLAs*; and some *Armees* established functional zones within their operational areas.

An example of the latter was the *1. Armee*, which on 10 January 1917 reported the following disposi-

AIRMEN ON A TETHER

◄ On calm days the men of a *Ballonzug* walked their balloons from one location to another. In turbulent weather valuable hydrogen had to be vented to make the balloon less buoyant and a lorry or team of horses was used to move the balloon envelope and basket.

▼ Whenever possible balloon units were accompanied by their own anti-aircraft batteries. The effect of rapid-fire *Flak* bursts around a balloon, as seen here, alerted enemy fighter pilots to the danger they faced in attacking.

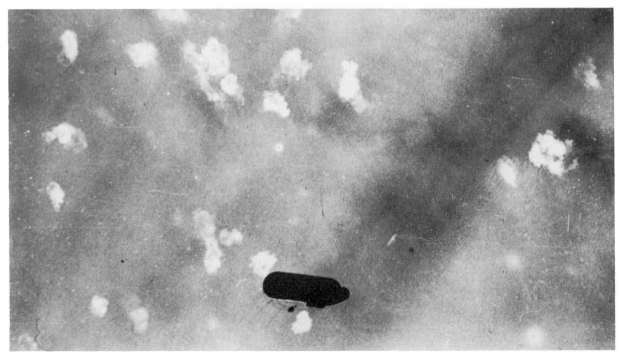

tion and strength, including numbers of balloons assigned to artillery and infantry:[26]

Gruppe	FLA	Key Point	Artillery	Infantry
Nord	31	Hendecourt	3	1
A	2	Queant	2	1
	3b	Pronville	2	1
B	17	Boursies	2	1
	29	Raperie	2	
C	7	Metz-en-Couture	4	
D	5	Epehy	3	

While the 6. Armee did not designate zones, by 15 April 1917 its Ballonzentral reported the following disposition, including integration of Ballonzüge:[27]

FLA	BZ	Key Point
27	71	Quesnoy
	72	Sequendin
	73	Sainghin
8b	21	Esterelles
	22	Harnes
	23	Meurchin
2	5	Fouquieres
	7	Sallaumines-North
43	106	Sallaumines-South
	110	Mericourt
3b	7b	Beaumont-North
	8b	Beaumont-South
	9b	Esquerchin
9	27	Brebieres-North
	79	Quiery la Motte
1b	1b	Lecluse
	2b	Fortequinne
	3b	Brebieres-West
	4b	Noyelle
37	6	Villers les Cagnicourt
	8	Baralle

The spring of 1917 brought other changes, as Peter Rieper noted:

'At the end of March we were detached from the [1. Armee] Front, received new [German-made "Ae"] balloons of the type used by the British and were moved up to Chemin des Dames [7. Armee Front]. There we also found an abundance of action, but it was on the whole better than on the Somme. The balloons were now systematically attacked by the enemy, as they were felt to be dangerous indeed [to the enemy].'[28]

Given the increasing importance of captive balloons, the office of the Kommandierende General der Luftstreitkräfte placed high emphasis on saving balloons from destruction. In a Kogenluft communiqué issued in April 1917, Feldflugchef Thomsen instructed all air units:

'Not to destroy enemy balloons that are torn loose when there is a possibility that they will drift over our territory; rather, to determine [their] whereabouts and the possibility of helping to salvage them intact.

'Not counting the value of the envelope (a new balloon would be 18,000–20,000 Marks) and the resultant loss of what is to us scarce rubber, is the futility of our balloon-makers in [having no] assessment of the [enemy's] manner of construction.'[29]

HAZARDS OF BALLOON OPERATIONS

Shortly after that Thomsen had high praise in the weekly Nachrichtenblatt for a Ballonzug 74 crew who saved their craft:

'On 15 April, at 1030 hours, as a flight of eight enemy aircraft approached from behind, Ballon 74 had to haul down a balloon. During the fast recovery using a winch and horses, the cable ripped on a ground mooring point. The balloon, 150 metres up, [which] had been making downward motions as a result of being hauled in, suddenly bolted up in a moderate wind. The leader of the groundcrew, Uffz Kuhn, instantly noticed the cable slipping away and called to six other men to hang on to it. This small team succeeded in wrapping the end of the cable around a tree, thereby saving the balloon before its strong buoyancy took effect. The enemy flier above the balloon was successfully warded off by M-Flakzug 62 [an anti-aircraft unit].'[30]

A few weeks later the Nachrichtenblatt reported success of a different nature on the 1. Armee Front:

'A balloon was torn away at [Feld-Luftschiffer-] Abteilung 29, [but] before it flew over enemy lines, it was shot down in flames by a German flier. The basket fell 1 kilometres north of La Fere about 200 metres beyond our barbed wire defence line and on the night of 4–5 May was salvaged by Uffz Fritsche and Luftschiffer Nolte [of FLA 30] with the help of infantrymen in the area.'[31]

It certainly was no disgrace for a balloon observer to use his parachute when he was threatened by enemy aircraft, which could cause only minimal damage to the balloon base. However, when a balloon came under artillery fire a successful hit on the balloon was sufficient to give an accurate range to the enemy guns, which could then do extensive damage to the launch area and adjacent anti-aircraft defences. Hence, a *6. Armee* observer who virtually duelled with an enemy artillery battery was singled out for praise in the *Nachrichtenblatt*, as noted in *General* von Hoeppner's citation:

'A balloon of *Ballonzug 110* was supposed to be hauled down due to hazardous weather conditions before 2000 hours on 28 June 1917 and had been cranked down to 50 metres when suddenly, at 2000 hours, unusually heavy enemy fire opened up. The observer, *Ltn d Res* Moeller, concluded from the observations of the preceding days and from the intensity of the enemy fire that the enemy intended to launch a major action. In spite of the dangerous situation, he gave the order to stop the recovery and to raise the balloon. In an almost hour-long observation *Ltn* Moeller determined [the location of] the batteries firing and continuously transmitted important reports about the site of the firing. Shortly before 2045 hours there was a glaring flash of an electrical discharge [near the balloon]. *Ltn* Moeller received a violent shock that paralyzed his left arm for several hours.'[32]

Fighter pilots and selected aircraft crews were widely acclaimed in the German popular press of the day. Balloon observers, who often went up in foul weather conditions, were largely ignored by the news media, but their bravery and hazard-laden achievements were publicized within the *Luftstreitkräfte*. The two-man crew of Balloon Ae 357 R of *BZ 53* on the *3. Armee* Front were the subject of a special report in the *Nachrichtenblatt*:

'On 15 October 1917 at 1530 hours lightning struck a balloon of [*Ballon-*] *Zug 53*. At the moment it happened the balloon was up at 850 metres. In the basket were *Ltn d Res* Gratz and Assistant Observer *Gefr* Menne. The lightning went sizzling through the cable and ground mooring into the earth. The winch was well earthed and felt no effects of the strong electrical charge; however, the telephone lines at the ground station were hit hard. Although damage to the balloon was not reported, either from the ground or from the balloon crew, the *Ballonzug* commander had it hauled down. Suddenly, when the balloon was at 500 metres altitude, it could be seen from the ground that it was on fire; at the same time the crew in the basket could see flames dipping into the belly of the balloon and just then, after the balloon had come down with relative speed, the two observers jumped out. In this connection *Ltn d Res* Gratz showed praiseworthy courage and sense of duty in that he first helped *Gefr* Menne – who had trouble due to the clumsiness of the winter clothing – to get out of the basket and free of entangled lines, waited until his parachute was fully deployed, and himself jumped

only after the first man was out of danger. Both parachutes were repeatedly endangered as the burning balloon plunged past them. However, both balloon observers landed on the ground unharmed and were ready for further service.

'The electrical charges also made themselves felt at the neighbouring balloons of *Züge 52* and *54* whose observers received violent shocks. Some minutes after the event it was noticed by observers of *BZ 54* that in the area of La Neuville (on the western edge of the Argonne Forest) French balloons there were likewise crashing in flames.

'The *3. Armee* weather station had, in fact, announced a storm warning nearly an hour before the occurrence, but as important assignments had been made, all balloons, even those of the French, remained in the sky; relatively cool, sunny weather prevailed, no signs of either lightning or thunder; it was appropriate for *Zug* commanders to wait longer for a possible storm. Appropriate lightning protection preparations as directed by the *Kommandierende General der Luftstreitkräfte* were carried out conscientiously.

'*Ltn d Res* Gratz was decorated with the *Eisernes Kreuz I. Klasse* and *Gefr* Menne with the *EK II*.'[33]

Nearby, on the *7. Armee* Front, *Ltn d Res* Peter Rieper had become commanding officer of *Ballonzug 19*. His unit opposed hard-pressed French forces which were still recovering from disastrous fighting along the Aisne earlier in the year. *General* Max von Boehn's *7. Armee* used the woods and undergrowth of the Chemin des Dames as a natural barrier to hamper the French *VIème Armée* of *Général* Charles Mangin in its advance northwards to Laon, but it was a hard battle every step of the way. Peter Rieper wrote:

'We were constantly bombarded, this time by 15cm incendiary shells which made a frightful crash when the explosions hit anywhere near the balloon. That was really not nice. One did not want to do the French a favour and haul down the balloon. There was nothing else to do but to have the balloon constantly raised and lowered between 700 and 1,500 metres to make it more difficult for the enemy battery commander to regulate the explosions.

'While I got off with twenty holes in the balloon in this manner, it did little good for my neighbour. He was shot down in flames. Both observers jumped out with parachutes and, while one came down smoothly, the other, hit in the carotid artery by a shell fragment, was a corpse when he hit the ground.

'The next day I had the same pleasure in the afternoon, when the enemy could observe better

▶ *Ltn d Res* Peter Rieper, with his telephone headset on, prepares for an ascent in the basket of this balloon at *Ballonzug 19*. Above him is the pouch for his Paulus parachute and to his left the map board.

with the sun at his back. Again, every few minutes an incendiary shell came. Simply horrible! After some searching, luckily I found the battery that had fired at me so that I could tell – by the flight time of the shots – that it would be exactly 37 seconds until the next incendiary explosion. Then we had a real duel until the setting sun broke it off.

'Another day, 17 October, was again dominated by a colossal artillery fight with the enemy. There were many new batteries firing from the hinterlands and there was conspicuously brisk traffic on the roads and railways. Something special seemed to be brewing. There was excellent visibility and therefore enormous work for me.

'Towards noon, half an hour before the relief crew came on, I was in the process of contending with the twelfth target of that morning, a newly observed battery near Braye [13 kilometres south of Laon], when I was informed by telephone from below that four enemy fliers were heading in the direction of the balloon. At a distance of barely 1½ kilometres I could see the fellows already, scarcely 2,000 metres up. I was at an altitude of 1,300 metres. They certainly gave the impression that they wanted to get "personal" and not let themselves be diverted by our revolving cannon, our balloon protection, the so-called "*Lichtspucker*" [Light Spitter]. Then it seemed to me to be expedient to be ready to travel. Therefore, I stripped off the telephone from my head, drew the constantly buckled parachute belt yet a notch tighter and sat myself out on the edge of the basket as one of the brutes came whistling down towards me in a dive.

'Lord Jesus! As I raised my head, an incendiary rocket came from the devil-knows-where. After the first missed the balloon by a few metres, another one came right through the belly of the balloon. It was time to get out.

'No doubt the highly inflammable hydrogen gas in the balloon above must have been set on fire, although the flame was invisible to me, hanging below in the basket. But now I had to stay calm. I let myself slide down from the basket and was about to let go when, at the last moment, I noticed that one of my parachute lines had snagged on a carbine mount, on which I used to hang the reserve telephone. That would have been a fine mess if I had let go and was unable to get free of the balloon. I therefore climbed energetically hand-over-hand back into the basket to free the fouled line. That was not so simple in a burning balloon, wearing heavy fur gloves to unhook a thin line from such a small mount. But it had to go and it did! Then it was high time for me to go. Legs overboard again and let go all at once!

'Through my body weight I pulled the 'chute from its pouch, which was attached to the balloon basket. After I made a free fall of about 50 metres and the 'chute opened, the falling speed diminished. The balloon went plunging past me, wrapped in flames, the heat of which I could feel in my face.'[34]

Peter Rieper's parachute descent lasted about three minutes. A slight wind carried him some 2 kilometres away from *BZ 19*'s base, but nearby troops helped him gather in the billowing parachute, to keep the observer from being dragged along the ground. He was returned to his unit within the hour and a replacement balloon was in the air, over the same spot where Rieper had been sent aloft.

BETTER BALLOON SUPPORT ORGANIZED

The quick replacement was due to continued improvements in the field balloon organization. Prompt resupply of both men and equipment was aided by the establishment of *Feld-Luftschiffer-Parks* in rear areas and effective communication between the various *AOK Stabsoffiziere der Luft-schiffer-Truppen (Stofl)*. *Hptmn* Stottmeister noted:

'The further enlargement of the *Feld-Luftschiffer-Truppen* and the increase of their importance in co-operation during the defensive battles made it necessary to replace the *Stofls*, whose areas of responsibility had become too big [for so low a level

of command] with *Kommandeure der Luft-Schiffer-Truppen (Koluft)* at the *AOK*. A *Koluft* was equipped with a *Ballonzentral*, a *Feld-Luftschiffer-Park*, a winch repair workshop and, starting in the spring of 1918, most of all at least one railway wagon fitted with a *Feldgasanstalt* [Field Gas Unit] with a daily output of 1,200 to 1,500m³ [of hydrogen]. This meant six to seven railway wagons per day to re-supply gas.'[35]

Thus, by the time of the Spring 1918 offensive, German balloon units were at the peak of their organization, disposition and strength. In May 1918 *Ltn* Peter Rieper's *Ballonzug 19* was stationed at a camp in the woods outside Laon. Nearby was the East Prussian *37. Infanterie-Division* commanded by *General* Walter von Eberhardt, the former commander of the *Fliegertruppe*, with whom Rieper had worked during the March 1918 offensive at St Quentin. Rieper called this time 'the nicest, if even the most strenuous of my life as a *Luftschiffer*'. He went on:

'Some hours after the observation, one had the opportunity to see for oneself that everything was in order, how the targets had been hit by the individual shots that one had observed, and what one had accomplished. Oh, what a joy to be going forward for once!

'We followed our infantry at the modest distance of 3 to 5 kilometres, while during the positional [trench] warfare we had been 6 to 10 kilometres behind the rearmost lines. At this distance we could easily spot the movements of enemy infantry and the artillery emplacements. The battalion's heavy artillery, at whose disposal *BZ 19* was placed, was a battery consisting of a 10cm cannon, a 15cm howitzer and a 21cm mortar battery.

'Alternately, I sent the balloons back and forth to each half of the battery, to stay as close as possible on the previously determined advance route and to maintain constant telephone contact with the balloon. On a road on which a great many army corps are moving forward, that is easier ordered than done, especially since the balloon was continually pulled along and, to maintain the telephone connection, the cable had to be reeled in and out all the time. Everything depended on the telephone cable. For, of what use were the nicest observations if one could not send them to the Division or the battery attached to it?'[36]

BZ 19 approached the forest at Villers-Cotterets on 3 June 1918. Rieper found it difficult to observe anything in the high stand of trees. Only the hits of the *37. Division*'s mortars could be spotted with certainty, as he had to peer into the sun. In short order, his opponents brought up long-range guns and began lobbing incendiary shells, which had a visible trajectory in the ribbons of smoke behind them. Rieper went up and down constantly, thanks to the horse-drawn winch, so as to not make it too easy for his opponents. But in all that motion he still had to pay careful attention to the small specks coming his way; the previous day five neighbouring balloons had been shot down.

Soon the long-range guns were silent and he could concentrate on directing his howitzers against machine-gun nests he had spotted in the woods nearby.

'Suddenly there was a "tack, tack, tack" – machine-gun fire right near me! "Jump, *Herr Leutnant*," comes the word from below. I saw nothing, but I got ready to travel just the same. As I lifted the basket lines overboard, there was again a "tack, tack – pang!" My raised right arm fell down and I could not lift it again. I had a gunshot fracture in the upper arm. It was a good thing that my legs were somewhat long and, without having to hoist myself up I could climb over the edge of the basket. And then I let go immediately.

'The parachute opened promptly after the usual 50-metre free fall and the balloon went crashing down past me. I had just made it – but then the fellow came storming down once more and rattled away in the immediate area, with me, a wretched creature, as his target. The parachute took a few holes, to be sure, but it did not burn, as it had been made fireproof. The fellow should have been ashamed of himself.

'The wind blew me towards the enemy. But I was lucky again and came down just ahead of our advance infantry lines. On to a freshly ploughed field! I could not pull in the shroud lines hand-over-hand without the use of my right arm. Due to a pendulum-like motion of the parachute as a result of the severe tubulence, on landing I broke my right leg. The strong wind did not let the 'chute collapse; instead it dragged me several hundred metres over the ploughed field. Finally, some infantrymen came over and freed me from the bad situation, during which they secured the 'chute and loosened the swivel on the waist belt.'[37]

RIEPER RECEIVES THE *POUR LE MÉRITE*

Ltn d Res Peter Rieper was sent to a field hospital. His broken leg was set, but he lost his right arm. After two months in a hospital in Hamburg, he was posted to the *Luftschifferschule* in Namur as an instructor. And Rieper came to that post laden with honour, as the only balloon observer to receive the *Orden Pour le Mérite*. While many other balloon observers were brave and conscientious, Peter Rieper had those qualities in abundance, as noted by *General* von Eberhardt when he proposed the observer for the high award:

'His reputation as one of the most daring and successful *Ballonzug* commanders, who indeed did not shrink from bad weather, [and] also went high up without a basket, secured only by ropes, is known far and wide on the Western Front. No one is worthier of the high decoration . . .'[38]

The German *Luftschiffertruppe* did not suffer from lack of brave men. Despite its superb organization and value to the German military effort, ultimately lack of supplies and replacements defeated the captive balloon observation force. Karl Kuster recalled:

'In the final months of the war rubber became an even more acute problem than ever. Later, when we lost a balloon, it took nearly a week, and sometimes two, to get a replacement . . . The artillery suffered from worn-out gun barrels and eventually we couldn't make an accurate shot. Replacement barrels came through for the guns, but not fast enough.'[39]

At the same time, German aircraft units were unable to secure spare parts, tyres and new aircraft to protect the diminishing number of balloons available. Thus, as fewer and fewer replacement balloons arrived at the Front, the capability of balloon observation deteriorated. On 21 October 1918 *Koluft 2. Armee* noted in a secret report that only three balloons had been launched in the sector that day. To be fair, unfavourable winter weather adversely affected balloon operations, but on the day in question two of the three balloons had to be hauled down due to intense Allied air attacks.[40]

BALLOON FORCE DESCENDS

At the time of the Armistice the breakdown in the German Army was such that the balloon units were virtually ineffective, but the victorious Allies were keenly aware of their potential importance. As one German air staff officer later wrote: 'At the end of the war a total of 56 *Abteilungs* staffs and 184 *Ballonzüge* had been deployed at the Front, [and] their total disbandment was demanded by the *Entente* [forces].'[41] Even after the war, when Germany was allowed a small *Reichswehr* national defence force with limited ground, naval and air units, not a single balloon unit was permitted.[42]

8
BACK-SEAT BATTLE STATION

ON 15 JULY 1918 a temporary weakness in the French forward lines near Rheims allowed the German *22. Infanterie-Division* and the Bavarian *12. Infanterie-Division* to regain lost ground in the Champagne sector. Within two days, however, the offensive was halted by stiff French resistance, which was supported by murderous artillery fire.

To take the pressure off his beleaguered forces, *Generalmajor Freiherr* von Nagel zu Aichberg, commander of the *12. Inf.-Div.*, ordered one of his aviation support units to provide an aerial observer to direct artillery fire against the two French batteries that had his troops pinned down. *Hauptmann* Häfner, commanding Bavarian *Flieger-Abteilung (A) 295*, was requested to provide an aircraft and crew for the mission. In view of the skill needed to pilot a two-seat reconnaissance aircraft amidst the raging artillery duel, and the steely nerve necessary to concentrate on the battle and transmit accurate wireless-telegraphy messages, Häfner selected one of his most capable and experienced aircrews for the mission.

Leutnant der Reserve George Hengl, the officer observer in charge of the aircraft, had served in the infantry from the beginning of the war until his transfer to the aviation service in February 1918. *Vizefeldwebel* Hans Baur had joined the Bavarian aviation service in 1915 and had flown a variety of aircraft prior to this assignment on the German *1. Armee* Front. As this was to be no ordinary reconnaissance mission, pilot Baur selected the smallest, most manoeuvrable two-seater available to him: a Hannover Cl IIIa. The aircraft's narrow fuselage and sturdy construction would be great assets in the tight turns which would surely be needed to avoid enemy ground fire or fighter aircraft.

▼*Ltn d Res* Georg Hengl (left) and his pilot, *Vzfw* Hans Bauer, of Bavarian *Fl-Abt (A) 295* fought off ten SPADs during a flight in this Hannover Cl IIIa. The aircraft was considered easy to fly and very manoeuvrable, which, together with its great structural strength, made it a superb air-fighting machine.

ATTACKED BY TEN SPADS

Hengl and Baur took off at 1000 hours, enjoying the great German advantage of having the morning sun at their backs to make them more difficult to see. Hengl later wrote:

'At the Front, heavy bombardment was going on; to our left Rheims was in flames; close ahead of us lay Epernay and the River Marne. To recognize the target precisely, I had to get right over the enemy batteries, which were about 4 kilometres behind their lines. We flew over the lines at 3,000 metres and the enemy anti-aircraft batteries discovered us immediately.

'It became significantly unpleasant when Baur and I, at almost the same time, spotted an enemy fighter squadron – right over our target, of course. As they got closer, the formation turned out to be ten French SPAD single-seat fighters. They saw us at almost the same time, although we stayed right at the edge of the cloud cover. They swung towards us, but, meanwhile, we disappeared into the clouds. It did not help, however, for we had to be able to stay over the target to carry out our mission. The initial feeling of cowardice that timidly surfaces was quickly overcome and I decided to attack.'[1]

They were hardly out of the mist and cloud layer when Hengl spotted the target battery just off to one side ahead. He also saw the ten SPADs, 100 metres beneath them, in tight formation. Apparently the Frenchmen did not see the Germans, who quickly took the advantage of surprise:

'With the sun at our backs, we whisked into the cumulus [Hengl wrote]. Ten rounds from my machine-gun and the first Frenchman lost his wings. The wings and other debris fluttered down amidst the squadron. While the gentlemen tried to make sense out of all this confusion, I set fire to Number Two. My pilot, an old hand at this, calmly steered us down through the confusion, but twisted and turned in such a way that we presented a poor target to the Frenchmen's guns.

'One SPAD made a wonderful loop so close to me that I could clearly see the pilot in his seat. Indeed, he almost collided with us! It was his last clever little trick. The trails from my tracer ammunition were clear in my sights and, as he went into his loop, he became Number Three and dropped straight down.

'Now it really became grim for us and bullets hit us from all sides. Scraps of fabric fluttered off the wings and bits of wood were knocked off the fuselage decking between Baur and me. We were locked in a seemingly endless fight with one SPAD in particular, while behind us and in all directions the remainder of the group circled around. We dared not let them out of our sight for a second. Apparently we were engaged with the squadron commander, as he had two streamers attached to his wings. As we constantly dashed by each other at dizzying speeds, I got lucky for an instant and caught him in my sights. Baur brought me into a splendid position to fire. The Frenchman was apparently badly hit; one moment the aircraft was very steady in the air and then I saw it begin to sway. Suddenly it went down in the steepest dive and landed just inside the French lines. As if on command, the remaining opponents broke off this aerial battle and in all haste slipped away to their own airfield.

'We finally had time to catch our breath. My pilot let out a cry of joy and I reached over and embraced him in the same spirit. For all that, we quickly became serious again. Things looked very bad inside our shot-up aeroplane. Would we get home in one piece without breaking up in the air? It would have taken only a few shots in the wing spars or more air pressure than the badly shot-up struts could withstand! Despite all that, we dared to think about making it all the way home. Even the slight wound in my arm, which I had not noticed at first, would not prevent me from completing our mission, irrespective of the fact that the aircraft was meanwhile falling apart. Under all circumstances we had to direct our artillery.'[2]

The 20-year-old observer's decision could well have cost him and Baur, who was the same age, their lives. But it had to be done. Hengl quickly discovered that the aircraft's wireless-telegraphy set, with which he would have communicated with the German artillery battery, was irreparably damaged. After each of the first few rounds, he would have tapped out a coded message, correcting the range and then, since the telegraphy was transmitted only one way, he would have focused his binoculars on the German position, looking for a white panel to acknowledge receipt of the message. And so it would go on until the first shot hit the mark. Then he would simply radio 'Fire for effect' and use his binoculars to witness the destruction of the target.

Now, with the wireless set out of commission, Hengl had to resort to an earlier method of communication: after each round was fired, he wrote down the correction and put it into a metal canister, and directed Baur to fly back over the German position so that the message could be dropped near the battery. Then they went back across the lines to watch for the next round to strike enemy territory.

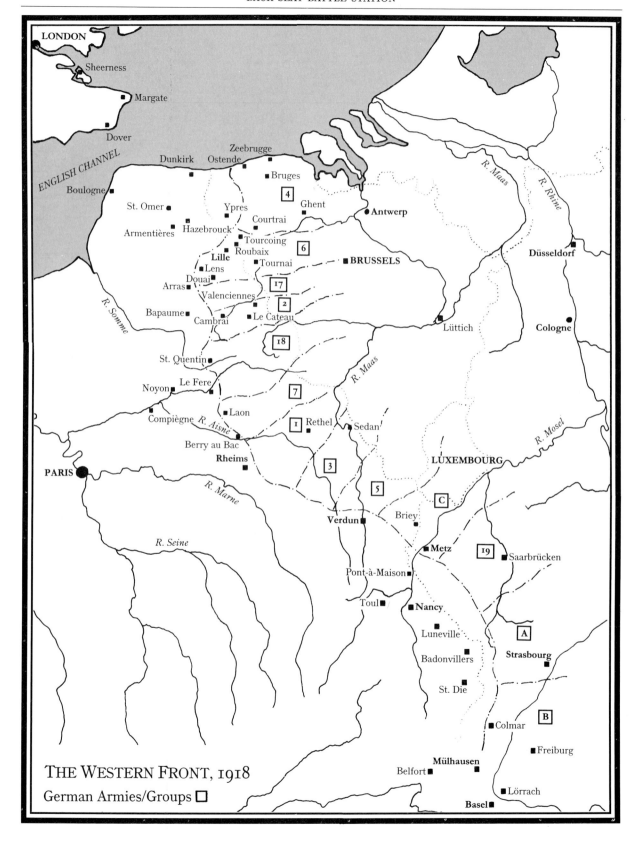

THE WESTERN FRONT, 1918

German Armies/Groups □

This nerve-racking procedure went on for nearly an hour, during which Hengl and Baur never knew whether a 'new' creaking sound in the badly strained struts and wings would signal their impending doom. With no parachutes to save them, the two airmen could only hope that the Hannover Cl IIIa would live up to its reputation for sturdiness.

It did and after they had dropped the final message and viewed the barrage that pounded the French target, they undertook one final portion of the mission. Hengl recalled:

'Finally, we flew down to the lowest altitude we could over the now devastated enemy battery emplacement and, with our machine-guns, finished off the place. In this way we provided the best service to our hardest-fighting element, the worthy infantry.'[3]

KNIGHTHOOD FOR HENGL

Although the official German Army register gave Hengl and Baur credit for shooting down only two of their four adversaries, the Kingdom of Bavaria offered far better rewards to its brave native sons. Georg Hengl was presented with Bavaria's highest bravery award for officers, the *Militär-Max-Joseph Orden* (Military Max-Joseph Order), which carried with it elevation to the nobility and lifelong use of the title *'Ritter'* (Knight). From that point on he was known as Georg *Ritter* von Hengl and enjoyed the distinction of being one of eleven Bavarian airmen (of whom only four were observers) to be so honoured. Hans Baur was presented with the *Silberne Tapferkeits-Medaille* (Silver Bravery Medal), the second-highest bravery award for a Bavarian NCO; he was one of only seventeen Bavarian pilots recognized in this manner.

Georg *Ritter* von Hengl and Hans Baur did not rest on their laurels. Four days after the hazardous flight near Epernay, they made low-level flights to drop ammunition to elements of the *12. Inf Div* that were completely cut off, and then made a series of strafing runs to keep the division's opponents off balance. They brought down a Bréguet 14B-2 two-seater on 20 August and another enemy aircraft on 5 October. During a long flight on 29 October, they fought off three SPAD two-seaters until their ammunition was totally expended and then managed to slip away.

The initiative and leadership that *Ritter* von Hengl and *Vzfw* Baur exhibited during their time with *Fl-Abt (A) 295* clearly set the stage for what was to come. Both men became general officers in World War II, *Ritter* von Hengl commanding a division of elite mountain troops and Baur displaying such skill that he was selected to be the personal pilot for Adolf Hitler, a fact that cost Baur ten years and an amputated leg in a Soviet prison camp.

CAVALRY IN THE SKY

From the outset of World War I it became apparent that aerial observers would have a crucial role in shaping events that took place during the ground fighting. The long network of trenches that soon developed from Flanders in the north to the Vosges mountains in the south quickly obviated a traditional role of the cavalry: lightning-quick dashes over the lines for reconnaissance and various disruptive purposes. The vast wastes of 'No Man's Land' created during the 1914–18 war made it virtually impossible to use horses in such a way. Thus, aerial reconnaissance – soon dubbed as 'the cavalry of the clouds' – became a prime source of intelligence-gathering. Although rarely as 'romantic' as the single-seat fighters whose proper role would have been to defend them, the two-seat reconnaissance crews were far more important to the daily running of the military machine on both sides. Indeed, that is why it became so important for fighters (if not defending their own reconnaissance machines) to pursue and bring down enemy reconnaissance aircraft before they could return with the military intelligence they had gleaned, or before they completed the artillery spotting activities that would lead to the destruction of one's own artillery batteries.

HAZARDS OF EARLY TRAINING

Retired *Generalleutnant* Erwin Jollasse, who left the infantry in 1916 to begin training as an observer, recalled some of the imprecise methods used during the early days of German aviation reconnaissance:

'At the aviation training centre at *Flieger-Ersatz-Abteilung 2* in Schneidemühl, crash landings passed more or less without repercussion as the order of the day. Forced landings due to engine trouble also took place frequently. Thus, whenever possible, we always sought out one of the big estates of the West Prussian nobility, where we would be taken in with great cordiality and hospitality.

'During my training at Schneidemühl, my longest excursion was a cross-country flight from there to Breslau. After several forced landings due to engine failure, we landed late in the evening, just before darkness set in. On reporting in, we were welcome somewhat brusquely by the base commander, *Hauptmann* Victor Carganico, one of the "old eagles" of German aviation who had set a number of aviation records before the war. He was worried about us, as there was no radio communication between airfields at that time.

'All the aircraft we used were over-aged. At Schneidemühl, there were only B-type machines, in which the pilot sat *behind* the observer. C-type aircraft, which I later found at the Front, did not come into the training sequence until I got to the observers' school in Warsaw. In that type of aircraft, the pilot sat forward, with a fixed, forward-firing machine-gun which fired through the propeller arc, and the observer sat in the back seat with a flexible, ring-mounted machine-gun which could be fired on all sides of the cockpit. Some of the pilots at Warsaw were experienced combat fliers. During a practice flight with one of these pilots, a carburettor fire broke out in our aircraft. The pilot put the fire out immediately and, from high altitude, glided down to a field, stopping ten metres from a barbed wire fence.

'At the observers' school in Warsaw we were trained to use wireless telegraphy for ranging artillery batteries. We also learned how to take aerial photographs and how to "read" them for intelligence-gathering purposes. To be sure, we used only the small camera, which one had to tilt "overboard" in order to hold it out far enough. The 50cm and 70cm focal-length cameras, respectively, were in use when I was assigned to *Feldflieger-Abteilung 32* at the Front. These cameras were suspended on rubber tracks back aft in the observer's compartment and pictures were "shot" through a hole in the floorboards. The observer needed only to direct the pilot to the object to be photographed.'[4]

▲ *Ltn* Erwin Jollasse was commissioned as a Regular Army officer in 1913 and spent two years in the infantry before applying for aviation training and gaining the Observer's Badge, which he wore just below his Iron Cross 1st Class.

RECONNOITRING OVER THE SOMME

On completion of his training, Erwin Jollasse reported to *Feldfl-Abt 32* at Bertincourt, west of Bapaume on the Somme Front. He arrived on 4 August 1916 and began a lengthy orientation to the squadron and the operational area. Three weeks later the unit was transferred to Sains-lez-Marquoin, between Bapaume and Cambrai.

There was heavy activity in that sector and when Jollasse, newly promoted to *Oberleutnant*, made his first flight on 31 August, enemy fighters were on hand to give him a vigorous baptism of fire. *Feldfl-Abt 32*'s total complement of four Albatros C V two-seaters was in the air, performing visual and photographic reconnaissance, when the flight was attacked several times by F.E.2b 'pushers'. Jollasse

and his comrades made morning and evening patrols that day and reported ten separate fights with British aircraft.

The following day's flight operations were cancelled due to heavy cloud, which made high-altitude reconnaissance almost impossible. But on 2 September 1916 three crews from *Feldfl-Abt 32* took off on a combined reconnaissance and fighter mission. Once over the Front, they were attacked by several F.E.2b's. Erwin Jollasse remembered the fight:

'Suddenly we saw two FEs not too far away from us and we attacked immediately. The enemy aircraft returned our machine-gun fire without scoring any hits. After making a wide turn, we attacked anew and, coming from above, my pilot got one of the FEs completely in his sights and opened fire, whereupon the opponent showed the effect immediately. Leaving a long smoke trail, it went straight down and crashed. The other enemy aircraft immediately turned away. We followed the one opponent in wide circles as it fell and we were able to observe the crash near the forward-most enemy positions. On returning to our airfield, my pilot, *Unteroffizier* Helmuth Wendroth, and I were welcomed by the commanding officer, *Hauptmann* Ritter. Beaming with joy, he told us that our victory had been confirmed by troops in the forward lines. In addition, the crew of *Leutnants* Dingel and Bartsch, in one of our other aircraft, observed our victory and likewise reported it.'[5]

Existing evidence strongly suggests that the F.E.2b brought down was aircraft 4290 of No 11 Squadron, Royal Flying Corps. That aircraft and its crew of 2nd Lts E. Burton and F. W. Griffiths were the only FE loss reported on 2 September 1916. British authorities subsequently learned that Burton and Griffiths were taken prisoner and sent to a camp in Osnabrück, Germany.

TO THE VICTOR . . .

At that stage in the war it was not uncommon for German two-seater squadrons to use one or more of their own machines – in this case the reliable Albatros C V – to go after enemy aircraft threatening the mission in hand. When they were successful, these reconnaissance crews were accorded the same honours as the single-seat fighter pilots, with one interesting distinction. *Obltn* Jollasse and *Uffz* Wendroth *each* received special certificates and an *Ehrenbecher* (Cup of Honour) for being the victors in their *first* aerial combat. This form of award invites confusion, as it might appear that each man was given separate credit for the victory, as a fighter pilot would be; in fact, the double presentation clearly acknowledged that the aerial victory was a joint effort.

At the end of 1916 Jollasse's unit was one of a number of *Feldflieger-Abteilungen* whose broad range of missions and mixture of aircraft were clarified after the *Fliegertruppe* was reorganized and expanded as the *Luftstreitkräfte*. Thus, on 31 December, his unit became one of the 93 units specifically identified with the artillery co-operation and support role; accordingly, the designation was changed to *Flieger-Abteilung (A) 263*, with the 'A' and the three-digit designation indicating the linkage to artillery. Under the same new enumeration system, the old *Feldflieger-Abteilung 64* became the 'new' *Flieger-Abteilung 32*, with an all-new mission

▲ Following their successful aerial combat on 2 September 1916, *Ltn* Erwin Jollasse and his pilot, *Uffz* Wendroth, were each awarded the *Ehrenbecher*. The commemorative goblet, nearly 8in tall, was presented to airmen on the occasion of their first aerial victory. Goblets presented in 1915, 1916 and early 1917, such as this one awarded to *Ltn* Jollasse, were silver; thereafter, they were made of iron.

(long-range reconnaissance) and no connection with the old '32'.

Even as the new *Fl-Abt (A) 263*, Erwin Jollasse's unit followed the general rule of keeping good pilot-observer teams together. Occasional temporary changes enabled experienced crewmen to work with men newer to wartime conditions. Thus, in January 1917, *Obltn* Jollasse was assigned to fly for a brief period with a new pilot, *Gefreiter* Otto Rosenfeld. As it turned out, Rosenfeld possessed talents and ambitions beyond the tedious and often monotonous duties of a reconnaissance squadron. While Rosenfeld *could* follow the observer's directions and ensure that the aircraft remained a stable platform for reconnaissance and artillery-spotting duties, his true calling was as a fighter pilot.

During a flight on 24 January, *Gefr* Rosenfeld skilfully brought *Obltn* Jollasse over important positions at Doullens, on the Somme Front, where encampments and railway lines were key targets in a primary staging area. On the way back to their airfield at Haynecourt with valuable photographs and written notes, their Albatros C V was attacked by Sopwith Pup fighters. Attempting to return fire, Jollasse discovered that his machine-gun had jammed. He recalled:

'My pilot also had a jam in his machine-gun after a short burst of fire. From about 5,000 metres, we went into a long dive in order to escape the stream of fire from the six Sopwith fighters. It was the first time that we had met enemy fighters at that altitude. Previously, we had been bothered only by anti-aircraft at this height.

'During the sudden nose dive, some of the already exposed film packets flew out of the aircraft through the trap door in the floor, where the 70cm camera usually protruded from my compartment. My only concern was that the Albatros would be unable to recover from the enormous overload of this dive. But it managed to pull out, even though it shook and shivered in every joint!

'Remarkably, the enemy fighters did not follow us down. Only anti-aircraft and well-aimed machine-gun fire from the British trenches accompanied us until we were at about 600 metres over the enemy trenches and crossed over in the direction of our own airfield. I could only show my appreciation by clapping my pilot on the shoulder. It was only thanks to him that we got out of that dangerous situation in one piece.'[6]

Rosenfeld tried to turn the tables during a fight on 8 February 1917. He spotted a British B.E.2c reconnaissance aircraft and went after it. Jollasse remembered:

'At about 4,000 metres altitude we were forced by excellently aimed anti-aircraft fire to give up pursuit of the BE, which had already done its job. We were forced to make a steep dive in order to evade the anti-aircraft fire and were tracked to the last by well-placed fire from the British trenches. But we were lucky! We landed back at our airfield with [only] several holes in the wings of our aeroplane.'[7]

A short time later Rosenfeld left *Fl-Abt (A) 263* and, after completing the course at the fighter pilots' school at Valenciennes, he was assigned to *Jagdstaffel 12*, commanded by the famous Bavarian fighter ace *Obltn* Adolf *Ritter* von Tutschek. While with *Jasta 12* Rosenfeld shot down 12 aircraft and one observation balloon. He was killed in combat following his last victory, on 7 July 1918.

Erwin Jollasse returned to flying with Helmuth Wendroth, by now promoted to *Vizefeldwebel*. They had several relatively uneventful combat flights and ended their partnership with a routine flight which turned out to be very eventful. On 2 April they flew

◄**Cockpits of early German C-type two-seaters were spartan in layout. Some, such as this Albatros, still used wheel control.**

their old Albatros C V to a nearby air replacement depot to exchange it for a new Rumpler C IV. Just after take-off, while still at low altitude, *Vzfw* Wendroth discovered that the elevator cables did not respond. Thus out of the pilot's control, the Rumpler came down and hit the ground. Erwin Jollasse recalled:

'Since I had not buckled myself in for the landing, as instructed, when the aeroplane bounded in, I was catapulted out and "landed" about 15 to 20 metres away from the aircraft. I lay there stunned for a moment. As the crash occurred almost at the edge of the airfield, groundcrew and other personnel came to the site immediately. I feared the worst for my pilot, with whom I had made so many successful combat flights. He was hanging in his badly demolished and crushed-together seat, between the wires. Thank God, his injuries were not as bad as at first feared.'[8]

Helmuth Wendroth received injuries to his upper and lower jaw, but was otherwise well enough

▲ The Albatros C I, powered by either a 160hp Mercedes or 150hp Benz engine, saw wide use among German two-seater units. Note the 'claw' brake mounted mid-way on the axle, which was activated by the pilot as the aircraft ended its landing run.

to return to his flying duties. On 13 July 1917 *Vzfw* Wendroth and his new observer, *Ltn* Konrad Blaufuss, were in a DFW C V which was hit by anti-aircraft fire and forced to land behind British lines. The two men were taken prisoner and the aircraft, assigned the identification number G 55, was in good enough condition to be studied by teams of British aviation engineers and evaluated for performance.

For Erwin Jollasse, however, severe body injuries caused him to be sent to hospital, after which he served as an instructor and then as an aviation staff officer before returning to the infantry in 1918. He had a distinguished career in World War II and was awarded the highest German decoration, the Knight's Cross of the Iron Cross.

FIRST *POUR LE MÉRITE* OBSERVER

While the various German states had their own ways of honouring the wartime achievements of their native sons, it was generally conceded that at least one award from the Kingdom of Prussia had a special aura. It was the *Orden Pour le Mérite*, established in 1740 as the highest Prussian award for bravery. Since the German *Kaiser* was also King of Prussia, 'his' orders and medals became all the more prized. In World War I the *Orden Pour le Mérite* was presented to 687 officers, of whom only 81 were assigned to aviation duties. Most of the aviation personnel – 62 in all – were fighter pilots. The next highest number was the eight observers who received the award for their continuous bravery in combat.

One of these *Pour le Mérite* recipients was former artillery officer *Obltn* Paul *Freiherr* von Pechmann, who joined the *Fliegertruppe* in 1915. By early 1917 he had become *Abteilungs-Führer* of *Fl-Abt (A) 215*. Even as squadron commander, von Pechmann led several routine reconnaissance missions per day, as well as night missions and special assignments ordered by the High Command. Small wonder, therefore, that on 31 July 1917 *Kaiser* Wilhelm II personally presented the *Orden Pour le Mérite* to von Pechmann and made him the first of the eight observers to receive the coveted award.

Subsequently Paul von Pechmann was given command of *Fl-Abt (A) 217* and he played an important role in the 21 March 1918 German offensive. *Freiherr* von Pechmann carried out a reconnaissance mission at such low altitude, hampered by ground fog, that he was under almost constant fire from the ground. He returned to his airfield with 125 holes in his aircraft.

Von Pechmann's tenacity and courage are evident in this account of a mission he undertook at a crucial point during the final months of the war:

'In order to direct the fire of a light and a heavy field howitzer battery, as well as a 15cm cannon, against three targets, I took off at 0600 hours on a wonderful cloudless and clear morning in June 1918. To the west there was one shell burst after another. We flew over the same territory where the Battle of the Somme took place in 1916, but nothing remained but a vast desert. Past Bourchavernes, Maurepas and Maricourt, we flew to the area around Albert. A British squadron of eighteen D.H.9s flew

Oberleutnant
Frhr. von Pechmann

▲ **Obltn Paul *Freiherr* von Pechmann was the first observer to receive the *Orden Pour le Mérite*. Previously, he had been awarded the Knight's Cross of the Royal Order** of the House of Hohenzollern with Swords, which for this formal portrait he wore directly below Prussia's highest bravery award.

over us at considerable altitude, swung to the south, eagerly followed by the fire of our anti-aircraft guns, and over Cappy on the Somme laid their late "Easter eggs", which shrouded the small village and the nearby airfield in dense clouds of smoke. With the brisk nature of the flight operations, it was especially important that day to keep friend and enemy in sight constantly, to avoid being surprised.

'The receiving station at Becourt-Becordel had long since laid out "Target 1 Ready to Fire" in giant white letters. Firing on the sugar refinery at Ribemont sur Ancre could begin. One battery had already drawn a bead on it and also just fired on the Ancre bridges and endangered the advance of the morning provisions for the comrades in the forward-most lines. A light tap on the Morse key of the wireless-telegraphy set and on the ground four flashes from a hedgerow. After 43 seconds, four bomb craters were in the garden on the east side of the refinery, about 200 metres short. The enemy batteries were silent. Two minutes later, in the next salvo, two were right on the refinery and two just off. After half an hour's firing, it went up in flames. Ammunition explosions gave proof that the Tommies had all sorts of supplies stored there. From the west there now approached five ugly birds of dirty [khaki] appearance with cockades. Mindful of the flight of Fokker triplanes flying over us as escorts, they left us alone and turned away.'9

Freiherr von Pechmann and his pilot flew over the second target and ranged a heavy field howitzer battery against a British battery concealed in a gorge on the south side of Bresle. German artillery fire continually interrupted the Bresle battery's work. Von Pechmann continues:

'After two hours we were finally ready and the receiving station laid out the sign "Target 3 Ready for Fire". Now came the nicest but also the most difficult target: the munitions dump on the edge of Marloy. Unfortunately, just then the triplanes were relieved by a flight of Albatros fighters and, during the change, the ugly Sopwiths tried coming out of the sun to surprise us and drive us away. Even before we could begin ranging the guns, twice we were chased from the Front to our own rear areas. A sinking feeling, certainly not unusual, but this time the obnoxious bees were especially tenacious. Then the Albatroses took on these gentlemen. Soon one fell headlong, enveloped in flames, and paid the price for his boldness. The others, slightly intimidated, flew back to their lines and so I could begin ranging the guns.

'The first shot landed in the middle of Marloy and a column of vehicles on the main road was chased out of the village at the quickest pace. That suited us fine because we were supposed to fire in that direction. The next round hit about 500 metres short of the munitions dump, but with powerful smoke and dust clouds only about 100 metres from the fleeing column. From the road downwards they could not turn at all into the gorge. Therefore, the people simply left the vehicles where they stood and headed for the most likely safe place.'10

Freiherr von Pechmann's LVG stayed beneath the Albatros formation and the observer looked through his binoculars to make sure that the vehicle column was not moving. Then he began directing

fire against the fifth target. Abruptly, he was interrupted by the clatter of machine-gun fire and saw that two Sopwiths were only 50 metres behind him and closing in for the kill.

The defence of the aircraft was entirely up to the observer. The pilot could only take evasive action. Even then, von Pechmann noted, 'occasionally the turns were so tight that I believed them to be involuntary and that perhaps my pilot had been badly wounded'.

The LVG went lower and lower in a tight spiral and still the Sopwiths hung on, riddling the two-seater's engine and radiator. Von Pechmann continues:

'We were only 50 metres above Albert. Both of the ugly birds would not let up at all. Therefore we had to go further eastwards.

'Without a drop of water the good old engine could not last long. It was very clear that we would land among the shell holes. Finally, our uninvited companions gave up on us and attempted to go after a nearby captive balloon, which of course they did not get. We flew towards Montauban and then the engine finally stopped. There was little time to seek a landing spot from 50 metres' altitude. One shell hole lay near the other. My pilot had let the aeroplane flatten out for a time, and then put it down in about 15 metres – completely undamaged and just ahead of a deep shell crater in the ruins of Montauban.

'While we were waiting to be picked up by a car from our squadron, we had the satisfaction of seeing what finally happened to one of our two targets. In the distance there were smoke clouds over the sugar refinery at Ribemont! Two days later my LVG, fitted with a new engine, proudly flew over our hosts at Montauban.'11

Paul *Freiherr* von Pechmann went on to fly many more such hazardous missions. During some of the heaviest fighting, he and his pilot flew at treetop level to drop food supplies and ammunition to German troops who had been cut off. He continued to fly right up to the end of the war, logging more than 700 combat missions, and remained in service until 1921.

FROM THE TRENCHES TO THE SKIES
'Glück muss' man haben' ('One has to have luck') would have been an appropriate motto for the airmen of World War I. A good example is Hanns-Gerd Rabe, who enlisted in the German Army on 2 August 1914 and, from the outset, was in continuous service and survived wounds suffered during

fierce ground fighting on both the Eastern and Western Fronts. A dedicated soldier, Rabe advanced through the ranks and was commissioned *Leutnant der Reserve* on 27 January 1916, the *Kaiser*'s birthday. His connection with 'the Supreme War Lord' was strengthened when on two occasions he received awards from the *Kaiser*'s own hand: the *Eisernes Kreuz I. Klasse* on 22 August 1917 and the *Ritterkreuz des königlichen Hausordens von Hohenzollern mit Schwertern* (Knight's Cross of the Royal Order of the House of Hohenzollern with Swords) on 23 December 1917; the latter often preceded the awarding of the *Orden Pour le Mérite*.

But, recognizing the futility of trench warfare, Rabe left his promising infantry career in January 1918 and began training as an aviation observer. He graduated from the aviation orientation course given at *Flieger-Ersatz-Abteilung 3* at Gotha and, on 4 March, reported to the *Beobachter-Schule* (Aviation Observers' School) at Schwerin. He was posted to *Armeeflugpark 6* in Tournai on 28 April and on 21 May was posted to *Fl-Abt (A) 253*.

Rabe's squadron carried out reconnaissance and artillery spotting flights along a section of the *6. Armee* Front in Flanders that was patrolled by some of the best RAF fighter squadrons. Despite warnings in intelligence reports and other despatches, which described enemy squadron markings and the personal insignia of some better-known fighter pilots, Hanns-Gerd Rabe almost waited too long to order his pilot to take evasive action and almost added his aircraft to an ace's victory score.

SURVIVING A FIGHT WITH BILLY BISHOP

Late in the morning of 28 May, *Ltn d Res* Rabe and his pilot, *Uffz* Peter Johannes, were on an artillery spotting mission over Ypres when the observer noted a lone British fighter trailing them. As Rabe told the author:

'He was quite far off and we were in a Rumpler C VII, the highest-flying aeroplane we had at the time, so I was not worried about one Tommy

fighterplane. Then he seemed to have disappeared, perhaps to find a more opportune target.

'I was looking back at the target area with my binoculars, watching for the next shell to hit. Suddenly an S.E.5 came between me and the target and filled my view. It was far back but gaining fast and I could see the aircraft as if I were next to it. The first thing I noticed was the white octagon insignia on the fuselage side and the big white letter next to it. I recognized it from a report I had read recently. *Mein Gott!* It was Bishop, the British Richthofen!

'I knew we were dead men if we didn't get out of there fast. No time to try to use the **Rumpler**'s superior altitude ability and climb away. We **would** have to make a fast dive for our lines. The engine was not at full power, so I leaned over to my pilot and yelled: "Dive for home! Right now or we are done for!"

'He gave full power and pushed the machine over into a streaking dive eastwards. I looked through the binoculars at Mr Bishop, who got smaller and smaller, and I was overjoyed that we had managed to elude this master airfighter. If given the choice, I would always avoid combat and the possible loss of the exposed photographic plates and notes I had made earlier in the flight. When we discussed the episode after dinner, my *Abteilungs-Kameraden* agreed there was no shame attached to declining a fight with such a formidable opponent.'[12]

Evidence indicates that Hanns-Gerd Rabe's opponent was Major William Avery Bishop, VC, DSO, MC, DFC, Commanding Officer of No 85 Squadron, RAF. The Canadian ace (who ultimately ranked second among all British Empire pilots) was angry at having been unable to surprise the Rumpler. The day before he had scored his 48th victory over a two-seater near Passchendaele, not far away. As the celebrated Canadian pilot's son, William Arthur Bishop, noted in his biography:

'Before lunch he spotted an enemy two-seater on artillery observation over the battered city of Ypres. Not a tree or building was left standing. It seemed to be the most ravaged spot on earth. The two-seater eluded him easily. The pilot [*sic*] saw

him in plenty of time, dived quickly and sped off east. Even with the S.E.5a's powerful Wolseley Viper engine Bishop could not catch him. At lunch he grumbled to "Lobo" Benbow about his upset and bad luck with the two-seater.'[13]

NIGHT RECONNAISSANCE

Ltn Rabe gained a reputation as a tenacious, hard-working observer. He never declined a mission and often volunteered for extra duty, driven by his earlier experiences to help his hard-pressed former comrades in the trenches. Consequently, he readily accepted challenges, even when asked to fly night reconnaissance missions. He later wrote:

'Night flights were a strange adventure. Starting out in the darkness towards an uncertain horizon, into the boundlessness of the atmosphere, the aircrews scarcely knew up from down. The only light came from the long darting flickers of flame streaming from the engine exhaust; ghostlike, they illuminated the softly vibrating contours of the machine and made the dark earth in the deepness appear even darker. Never were pilot and observer more alone than in the uncertainty of the night with its threatening perils. The dark ribbons of canals, the bright streaks of roads and the straight lines of the railways offered certain reference points for orientation, but we flew out of intuition, having learnt by heart the landscape and maps which the observer simply has to have in his head; for the few and still primitive instruments – such as compass, tachometer, altimeter and airspeed indicator – were of little help.

'Once over the lines, the zones protected by anti-aircraft fire and searchlight emplacements were no real obstacles as an able pilot could quickly evade both. Serious trouble could be brought about only by a mechanical breakdown such as engine failure, lack of fuel, and the like. Had any of these unfortunate circumstances arisen and required a night-time landing on unfamiliar ground, almost certainly it would have resulted in the destruction of the aircraft and probably the deaths of the pilot and observer.

'There were many night flights of little significance other than to drop bombs somewhere or to fly low over enemy billets at night, disturbing the troops with machine-gun fire. When we were assigned such tasks, my pilot, [recently promoted] *Feldwebel* Peter Johannes, did not worry. I was able to make out the objects which I had committed to memory during our daytime flights and was, therefore, orientated to the darkness. My faithful "Emil" always set the steady DFW C V down in a smooth landing at the conclusion. To be sure, every flight at night made the heart beat a little faster, for

◀ *Ltn d Res* Hanns-Gerd Rabe (left) and his pilot, *Feldwebel* Peter Johannes, and mechanic, *Uffz* Noll, pose by Hannover Cl IIIa 2714/18 at a *Fl-Abt (A) 253* hangar at Pont-à-Marque, France in the summer of 1918. The fuselage insignia is the '*Wandervogel*' emblem of a popular pre-war German youth group. It was also appropriate as Rabe's name is the German word for 'raven'.

◀ *Ltn d Res* Hanns-Gerd Rabe (right) and fellow observer *Ltn d Res* Willy Hentschel by the *Fl-Abt (A) 253* Hannover Cl IIIa in which Hentschel and his pilot, *Uffz* Braunger, shot down a Sopwith Camel west of Givenchy on 1 August 1918.

an engine failure would have meant the end – but we tried not to think about the whims of chance.'[14]

By midsummer 1918, as the impact of American divisions was finally being felt, the German High Command directed all aerial reconnaissance units to pay close attention to Allied troop and matériel concentrations. It was thought that unusually heavy activity would signal preparations for the counter-punch to the Germans' spring offensive.

ALLIED BUILD-UP
SPOTTED AND IGNORED

The astute observations offered were, however, not heeded. Hanns-Gerd Rabe told the author:

'The Supreme High Command persisted in the notion that the anticipated *Entente* grand attack must come on the southern part of the Flanders Front. We observers rejected that idea, based on the results of our reconnaissance. We looked more to the area south of the Somme region and the forests of Compiègne and Villers-Cotteret, because the transports seemed to be concentrating there daily and because an army could begin massing for an attack unobserved. Indeed, that area proved to be the source of the decisive attack on 8 August 1918.

'In any event, we observers who held the divergent viewpoint were ignored. Our prophetically precise conclusions were not appreciated – even when our continuous surveillance showed that rail traffic, which poured into the staging area inland from the coast, became even more concentrated.'[15]

Finally, to clarify the situation, *6. Armee* HQ assigned *Fl-Abt (A) 253* to carry out an extensive aerial reconnaissance on the evening of 25 July, a day marked by clear weather with occasional summer showers. The proposed route was from the *Abteilung*'s airfield at Pont-à-Marque to the Channel coast and back. *Ltd d Res* Rabe, the unit's most experienced night observer, volunteered for the mission, even though he had already flown three times that day, beginning with the 'baker's boy flight' at 0500 hours. On returning from the third flight, Rabe's regular pilot, *Fwbl* Johannes, made a hard landing and broke the undercarriage axle. Johannes was quite distressed about the accident and so Rabe selected another pilot, *Uffz* Braunger. Rabe recalled:

'Our DFW C V was carefully checked and prepared for take-off: the fuel tanks were filled to the brim, flares were loaded aboard in quantity, the 25cm hand-held camera was accompanied by the most light-sensitive photographic plates, the wireless telegraph was set for a common frequency as a communications link in case we had to make a forced landing anywhere, and there was a pocket flashlight, good maps and a piece of stiff cardboard on which I could write. Everyone stood around the aeroplane as the engine was revved up to make sure that it sounded just right.'[16]

Soon the DFW crew were under way and approaching the Front, which Rabe recalled was 'ablaze with the flashes of shots and hits. Once a searchlight groped wearily for us in the distance, but its slender silver dagger did not find us.' They headed west over La Bassée, Béthune, St Pol, Hesdin, Montreuil, Etaples and on to Boulogne-sur-Mer, where the shimmering surface of the sea and the coastline could be seen. Braunger dipped down to 50 metres when they were over busy railway lines, so Rabe could determine whether the trains were full or empty. He goes on:

'Occasionally, for encouragement and to bring a dramatic element to my work, I fired a series of rounds at the train – especially at the locomotive – but without special excitement, without emotion. This stern action was some relief in my essential work of investigation and observation. I could not have cared less whether I was successful in making the locomotive lose steam or come to a halt.'[17]

Such diversions aside, the work was hectic and tedious, trying to write information to complement each exposed photographic plate. Without such notations, the photos would have less value.

'I was only barely conscious of our smooth running engine . . . Now and then I shone my flashlight on the fuel gauge, to which the pilot nodded assuringly. But I knew he was relieved when, at Boulogne, I set the course eastwards. We had trouble with anti-aircraft fire and searchlights over Boulogne, but we were disturbed for only a few minutes.

'Later, back over Béthune, I became more relaxed. We had done it! I had the pilot climb to 2,000 metres in order to cross the Front undisturbed. North of us, a *Bombengeschwader* must have been on the return flight from London; for, there the probing fingers of the searchlights struck into the heavens. Red flares exploded against the backdrop of cloud there and hid the moon from sight. I pointed out to Braunger the directional signals from Lille in the north and Douai in the south which were 3.7cm flare shells fired into the sky at certain intervals. These were comforting help for the safe return of the bomber groups.

'At Wingles, east of the Front, a big illuminated cross lay on the ground. The directional signal was visible from the sky and remained illuminated as long as the bombers were under way. "Now stay with the cross, then further east to our airfield at Pont-à-Marque," I yelled into the pilot's ear. Then I sat back on the folding seat and, by the light of the flashlight, made more precise notes about my observations, which were not always possible during the flight on the other side of the lines.'[18]

DISORIENTATED AND LOW ON FUEL

About 20 minutes later, Rabe's relaxation turned to concern. The previously open night sky was now covered with clouds and there were no discernible landmarks below. Worst of all, the pilot had become disorientated and a check of the fuel gauge showed about half an hour's worth of petrol left. Rabe ordered Braunger to fly straight ahead, making no turns, while he sorted out the situation.

▶ **For high-altitude flights** *Flieger-Abteilung* **crews wore heavy flying suits, thick boots and face protection. Electrically heated flying suits were available, but were powered by a wind-driven generator that could malfunction; hence the thick suits were considered more reliable.**

▲ High above the clouds, a DFW C V of *Fl-Abt (A) 240* crosses the lines unescorted, with the observer at his machine-gun, ready to defend the aircraft.

◄ Climbing to altitude, this DFW C V of *Fl-Abt 33* was captured by the aerial camera of another aircraft of the same unit.

► The vantage point of aerial reconnaissance can be seen in this view of a poison gas attack launched on the Flanders Front during heavy fighting for Ypres on 6 September 1917. According-ing to the information etched into the original glass-plate negative, at the top of the frame, observer *Ltn* Oscar Bechtle took this photo at 0830 hours at 1,500 metres altitude west of Becelaere on the approach to Ypres.

'Then it occurred to me to use my wireless telegraph. Quickly, I unreeled the aerial wire and tapped out the uncoded message: "S-O-S . . . DFW C V 490/17 looking for landing place . . . S-O-S." A long, heart-pounding wait. Finally a searchlight flared up, groped towards us and then shone on a landing field, where green and red landing lights were quickly set up. I sent this message in German and English, hopeful as ever: "*Danke* . . . Thank you . . . *ich lande*."

'I gave my uncertain pilot precise orders: "Set down at the first landing light – tail low. Keep the crate level and keep the engine running. If we are with the Tommies, immediately give it the gas and then try to find an easterly heading."

'I buckled my safety belt. In cautious turns he brought the machine down to the ground. A searchlight behind us laid a wide stream of light along the ground and the pilot slowly let the aircraft flatten out, still above the landing strip. My heart beat wildly. The machine hung like a ripe plum just above the ground. The tail skid whizzed along the grass, then the wheels rumbled as the aeroplane skipped along lazily. We were right at the edge of the airfield. There was a period of silent waiting, with the propeller spinning as the engine idled. I stood, with the safety catch off the machine-gun, ready for anything . . . waiting, tensely waiting.

'Then, like heavenly music to my ears, there came a flat singing German voice with an especially strong Saxon accent: "Oh, dear God, where did you come from?"

'"From your King Friedrich August in Dresden," I replied sarcastically.

'"Then you have come a long way," he answered.'[19]

Despite reports from Hanns-Gerd Rabe and numerous other observers, two weeks later German Army units were caught virtually unprepared by the great offensive of 8 August 1918. At 0420 hours (British time) a massive bombardment opened up all along the German *2. Armee* Front and, operating under a providential thick ground mist, British tanks, armoured cars, armed lorries and infantry advanced. By the end of the day British troops had advanced 7 miles and regained all the Amiens outer defences except those at Le Quesnel.

For German ground and air units, operations over the next few months were hampered continually by gradual moves to the east. Compounding matters, an outbreak of influenza on both sides of the lines was an especially hard blow to weary German forces.

Hanns-Gerd Rabe witnessed this disintegration when, shortly after arriving home for leave in late September, he was recalled to the Front. A cryptic telegram directed him to report to what was once an auxiliary airfield at Maubray. There he found a new but dispirited *Abteilungs-Führer*, *Hptmn* Zimmermann, presiding over a unit with few pilot-observer teams fit for combat flying.

The observer's pilot, now *Vzfw* Johannes, had been wounded in an air fight on 17 September during which Rabe suffered only a minor flesh wound. He was assigned a new pilot, *Uffz* Mühlke, who appeared to have had deficient training, as Rabe noted:

'I had problems with my young pilot and often chewed him up when he made mistakes in the air. Once I gave him a resounding smack on the ear when, during heavy anti-aircraft fire near Tournai, instead of diving the crate *down* at 230 kilometres per hour, he pulled *up* into a hard climb in which we lost forward airspeed and ended up right in the thick of all the shell bursts. From my rear cockpit I bent over him, grasped the control column and pushed the LVG C VI into a screaming dive that carried us through the clouds of anti-aircraft fire.'[20]

After a few flights the new pilot improved. Rabe wrote:

'During a moment of high spirits, I had *Uffz* Mühlke fly far out of our assigned area, at rooftop height, to our old airfield at Pont-à-Marque. Arranged out on the airfield now was a British fighter squadron. Since it was still early in the morning, three Sopwith Camels stood in a row before their tent hangars. I suitably sprayed the bewildered Englishmen in all of their crates and tents. My pilot, by now completely attuned to my perilous brand of flying, pulled into a steep turn over the 'field so that with my machine-gun, hand grenades and gas bombs, I left behind a scattered anthill. On the ground, the brown "ants" fled into their holes.'[21]

Despite such antics, Rabe felt weaker and more feverish after each successive flight. He knew that he was in the early stage of influenza, but out of loyalty to his former comrades in the trenches, he continued to fly. Finally, in early October, the flu got the best of Rabe right in the middle of a mission. He and Mühlke were reconnoitring Barry-Maulde,

▲Later in the war the *Flieger-Abteilungen* were called on to provide *Infanteriefliegerdienst* (close ground-support for infantry units). Given the hazards of enemy ground fire, these 'Iff' crews were usually provided with J-type aircraft which had armour plate along the bottom of the fuselage and control surfaces, such as this Junkers J I.

near their recently abandoned airfield at Maubray, when they were attacked by five Sopwith Camels. At the height of the fighting, Rabe fainted and dropped to the cockpit floor. Thinking that his observer was dead, Mühlke took the LVG into a steep dive and headed for the ground, trailing smoke. The Camel pilots must have thought that they had killed the observer and finished off the aircraft, as they climbed away from the falling two-seater.

Hanns-Gerd Rabe's next recollection was the scene back at Lessines airfield:

'I felt nothing of the landing. When I came to I was lying on a stretcher; mechanics, pilots and officers stood around me, a doctor knelt near me and opened up my flying suit and asked: "Where have you been wounded?"

'I shook my head and said: "I passed out. This damned flu did me in."

'*Uffz* Mühlke came over and said proudly: "Thirty-seven hits in the old crate!"

'"Did it burn?"

'"Of course, *Herr Leutnant*, right down to a heap of ashes," he grinned.

'"Then it is good," I said before exhaustion caused me to slip back into unconsciousness. When

I awoke, I was undressed and in bed in my quarters on the Flanders farm the *Abteilung* used as a base. Near the bed stood the doctor and the farmer's wife, who fed me warm milk. It tasted as bitter as medicine.

'The doctor said: "Such madness that you continued to fly and tried to win the war while running a fever with a temperature of 39.5 degrees [Celsius]. That was your last combat flight."'[22]

ARMISTICE AND REVOLUTION

After a short recuperation, *Ltn* Hanns-Gerd Rabe spent the final weeks of World War I as an Aviation Liaison Officer to the *XXXX Armeekorps*. He was at a chateau in Gaesbeek, Belgium, when the armistice went into effect on 11 November 1918. The formal announcement led to almost complete dissolution of the forces that remained in the area, so Rabe was granted his request for a staff car and sufficient fuel to rejoin *Fl-Abt (A) 253*, then near Brussels. Given a Mercedes touring car and a radio lorry, Rabe's official task was to distribute demobilization orders to units along the way to his destination.

His driver asked why the Mercedes and lorry were so heavily armed – each with a fully loaded light machine-gun and hand grenades – within their own lines and Rabe replied: 'Because we are driving to Brussels, where there is a revolution going on and everything is in an uproar. We are going to need more than a walking stick to get through all that.'[23]

The abdication of the *Kaiser* and the collapse of the Imperial government had made it increasingly difficult to maintain order in the German armed forces. Communist-inspired mutinies in the Navy led to a breakdown in discipline in many Army units and the formation of Soldiers' and Workers' Councils.

Such was the case when *Ltn* Rabe arrived at *Fl-Abt (A) 253*'s airfield at Beerthem-Meerbeck, near Louvain, on the evening of 12 November. The *Abteilungs-Führer* was sick in bed and the other officers had been stripped of their rank and told to stay out of the way while members of the *Soldaten-rat* (Soldiers' Council) plundered and destroyed at will. 'Many aircraft and tents were on fire, casting an eerie glow against the night sky like some gloomy scene from Dante's *Inferno*,' Rabe recalled.[24]

Cautiously and quietly, Rabe located friendly mechanics and officers, and armed them with rifles from the lorry. Then they confronted and disarmed the *Soldatenrat* leaders – all rear-echelon types – and ordered them to help load the remaining lorries for a convoy to get under way that evening. Rabe's car would be last, they were told, to ensure against stragglers.

They travelled through the night, stopping only to pick up three nurses who were stranded when another *Soldatenrat* group seized the convoy they were in. After a few hours' pause in the morning, the remnants of *Fl-Abt (A) 253* set out for Cologne. Rabe was not surprised to learn that the brief stop had given the 'revolutionaries', whose number included the paymaster's clerk, a chance to slip away with the *Abteilung*'s cash reserves and a car before the convoy set out again.

Late in the afternoon of 15 November, Rabe's convoy reached Cologne and the River Rhine. It was a chaotic scene, with assortments of military units pouring into the city's main railway station in the hope of getting rides home. Still in charge, Rabe arranged for the local military district commander to take charge of the vehicles and weapons. Then he secured billets for the officers and men, as well as the nurses.

The following morning he assembled the group at the railway station and made his final speech to them:

'Former heroes, drunkards, combat fliers, rear-echelon warriors and revolutionaries! In your homeland at last, you are herby discharged from the Royal Prussian Army.'[25]

As Rabe's group went their different ways and *Fl-Abt (A) 253* passed into history, other units of the German *Luftstreitkräfte* burned their aircraft at their last front-line airfields or purposely crashed them when landing at Allied airfields.

In an attempt to 'beat swords into ploughshares', many salvable German aircraft were demilitarized and sold to private parties to help create a fledgling civil air transport industry. Unfortunately, rigorous demands by the Treaty of Versailles, a weak German economy, the resultant social and political chaos, and international apathy all conspired to reverse many of the positive directions in which Germany's former military aviators might have taken.

Thus, Germany's first air force became the training ground for the senior members and the role model that inspired the development of the second German air arm to fly combat missions over Europe and beyond.

REFERENCES

Introduction

1 Cuneo, *Winged Mars Vol I: The German Air Weapon 1870–1914*, (1942), p. 9
2 Ibid, pp. 39–41
3 Neumann (ed), *Die deutschen Luftstreitkräfte im Weltkriege*, (1920), pp. 59–61
4 Ibid, p. 61
5 Plettschacher, *Die Königlichen Bayerischen Fliegertruppen 1912–1919*, (1978), pp. 19, 22
6 Neumann (ed), *Die deutschen Luftstreitkräfte im Weltkriege*, (1920), p. 62
7 Ibid, p. 62
8 Neumann (ed), *In der Luft unbesiegt*, (1923), pp. 12–13
9 Ibid, p. 15
10 Cuneo, *Winged Mars Vol II: The Air Weapon 1914–1916*, (1947), p. 128
11 Neumann (ed), *Die deutschen Luftstreitkräfte im Weltkriege*, (1920), p. 64
12 Duiven, *German Jasta and Jagdgeschwader C.O.s 1916–1918*, (1988), pp. 144–145
13 von Hoeppner, *Deutschlands Krieg in der Luft*, (1921), p. 82
14 Plettschacher, *Die Königlichen Bayerischen Fliegertruppen 1912–1919*, (1978), pp. 43–44
15 Nowarra, *Eisernes Kreuz und Balkenkreuz*, (1968), pp. 37–39
16 Duiven, *German Jasta and Jagdgeschwader C.O.s 1916–1918*, (1988), p. 160
17 Neumann (ed), *Die deutschen Luftstreitkräfte im Weltkriege*, (1920), pp. 74–75
18 Ibid, p. 78

Chapter 1

1 Cuneo, *Winged Mars Vol II: The Air Weapon 1914–1916*, (1947), p. 16
2 Supf, *Das Buch der deutschen Fluggeschichte Vol II*, (1958), p. 286

3 Ibid, p. 283
4 Ibid, p. 286
5 von Hoeppner, *Deutschlands Krieg in der Luft*, (1921), pp. 20–21
6 Hug, *Carrier Pigeon Flieger*, (1972), p. 304
7 Ibid, p. 304
8 Neumann, *In der Luft unbesiegt*, (1923), p. 26
9 Neumann, *Die deutschen Luftstreitkräfte im Weltkriege*, (1920), p. 439
10 Jones, *The War in the Air Vol II*, (1928), p. 136
11 Hug, *Carrier Pigeon Flieger*, (1972), p. 305
12 Neumann, *In der Luft unbesiegt*, pp. 25–26
13 Ibid, p. 27
14 Jones, *The War in the Air Vol II*, (1928), p. 342
15 von Langsdorff, *Flieger am Feind*, (1934), p. 26
16 Ibid, pp. 28–29
17 Ferko, *Fliegertruppe 1914–1918*, (1980), pp. 2–3
18 von Eberhardt, *Unsere Luftstreitkräfte 1914–1918*, (1930), p. 371
19 Ibid, p. 372
20 Ibid, p. 374
21 Ibid, p. 376
22 Ferko, *Fliegertruppe 1914–1918*, (1980), p. 4
23 von Eberhardt, *Unsere Luftstreitkräfte 1914–1918*, (1930), p. 378
24 Ibid, p. 380
25 von Hoeppner, *Deutschlands Krieg in der Luft*, (1921), p. 40
26 von Richthofen, *The Red Baron*, (1969), pp. 34–35
27 Ibid, pp. 33–34
28 *AOK 3. Armee Bericht Nr Ia 5515*, 12 September 1915
29 *AOK 3. Armee Bericht Nr Ia 5821*, 28 September 1915
30 von Richthofen, *The Red Baron*, (1969), p. 36
31 Ibid, pp. 36–37
32 *AOK 3. Armee Bericht Nr Ia 6524*, 3 November 1915

33 Werner, *Briefe eines deutschen Kampffliegers an ein junges Mädchen*, (1930), p. 14
34 Ibid, pp. 15–17
35 Ibid, pp. 17–18
36 *Kampfgeschwader 2 OHL Anlage zu I 3797*, 22 May 1916
37 von Richthofen, *The Red Baron*, (1969), p. 49

Chapter 2

1 von Hoeppner, *Deutschlands Krieg in der Luft*, (1921), p. 39
2 Immelmann, *Immelmann der Adler von Lille*, (1934), p. 93
3 Bruce, *The Fokker Monoplanes*, (1965), p. 5
4 Pardee, *Eindeckers of World War I*, (1981), p. 133
5 Immelmann, *Immelmann der Adler von Lille*, (1934), pp. 103–104
6 *AOK 3. Armee Stabsoffizier der Ballon-Abwehrkanonen Bericht Nr 101*, 27 August 1915
7 Jones, *The War in the Air Vol II*, (1928), p. 150
8 Supf, *Das Buch der deutschen Fluggeschichte Vol II*, (1958), p. 308
9 *Stabsoffizier der Fliegertruppen der 6. Armee Bericht Nr 16981*, 31 July 1916, p. 3
10 *Feldflieger-Abteilung 32 Bericht Nr 4752/15*, 10 November 1915
11 Welkoborsky, *Vom Fliegen, Siegen und Sterben einer Feldflieger-Abteilung*, (1939), p. 79
12 *Feldflieger-Abteilung 32 Luftkampf-Bericht*, 29 December 1915
13 *AOK 2. Armee Besondere Anordnung Nr 105*, 1 January 1916
14 Jones, *The War in the Air Vol II*, (1928), pp. 156–157
15 Welkoborsky, *Vom Fliegen, Siegen und Sterben einer Feldflieger-Abteilung*, (1939), p. 88

16 Cuneo, *Winged Mars Vol II: The Air Weapon 1914–1916*, (1947), p. 231
17 Lewis, *Sagittarius Rising*, (1936), pp. 53–54
18 *Feldfl.-Abt. 32 Luftkampf-Bericht*, 20 February 1916
19 *Feldfl.-Abt. 32 Luftkampf-Bericht*, 14 March 1916
15 Welkoborsky, *Vom Fliegen, Siegen und Sterben einer Feldflieger-Abteilung*, (1939), p. 99
21 *Bericht Boelckes über 160er E-Flugzeuge* (to the Feldflugchef), 23 March 1916
22 *AOK 7. Armee Bericht Nr 4238*, 21 March 1916
23 *Stabsoffizier der Flieger der 7. Armee Bericht Nr 5876*, 22 March 1916
24 Woodman, *Early Aircraft Armament – The Aeroplanes and the Gun up to 1918*, (1989), p. 187
25 *Chef des Feldflugwesens Anweisung Nr 16170*, 11 May 1916
26 *Feldfl.-Abt. 32 Bericht Nr 739/16*, 24 May 1916
27 *Feldfl.-Abt. 32 Bericht Nr 831/16*, 11 June 1916
28 *AOK 6. Armee Bericht Nr 54749 Besondere Anordnungen*, 12 June 1916
29 Immelmann, *Immelmann der Adler von Lille*, (1934), p. 178
30 Ibid, p. 181
31 *Feldfl.-Abt. 32 Bericht Nr 1379/16*, 1 August 1916
32 Welkoborsky, *Vom Fliegen, Siegen und Sterben einer Feldflieger-Abteilung*, (1939), p. 117
33 Ferko, *The Origin of the First Jagdstaffeln*, (1965), p. 342
34 *AOK 1. Armee Bericht Ia/Ib Nr 3156*, 29 August 1916
35 *Jagdstaffel 12 Flugzeuge-Bericht Nr. 72/16*, 6 November 1916

Chapter 3

1 Cuneo, *Winged Mars Vol II: The Air Weapon 1914–1916*, (1947), pp. 402–403
2 Ibid, p. 110
3 Ibid, p. 110
4 Nowarra and Duvall, *Russian Civil and Military Aircraft 1884–1969*, (1971), p. 33
5 von Hoeppner, *Deutschlands Krieg in der Luft*, (1921), p. 15
6 Supf, *Das Buch der deutschen Fluggeschichte Vol II*, (1958), pp. 277–278
7 Ibid, p. 281
8 von Eberhardt, *Unsere Luftstreikräfte 1914–1918*, (1930), p. 147
9 Ibid, p. 147
10 Ibid, pp. 147–148
11 von Loewenstern, *Der Frontflieger*, (1937), p. 35
12 Robertson, *Air Aces of the 1914–1918 War*, (1959), p. 152
13 von Loewenstern, *Der Frontflieger*, (1937), p. 76
14 Kuppinger, *Bomber Observer: The Reminiscences of Oskar Kuppinger Part 1*, (1978), p. 113
15 Ibid, p. 114
16 Ibid, pp. 117–119
17 Ibid, p. 119
18 Ibid, p. 120
19 Neumann, *In der Luft unbesiegt*, (1923), pp. 101–102
20 Ibid, pp. 103–104
21 Ibid, pp. 105–106
22 Ibid, pp. 119–120
23 *Nachrichtenblatt der Luftstreitkräfte Vol 2, No 2*, (1918), p. 20
24 Neumann, *In der Luft unbesiegt*, (1923), p. 126
25 Ibid, pp. 127–128

Chapter 4

1 Braun, *Bombing Missions on Two Front*, (1982), pp. 37–38
2 Ibid, pp. 39–41
3 Ibid, p. 42
4 *Kriegsministerium Bericht Nr 439/4.17.A7L*, 25 April 1917
5 Braun, *Bombing Missions on Two Fronts*, (1982), pp. 47–48
6 Kilduff, *Bogohl 3 Combat Log*, (1982), p. 67
7 Ibid, p. 67
8 Jones, *The War in the Air Vol V*, (1935), p. 28
9 von Hoeppner, *Deutschlands Krieg in der Luft*, (1921), pp. 111–112

10 Delang, letter to author dated 21 February 1982
11 Jones, *The War in the Air Vol V*, (1935), p. 28
12 Fredette, *The First Battle of Britain 1917/18*, (1966), p. 59
13 *Nachrichtenblatt der Luftstreitkräfte Vol 1, No 20*, (1917), p. 81
14 Wolff'schen Telegr.-Bureaus, *Amtliche Kriegs-Depeschen nach Berichten des*, Vol 6, (no date), p. 2269
15 Kilduff, *Bogohl 3 Combat Log*, (1982), p. 68
16 *Nachrichtenblatt der Luftstreitkräfte Vol 1, No 17*, (1917), p. 34
17 Fredette, *The First Battle of Britain 1917/18*, (1966), p. 61
18 Jones, *The War in the Air Vol V*, (1935), p. 35
19 Kilduff, *Bogohl 3 Combat Log*, (1982), p. 68
20 Delang, letter to author dated 21 February 1982
21 Ibid
22 Ibid
23 *Royal Flying Corps War Diary*, 1 October 1917, Air 1/1186/204/5/2595, p. 3A
24 *No 1 Squadron, RFC, Combat Reports*, 12 December 1917, Air 1/204/5/2634, p. 60
25 Imrie, *Pictorial History of the German Army Air Service 1914–1918*, (1971), p. 46
26 *Kriegsministerium Bericht Nr 1010/17.g.A7L*, 18 December 1917
27 Kuppinger, *Bomber Observer: The Reminiscences of Oskar Kuppinger Part 2*, (1978), pp. 208–209
28 Keller, letter to author dated 15 October 1968
29 Kuppinger, *Bomber Observer: The Reminiscences of Oskar Kuppinger Part 2*, (1978), p. 208
30 Ibid, p. 214
31 Ibid, p. 216
32 Knauer, *Flying the AEG G IV*, (1974), pp. 121–123
33 Ibid, p. 124
34 Ibid, p. 125
35 Köhl, *Bremsklötze weg!*, (1932), pp. 61–62
36 *Nachrichtenblatt der Luftstreitkräfte Vol 2, No 14*, (1918), p. 198
37 Jones, *The War in the Air Vol V*, (1935), pp. 130–131
38 Kuppinger, *Bomber*

Observer: The Reminiscences of Oskar Kuppinger Part 2, (1978), pp. 218–219
39 Ibid, p. 221
40 *Kofl 18. Armee Bericht Nr 5207*, 26 August 1918
41 Kuppinger, *Bomber Observer: The Reminiscences of Oskar Kuppinger Part 2*, (1978), pp. 222–223
42 Ibid, pp. 223–225
43 Braun, *Bombing Missions on Two Fronts*, (1982), p. 64
44 Knauer, *Flying the AEG G IV*, (1974), p. 125

Chapter 5

1 Neumann, *Die deutschen Luftstreitkräfte im Weltkriege*, (1920), p. 118
2 Ibid, p. 120
3 Gamble, *The Story of a North Sea Air Station*, (1928), p. 113
4 Miller, *The Hornets of Zeebrugge*, (1970), p. 9
5 Neumann, *Die deutschen Luftstreitkräfte im Weltkriege*, (1920), p. 123
6 Jones, *The War in the Air Vol III*, (1931), p. 150
7 Ibid, p. 97
8 Gamble, *The Story of a North Sea Air Station*, (1928), p. 159
9 Kilduff, *Combat Fliers of Baden*, (1989), pp. 335–336
10 Cole, *Royal Flying Corps 1915–1916*, (1969), p. 127
11 Miller, *The Hornets of Zeebrugge*, (1970), p. 13
12 Jones, *The War in the Air Vol II*, (1928), p. 430
13 von Langsdorff, *Flieger am Feind*, (1934), p. 42
14 Ibid, p. 44
15 Stormer, *Seaplanes in Combat*, (1980), p. 118
16 von Langsdorff, *Flieger am Feind*, (1934), pp. 47–48
17 Eisenlohr, *Marineflieger!*, (1984), p. 52
18 Ibid, pp. 53–54
19 Ibid, p. 54
20 Ibid, p. 54
21 Stormer, *Seaplanes in Combat*, (1979), pp. 109–110
22 *Gruppenkommandeur der Seeflieger G Bch Nr 386*, 25 February 1918
23 Paine, *The First Yale Unit Vol II*, (1925), p. 107
24 Stormer, *Seaplanes in Combat*, (1979), pp. 121–123
25 Jones, *The War in the Air Vol VI*, (1934), p. 377

26 Stormer, *Seaplanes in Combat*, (1979), p. 119
27 Ibid, pp. 128–129
28 Ibid, p. 129

Chapter 6

1 Gibbons, *The Red Knight of Germany*, (1927), p. 103
2 Ibid, p. 152
3 von Richthofen, *The Red Baron*, (1969), p. 103
4 Ibid, pp. 103–104
5 Ibid, pp. 125–126
6 Gibbons, *The Red Knight of Germany*, (1927), p. 238
7 Ibid, pp. 245–246
8 Jones, *The War in the Air, Vol III*, (1931), p. 376
9 Ibid, p. 377
10 Nowarra, *Capt Ball's Last Flight*, (1963), pp. 223–244
11 Gibbons, *The Red Knight of Germany*, (1927), p. 272
12 'Vigilant', *Richthofen – The Red Knight of the Air*, (no date), p. 181
13 Gibbons, *The Red Knight of Germany*, (1927), p. 280
14 Ibid, pp. 317–318
15 von Richthofen, *The Red Baron*, (1969), p. 138
16 Ibid, p. 139
17 Ibid, p. 129
18 *RFC War Diary*, (1918), pp. 180–181
19 Gibbons, *The Red Knight of Germany*, (1927), p. 330
20 Dickhuth-Harrach, *Im Felde unbesiegt, Vol I*, (1921), p. 278
21 Ibid, p. 281
22 Ibid, p. 288
23 Ibid, p. 289
24 Ibid, p. 292

Chapter 7

1 *Nachrichtenblatt der Luftstreitkräfte Vol 1, No 4*, (1917), p. 4
2 von Hoeppner, *Deutschlands Krieg in der Luft*, (1921), p. 26
3 Neumann, *Die deutschen Luftstreitkräfte im Weltkriege*, (1920), pp. 7–8
4 Ibid, pp. 8–9
5 Ibid, p. 9
6 Ibid, pp. 217–218
7 von Hoeppner, *Deutschlands Krieg in der Luft*, (1921), p. 28
8 Neumann, *Die deutschen Luftstreitkräfte im Weltkriege*, (1920), p. 10
9 Ibid, p. 10
10 Cuneo, *Winged Mars Vol II:*

The Air Weapon 1914–1916,
(1947), p. 209
11 Kuster, *Kuster und der
Drachen*, (1964), p. 246
12 Ibid, p. 248
13 *Kriegs-Echo Nr 93*, (1916),
p. 7
14 Cuneo, *Winged Mars Vol II:
The Air Weapon 1914–1916*,
(1947), p. 209
15 Neumann, *Die deutschen
Luftstreitkräfte im Weltkriege*,
(1920), p. 318
16 *Chef des Feldflugwesens
Ausarbeitung Nr 17833/16L*, 3
July 1916, p. 1
17 Ibid, pp. 1–2
18 Ibid, pp. 2–3
19 von Hoeppner,
Deutschlands Krieg in der Luft,
(1921), pp. 79–80
20 Ibid, p. 80
21 *Preussische Luftschiffer-
Abteilung 2 Bericht Nr 3437.16*,
14 September 1916
22 Neumann, *Die deutschen
Luftstreitkräfte im Weltkriege*,
(1920), p. 320
23 Rieper, unpublished

manuscript (no date)
24 Ibid
25 von Hoeppner,
Deutschlands Krieg in der Luft,
(1921), p. 93
26 *Ballonzentral 1. Armee
Bericht Nr 41/17*, 10 January
1917
27 *Ballonzentral 6. Armee
Bericht Nr 499/17*, 15 April
1917
28 Rieper, unpublished
manuscript (no date)
29 *Kommandierende General
der Luftstreitkräfte Bericht Nr
38620.L*, 12 April 1917
30 *Nachrichtenblatt der
Luftstreitkräfte Vol 1, No 10*,
(1917), p. 5
31 *Nachrichtenblatt der
Luftstreitkräfte Vol 1, No 13*,
(1917), p. 2
32 *Nachrichtenblatt der
Luftstreitkräfte Vol 1, No 22*,
(1917), p. 3
33 *Nachrichtenblatt der
Luftstreitkräfte Vol 1, No 36*,
(1917), p. 355
34 Rieper, unpublished

manuscript (no date)
35 Neumann, *Die deutschen
Luftstreitkräfte im Weltkriege*,
(1920), p. 14
36 Rieper, unpublished
manuscript (no date)
37 Ibid
38 Zuerl, *Pour le Mérite-
Flieger*, (1938), p. 386
39 Kuster, *Kuster und der
Drachen*, (1964), p. 253
40 *Kgl Sachs Kommandeur der
Luftschiffer 2. Armee Ballonzentrale Bericht Nr 2574/III*, 21
October 1918
41 von Eberhardt, *Unsere
Luftstreitkräfte 1914–1918*,
(1930), p. 78
42 Ibid, p. 78

Chapter 8
1 Neumann, *In der Luft
unbesiegt*, (1923), p. 198
2 Ibid, pp. 198–199
3 Ibid, p. 199
4 Jollasse, *Aerial Observer in
Combat*, (1984), pp. 20–21
5 Ibid, pp. 22–23
6 Ibid, p. 26

7 Ibid, pp. 27–28
8 Ibid, p. 29
9 von Langsdorff, *Flieger am
Feind*, (1934), pp. 251–252
10 Ibid, pp. 252–253
11 Ibid, pp. 254–255
12 Rabe, interview with the
author, 10 September 1984
13 Bishop, *The Courage of the
Early Morning*, (1966), p. 149
14 Rabe, *Night
Reconnaissance: A Personal
Memoir*, (1973), pp. 66–67
15 Ibid, p. 67
16 Ibid, pp. 67–68
17 Ibid, p. 69
18 Ibid, p. 69
19 Ibid, p. 70
20 Rabe, *My Last Combat
Flight*, (1977), p. 232
21 Ibid, p. 233
22 Ibid, p. 235
23 Rabe, *The Collapse of
Flieger-Abteilung (A) 253*,
(1978), p. 362
24 Ibid, p. 364
25 Ibid, p. 367

BIBLIOGRAPHY

Books

COLE, C. (ed), *Royal Flying Corps 1915–1916*, London, 1969

CUNEO, J., *Winged Mars Vol I: The German Air Weapon 1870–1914*, Harrisburg, Pa., 1942

— *Winged Mars Vol II: The Air Weapon 1914–1916*, Harrisburg, Pa., 1947

DICKHUTH-HARRACH, G. (ed), *Im Felde unbesiegt, Vol I*, Munich, 1921

VON EBERHARDT, W. (ed), *Unsere Luftstreitkräfte 1914–1918*, Berlin, 1930

FREDETTE, R., *The First Battle of Britain*, London, 1966

GAMBLE, C., *The Story of a North Sea Air Station*, London, 1928

GIBBONS, F., *The Red Knight of Germany*, New York, 1927

VON HOEPPNER, E., *Deutschlands Krieg in der Luft*, Leipzig, 1921

IMMELMANN, F. (ed), *Immelmann der Adler von Lille*, Leipzig, 1934

IMRIE, A., *Pictorial History of the German Army Air Service 1914–1918*, London, 1971

— *German Naval Air Service*, London, 1989

JONES, H., *The War in the Air*, Vol II, Oxford, 1928

— *The War in the Air*, Vol III, Oxford, 1931

— *The War in the Air*, Vol IV, Oxford, 1934

— *The War in the Air*, Vol V, Oxford, 1935

— *The War in the Air*, Vol VI, Oxford, 1937

KÖHL, H., *Bremsklötze weg!*, Berlin, 1932

VON LANGSDORFF, W., *Flieger am Feind*, Gütersloh, 1934

LEWIS, C., *Sagittarius Rising*, London, 1936

VON LOEWENSTERN, E., *Der Frontflieger*, Berlin, 1937

NEUMANN, G. (ed), *Die deutschen Luftstreitkräfte im Weltkriege*, Berlin, 1920

— *In der Luft unbesiegt*, Munich, 1923

NOWARRA, H., *Eisernes Kreuz und Balkenkreuz*, Mainz, 1968

— and DUVAL, G., *Russian Civil and Military Aircraft 1884–1969*, London, 1970

PAINE, R., *The First Yale Unit*, Vol II, Cambridge, 1925

PLETSCHACHER, P., *Die Königlichen Bayerischen Fliegertruppen 1912–1919*, Stuttgart, 1978

VON RICHTHOFEN, M. (translated by P. Kilduff), *The Red Baron*, New York, 1969

ROBERTSON, B., *Air Aces of the 1914–1918 War*, Letchworth, 1959

SUPF, P., *Das Buch der deutschen Fluggeschichte*, Vol II, Stuttgart, 1958

'VIGILANT' [C. Sykes], *Richthofen – The Red Knight of the Air*, London

WELKOBORSKY, N., *Vom Fliegen, Siegen und Sterben einer Feldflieger-Abteilung*, Berlin, 1939

WERNER, J. (ed), *Briefe eines deutschen Kampffliegers an ein junges Mädchen*, Leipzig, 1930

WOLFF'SCHEN TELEGR.-BUREAUS, *Amtliche Kriegs-Depeschen nach Berichten des*, Vol 6, Berlin

WOODMAN, H., *Early Aircraft Armament – The Aeroplanes and the Gun up to 1918*, London, 1989

ZUERL, W., *Pour le Mérite-Flieger*, Munich, 1938

Documents

AOK 1. Armee Berichte, published in the field, 1916

AOK 2. Armee Berichte, 1916

AOK 3. Armee Berichte, 1915

AOK 3. Armee Stabsoffizier der Ballon-Abwehrkanonen Berichte, 1915

AOK 7. Armee Berichte, 1916

Feldflieger-Abteilung 32 Berichte, 1915

Gruppenkommandeur der Seeflieger Berichte, 1918

Jagdstaffel 12 Flugzeuge-Berichte, 1916

Kampfgeschwader 2 OHL Berichte, 1916

Kommandeur der Flieger der 18. Armee Berichte, 1918

Kommandeur der Luftschiffer der 2. Armee Berichte, 1918

KOGENLUFT, *Chef des Feldflugwesens Berichte*, Berlin, 1916

— *Nachrichtenblatt der Luftstreitkräfte Vol I*, Berlin, 1917

— *Nachrichtenblatt der Luftstreitkräfte Vol II*, Berlin, 1918

Kriegsministerium Berichte, Berlin, 1917

No 1 Squadron, RFC, Combat Reports, in the field, 1917

Preussische Luftschiffer-Abteilung 2 Berichte, 1916

ROYAL FLYING CORPS, *War Diary*, London, 1917

— *War Diary*, London, 1918.

Stabsoffizier der Fliegertruppen der 6. Armee Berichte, 1916

Stabsoffizier der Flieger der 7. Armee Berichte, 1916

Articles and Monographs

BRAUN, I., 'Bombing Missions on Two Fronts' (transl. A. von Krusenstiern), *Cross & Cockade Journal*, 1982

BRUCE, J., *The Fokker Monoplanes*, Profile Publications, 1965

DUIVEN, R., 'German Jasta and Jagdgeschwader C.O.s 1916–1918', *Over the Front*, 1988

EISENLOHR, W., 'Marineflieger! The Reminiscences of —' [transl. P. Kilduff], *Cross & Cockade Journal*, 1984

FERKO, A., *Fliegertruppe 1914–1918*, Salem, Ohio, 1980

— 'The Origin of the First Jagdstaffeln', *Cross & Cockade Journal*, 1965

HUG, A., 'Carrier Pigeon Flieger: The World War I Experiences of —' [ed. N. Shirley], *Cross & Cockade Journal*, 1972

KILDUFF, P. (ed.), 'Bogohl 3 Combat Log', *Cross & Cockade Journal*, 1982

KILDUFF, P. (ed.), 'Combat Fliers of Baden', *Over the Front*, 1989

KNAUER, J., 'Flying the AEG G IV' [ed. P. Kilduff], *Cross & Cockade Journal*, 1974

KUPPINGER, O., 'Bomber Observer: The Reminiscences of – Part 1' [transl. P. Kilduff], *Cross & Cockade Journal*, 1978

— 'Bomber Observer: The Reminiscences of – Part 2' [transl. P. Kilduff], *Cross & Cockade Journal*, 1978

KUSTER, K., 'Kuster und der Drachen' [ed. E. Swearingen], *Cross & Cockade Journal*, 1964

MILLER, T. (ed.), 'The Hornets of Zeebrugge', *Cross & Cockade Journal*, 1970

PARDEE, D., 'Eindeckers of World War I', *Cross & Cockade Journal*, 1981

STORMER, F., 'Seaplanes in Combat: The Reminiscences of –' [transl. P. Kilduff], *Cross & Cockade Journal*, 1979

Other Sources

BAUR, H., Correspondence

DELANG, K., Correspondence

JOLLASSE, E., Correspondence

KELLER, A., Correspondence

KUPPINGER, O., Correspondence

RABE, H., Correspondence and interviews

RIEPER, P., Unpublished manuscript, privately held

INDEX